FAVORITE RECIPES® PRESS

RECIPES WORTH SHARING

RECIPES WORTH SHARING

Recipes and Stories from America's
Most-Loved Community Cookbooks

Copyright© 2008 by

FRP

Favorite Recipes® Press
P.O. Box 305142
Nashville, Tennessee 37230
1-800-358-0560

Cover images © by Jeffery M. Horler and Stockbyte
Illustrations © by Barbara Ball
Cover Design: Rikki Campbell Ogden

Library of Congress Control Number: 2008931808
ISBN: 978-0-87197-543-0

Favorite Recipes® Press is an imprint of FRP, Inc., a wholly-owned subsidiary of
Southwestern/Great American, Inc.

Executive Editor: Sheila Thomas
Art Director: Steve Newman
Book Design: Travis Rader
Project Editor: Tanis Westbrook

Manufactured in the United States of America
First Printing: 2008

This cookbook is a collection of favorite recipes generously shared by the committee
members of community cookbooks across America. We would have loved to include
every recipe and story submitted; however, due to limited space, duplications, and
similarities, it was impossible to include them all. The FRP team worked diligently to
verify the proper names and spellings of the many organizations and individual
contributors. Should there be an error, please accept our sincere apologies, and let us
know so that we can correct it for subsequent printings.

 This symbol denotes recipes that are Too Good to Be Forgotten classics.

Acknowledgments

In developing this book, I put out a call for recipes and stories from organizations that have published community cookbooks. Nothing could have prepared me for the flood of responses I received. Many of the groups called special meetings to choose their most prized and trusted recipes, discussing the details with past and present committee members to be sure they were submitting only the best of the best. Beyond the recipes, they shared their experiences of developing their cookbooks and, of particular importance to many of the members, recounted all the community needs met through sales of their cookbooks. In turn, I'm thrilled to be able to present recipes from more than eighty regional cookbooks, representing sixty-three organizations and sixty-one communities throughout twenty-six states. My sincere thanks to the many contributors who recommended recipes and shared their stories with FRP Publishing on behalf of their organizations.

I have always loved recipe cards, you know, the handwritten ones that were used to share recipes before the personal computer. I treasure my grandmother's recipe boxes, stuffed with recipes shared by friends and family. Most handwritten, some neatly typed (in the uneven letters suggesting the use of a typewriter) on index cards—many splattered with memories from long-ago meals. The design for *Recipes Worth Sharing* was conceived with this in mind. Thank you to Rikki Campbell Ogden, for her incredible ability to read my mind and create the perfect cover; to Barbara Ball, for her wonderful drawings that are reminiscent of the artwork found on those recipe cards of the past; to Martha Hopkins, for her never-ending support and friendship; and to the entire team at FRP, who care about community cookbooks as much as I do.

And thank you to all the community cookbook collectors out there. Your continued support of this book form helps not only to preserve a slice of history—and what a rich slice it is—but to foster a vibrant, living snapshot of America's dinner table.

Sheila Thomas
FRP Publishing
A division of FRP, Inc.

Foreword

Community cookbooks are much more than just a collection of recipes. Published by volunteers from charitable organizations, community cookbooks represent people, places, and causes and allow us a glimpse of the regional, ethnic, family, and societal traditions of the contributors. Proceeds from these literary treasures are given back to the community, helping to change the lives of those most in need.

In this, our tribute to community cookbooks, you will discover how the resources generated by community cookbook sales touch the lives of volunteers, individuals, and their communities.

"I believe in the power of paying it forward and wish that all humankind would incorporate it into their lives. This practice encourages people to help others by paying good deeds forward rather than simply paying them back. Helping familiar people is wonderful, but helping complete strangers is truly inspirational.

This is exactly what the Newnan Junior Service League has done for me. They have payed it forward, helping me finance my education so that I could, in turn, help others as a nurse in the future. As a student in the nursing program at Georgia College and State University, I know that I would not be where I am today without the aid of Newnan Junior Service League, funded in part through the sales of their cookbooks, *A Taste of Georgia* and *A Taste of Georgia, Another Serving*. I plan on showing my appreciation by helping others in their time of need."

Ashley McKowen
Scholarship Recipient
Newnan Junior Service League

Introduction

Since 1961, FRP, or Favorite Recipes Press as we were known then, has been blessed to work with hundreds of women's organizations of all kinds, some large, some small, from all corners of America and even a few in other countries. To work as a partner alongside these volunteers, who give so much of their time, sweat, and tears to the development of a community cookbook, is an honor. These women who take on the task of chairperson or a position on the cookbook committee are passionate about collecting only the very best recipes from their memberships and communities, showcasing their regional cuisines and traditions, telling the story behind their charitable causes, and raising money so that the good work of their organizations can be carried on, even expanded.

Community cookbooks are some of the most loved and most treasured cookbooks. Containing recipes that are tested (sometimes three or four times) and tasted in homes by ordinary cooks and ordinary families, they are the most trusted. And since each cookbook comes from within a community, the reader can glimpse what it would be like to live there. The community cookbook often goes underappreciated, when readers (or even members) don't realize the number of ways the cookbooks have contributed to their communities. That is what we hope to do here, in *Recipes Worth Sharing ... Recipes and Stories from America's Most-Loved Community Cookbooks:* to pay homage to the community cookbook form and to the volunteers and communities from which they hail.

Contents

Appetizers and Beverages

"During the development of *Marshes to Mansions*, we were interrupted when Hurricane Katrina ravaged our beloved neighbors in New Orleans and Southeast Louisiana on August 29, 2005. Cookbook production came to a halt as members of the Junior League of Lake Charles sprung into action, volunteering countless hours to shelter and care for displaced neighbors and friends.

Before that catastrophe was over, Hurricane Rita battered Southwest Louisiana just as cruelly on September 24, 2005. This time, our own region was evacuated as the storm raged, and Rita left behind immeasurable destruction and despair in her wake. When we all returned home, we learned that the recipe committee members had evacuated with their recipes and testing notes for our League cookbook, leaving behind many of their own family treasures in the process. While everyone returned safely with their cookbook documents intact, many of their kitchens and homes had not survived the storm.

Two years later, *Marshes to Mansions* emerged from the rubble of Rita, a testament to the determination of the people of Lake Charles and the commitment of the Junior League to helping others weather life's storms, both literally and figuratively."

Karen Chamberlain
Junior League of Lake Charles, Louisiana

Palmiers with Prosciutto

Makes 20 palmiers

1 (11×18-inch) sheet puff pastry
3 tablespoons honey mustard
4 ounces thinly sliced prosciutto
3/4 cup freshly grated Parmesan cheese
1 egg
2 teaspoons water

Place the puff pastry on a hard surface. Spread with the honey mustard. Arrange the prosciutto over the mustard. Sprinkle with the cheese. Press the cheese lightly into the prosciutto with a rolling pin. Start at 1 long end, roll as for a jelly roll just to the middle of the pastry. Roll the other side to make 2 rolls that meet in the center. Cut down the center using a serrated knife. Cut each roll into 1/2-inch slices.

Arrange the slices cut side up on a baking sheet lined with parchment paper. Press lightly to flatten. Chill for 15 minutes. Whisk the egg and water in a bowl. Brush the top of each with the egg wash. Bake at 400 degrees in a preheated oven for 10 minutes or until puffed and golden brown. Serve warm or at room temperature.

Beginnings: A Collection of Appetizers
The Junior League of Akron, Inc., Akron, Ohio

The Junior League of Tampa Culinary Collection includes three titles: *The Life of the Party,* *EveryDay Feasts,* and *Savor the Seasons.* In its first five years, the series has generated $750,000, with net profits totaling more than $300,000. With that level of commitment to the Tampa Bay community, The Junior League of Tampa Culinary Collection lives up to its slogan, "Helping Families Taste the Best in Life."

Sausage Blossoms

2 pounds Italian sausage, casings removed
2 cups shredded Colby Jack Cheese
2 cups salsa

1 package won ton wrappers
Sour cream
Chopped green onions

Brown the sausage in a skillet, stirring until crumbly. Remove from the heat and add the Colby Jack cheese and salsa, stirring until the cheese is melted. Press the won ton wrappers into miniature muffin cups, leaving the edges extending upward. Spoon a heaping tablespoon of the sausage mixture into each cup. Bake at 350 degrees for 10 minutes or until won ton edges begin to brown. Remove to a serving platter and let stand for 5 minutes. Spoon a small amount of sour cream on top of each sausage blossom and sprinkle with chopped green onions. Serve immediately.

The Life of the Party
The Junior League of Tampa, Inc., Tampa, Florida

Sausage Cups

1 pound hot bulk pork sausage
1 pound fresh mushrooms, finely chopped
4 green onions, finely chopped

8 ounces cream cheese
Salt and pepper to taste
3 (15-ounce) packages mini phyllo shells

Brown the sausage in a skillet, stirring until crumbly; drain. Add the mushrooms and green onions and sauté until the vegetables are tender. Add the cream cheese. Cook until the cream cheese melts, stirring often. Season with salt and pepper. Spoon into the phyllo shells and arrange on a nonstick baking sheet. Bake at 350 degrees for 10 to 15 minutes.

Note: These may be made ahead and frozen before baking. Remove as many as you need directly from the freezer and bake at 350 degrees for 20 minutes.

A League of Our Own: From Blue Jeans to Ball Gowns
Rockwall Women's League, Rockwall, Texas

Ham and Okra Roll-Ups

8 ounces Herb Cheese Spread, softened
1 tablespoon dried minced onion
1 teaspoon seasoned salt
1 (12-ounce) package sliced rectangular ham, patted dry
1 (16-ounce) jar pickled okra, drained and stems removed

Combine the Herb Cheese Spread, onion and seasoned salt in a bowl and mix well. Spread the cheese mixture evenly over the ham slices. Place 1 or 2 okra pods lengthwise at one side of each of the ham slices and roll tightly. Chill, covered, until firm. Slice horizontally.

Variation: Substitute pickled asparagus for the okra.

Herb Cheese Spread

Makes 3 cups

1 cup (2 sticks) butter, softened
16 ounces cream cheese, softened
2 garlic cloves, minced
1 teaspoon cracked pepper, or more to taste

1/2 teaspoon oregano
1/2 teaspoon basil
1/2 teaspoon thyme
1/2 teaspoon marjoram

Whip the butter in a mixing bowl until light and fluffy. Add the cream cheese and mix well. Stir in the garlic, pepper, oregano, basil, thyme and marjoram. Chill, covered, until serving time.

The Cook's Canvas 2
Cameron Art Museum, Wilmington, North Carolina

To us, entertaining can mean anything from feeding your family a simple meal or serving friends an elegant dinner. *The Cook's Canvas 2* reminds us of the importance of sitting at the dinner table, laughing with friends and family, and slowing down to enjoy the moment.

Sauerkraut Balls

Makes variable amount

1 pound bulk sausage
4 ounces ground beef
1/2 cup chopped onion
3 tablespoons snipped fresh parsley
1 teaspoon each garlic powder, salt and sugar
1/2 teaspoon dry mustard
1/8 teaspoon pepper

1 to 2 pounds drained sauerkraut, chopped
1/2 cup bread crumbs
1 egg, beaten
1/4 cup milk
2 eggs, beaten
Seasoned bread crumbs
Hot Sweet Mustard Sauce

Brown the sausage and ground beef with the onion, parsley, garlic powder, salt, sugar, dry mustard and pepper in a skillet, stirring until the sausage and ground beef are crumbly; drain. Stir in the sauerkraut. Add 1/2 cup bread crumbs and 1 egg and mix well. Chill, covered, in the refrigerator. Shape the sausage mixture into 1-inch balls. Dip the balls in a mixture of the milk and 2 eggs. Coat with seasoned bread crumbs. Arrange the balls on a broiler rack in a broiler pan. Broil in a preheated oven until golden brown; drain. Serve with Hot Sweet Mustard Sauce. May freeze the sauerkraut balls before broiling for future use.

Hot Sweet Mustard Sauce

Makes 1 cup

1/4 cup dry mustard
2/3 cup water
1/4 cup sugar

1 1/2 tablespoons cornstarch
1/2 teaspoon salt
1/3 cup white vinegar

Combine the dry mustard with just enough of the water in a bowl until the mixture is of a pasty consistency. Let stand for several minutes. Combine the sugar, cornstarch and salt in a saucepan and mix well. Stir in the remaining water. Add the vinegar; mix well. Cook over low heat for 5 minutes, stirring constantly. Remove from heat. Let stand until cool. Stir in the mustard mixture.

Beginnings: A Collection of Appetizers
The Junior League of Akron, Inc., Akron, Ohio

Cherry-Sauced Meatballs

MEATBALLS
2 cups loosely packed torn white bread
1/2 cup milk
1 teaspoon soy sauce
1 teaspoon garlic salt

1/4 teaspoon onion powder
8 ounces ground beef
8 ounces hot bulk pork sausage
1 (8-ounce) can sliced water chestnuts, drained
   and chopped

CHERRY SAUCE
1 (21-ounce) can cherry pie filling
1/3 cup dry sherry
1/4 cup white vinegar

1/4 cup steak sauce
2 tablespoons brown sugar
2 tablespoons soy sauce

To prepare the meatballs, combine the bread, milk, soy sauce, garlic salt and onion powder in a bowl and stir to mix well. Mix the ground beef and sausage together in a bowl. Add to the bread mixture and mix well. Add the water chestnuts and mix well. Shape into 3/4-inch balls and place on a lightly greased rack in a broiler pan. Bake at 350 degrees for 20 minutes.

To prepare the sauce and assemble, combine the pie filling, sherry, vinegar, steak sauce, brown sugar and soy sauce in a saucepan and mix well. Cook over medium heat until heated through, stirring constantly. Place the meatballs in a chafing dish. Pour the sauce over the meatballs and stir to coat.

Great Women, Great Food
The Junior League of Kankakee County, Inc., Kankakee, Illinois

When our Junior League of Kankakee County decided to publish a new cookbook in 2006, we knew it would be no small undertaking. With just thirty-six active members, we didn't have all the luxuries of larger clubs with seemingly unlimited testers, editors, and other volunteers needed to bring a book to fruition.

For our cookbook, we wanted to showcase the rich, historical locations in Kankakee, including the League's headquarters, the Stone Barn. As the oldest building in downtown Kankakee, the Stone Barn seemed a natural fit for the cookbook and we decided to use color photos on the front of the chapter openers and black and white historical photos on the back. The historical society helped us acquire the black and white photos, and we arranged for a photographer to shoot the color photos. Unfortunately, we failed to remember the season: it was winter and the pictures would not include the bright, sunny pictures full of flowers we envisioned, but would be cloudy, dreary, and full of snow. Ooops! Our local visitor's bureau graciously donated lovely, spring and summertime color photos to use in our pages. As with so many of our projects, when we work together with the community for the community, beautiful things happen. And in this case, they taste fabulous, too!

The Junior League of Kankakee, Illinois

Apple Sausage Jumble

Serves 8 to 10

2 pounds kielbasa (sausage)
3/4 cup packed brown sugar
1 (35-ounce) jar chunky applesauce

1/4 cup finely chopped onion,
   or 1 tablespoon dried onion flakes

Cut sausage into 1/2-inch pieces. Combine sugar, applesauce, and onion in an ovenproof casserole. Mix in sausage pieces. Bake at 325 degrees for 1 1/2 to 2 hours. Transfer to a chafing dish or fondue pot at serving time.

Applehood & Motherpie
The Junior League of Rochester, Inc., Rochester, New York

Bacon Cheese Bites

Serves 8

3 cups (12 ounces) shredded sharp Cheddar cheese
1 (4-ounce) can sliced black olives
1 cup finely chopped green onions
1/4 to 1/2 cup chopped jalapeño chiles

1 cup mayonnaise
1 cup crumbled crisp-cooked bacon
1 package cocktail rye bread

Combine the cheese, olives, green onions, jalapeño chiles, mayonnaise and bacon in a bowl and mix well. Spread on the bread. (At this point, you may freeze on baking sheets, stack in sealable plastic bags and store in the freezer.) Place on a baking sheet. Bake at 300 degrees for 15 to 20 minutes or until bubbly.

Note: Make ahead and store in the freezer so you can pop as many as you need into the oven to serve unexpected guests or for a little snack.

Roux To Do
The Junior League of Greater Covington, Inc., Covington, Louisiana

Melon Manchego Wraps

8 dried pitted dates
3 ounces manchego cheese, cut into
   16 (1/2-inch-thick) slices

16 cantaloupe slices
8 slices prosciutto, cut into halves lengthwise

Cut the dates into halves lengthwise. Place a date half and slice of manchego cheese on each cantaloupe slice. Wrap with a slice of prosciutto, securing with wooden picks. You may substitute two Granny Smith apples for the cantaloupe, if desired. Slice the apples into 16 wedges and sprinkle with lemon juice to prevent them from turning brown.

Savor the Seasons
The Junior League of Tampa, Inc., Tampa, Florida

Gauguin's Coconut Chicken

Serves 8

PLUM SAUCE
1 jar plum jelly

1/4 cup fresh orange juice
1 tablespoon sherry

CHICKEN
1/2 cup milk
1 egg, beaten
1/2 cup plus 2 tablespoons flour
1 1/2 teaspoons seasoned salt

1/2 teaspoon white pepper
2 boneless skinless chicken breasts,
   cut into bite-size pieces
1 (7-ounce) package shredded coconut
Peanut oil for deep-frying

For the sauce, whisk the jelly in a bowl until frothy. Add the orange juice and wine gradually, whisking constantly until blended.

For the chicken, whisk the milk and egg in a bowl until blended. Stir in the flour, seasoned salt and white pepper. Dip the chicken in the egg mixture. Coat with the coconut. Deep-fry the chicken in the peanut oil in a skillet until golden brown; drain. Serve from a heated tray or chafing dish with the plum sauce.

Note: May prepare the chicken in advance and store, covered, in the refrigerator. Reheat in a 400-degree oven for 5 minutes.

Art Fare
Toledo Museum of Art Aides, Toledo, Ohio

Spicy Chicken on Pita Wedges

2 chicken breasts
Lemon pepper to taste
12 ounces cream cheese, softened
1 1/2 cups shredded Monterey Jack cheese
1/4 cup sour cream
1/4 cup chopped red onion
3 green onions, chopped
2 tablespoons chopped pickled jalapeño chiles
2 cloves garlic, minced

1 teaspoon cumin
1 teaspoon chili powder
1/2 teaspoon coriander
Salt and pepper to taste
4 pita bread rounds, split into halves horizontally
Sliced black olives
Sliced green onions
Shredded Monterey Jack cheese

Sprinkle the chicken with lemon pepper and place in a 2-quart saucepan. Add enough water to cover the chicken and bring to a boil. Reduce the heat. Cook, covered, until the chicken is cooked through; drain. Let stand until cool. Finely chop the chicken, discarding the bones. Combine the chicken, cream cheese, Monterey Jack cheese, sour cream, red onion, green onions, jalapeño chilies, garlic, cumin, chili powder, coriander, salt and pepper in a bowl and mix well. Spread 1/8 of the chicken mixture on each pita half. Cut each into eight wedges with a sharp knife or pizza cutter. Place on baking sheet. Bake at 375 degrees for 5 to 7 minutes or until bubbly. Arrange on a serving platter and top with olives, green onions and shredded Monterey Jack cheese.

Note: The chicken mixture can be prepared in advance and frozen in a sealed freezer-safe container.
Thaw in refrigerator. Spread on the pita halves and bake as directed.

Be Present At Our Table
Germantown United Methodist Women,
Germantown, Tennessee

The concept of an art museum cookbook began not just as a fund-raiser, but as an opportunity to promote the Toledo Museum of Art's collection to the public. After working on the book for one year, we were forced to table our plans and dreams due to changes in museum administration.

Fast forward ten years . . . the Museum Aides never lost hope. Our enthusiasm for the prospect of a museum cookbook resurfaced and felt even stronger than it had been a decade before. Our persistence outlived three Museum Directors and ten Aides Presidents. *Art Fare* went to press in 1999 and came out on top with a National Tabasco Community Cookbook Award. Our financial goals were reached. The earnings were used to inaugurate the TMA Aides Endowment Fund, which continues to benefit the museum.

Marilyn Arbaugh
Toledo Museum of Art
Toledo, Ohio

Crispy Crab Cakes with Mango and Green Onion Relish

Serves 6

MANGO AND GREEN ONION RELISH
2 large mangoes, chopped
1/2 red onion, finely chopped
2 green onions, minced
1 jalapeño chile, seeded and minced

2 tablespoons finely chopped red bell pepper
1 tablespoon chopped fresh cilantro
2 tablespoons lime juice
2 tablespoons olive oil
Salt and pepper to taste

CRAB CAKES
8 ounces lump crab meat, drained
8 ounces claw crab meat, drained
1/2 cup panko
2 tablespoons minced red bell pepper
1 tablespoon minced green onion

1 egg, lightly beaten
3 tablespoons cream cheese, softened
2 tablespoons Dijon mustard
1 tablespoon prepared horseradish
1 teaspoon Old Bay seasoning
Olive oil for sautéing

To prepare the relish, combine the mangoes, red onion, green onions, jalapeño chile, bell pepper and cilantro in a bowl and mix well. Stir in the lime juice and olive oil and season with salt and pepper. Chill, covered, for 1 to 10 hours.

To prepare the crab cakes, gently mix the crab meat, bread crumbs, bell pepper and green onion in a bowl. Add the egg, cream cheese, Dijon mustard, horseradish and Old Bay seasoning and mix well. Shape the crab meat mixture into twelve patties.

Heat a small amount of olive oil in a large skillet over medium-high heat. Sauté the crab cakes in the hot oil for 3 minutes per side or until light brown and crisp; drain. Serve with the mango and green onion relish.

Starfish Café: Changing Lives One Recipe at a Time ...
Union Mission/Starfish Café, Savannah, Georgia

Established in 1990 on behalf of the McIlhenny Company, the Tabasco Community Cookbook Awards recognize the achievements of community cookbooks and encourage the preservation of the vast array of regional food traditions. It is the only program solely created to recognize the best of the thousands of cookbooks issued annually to generate money for charitable causes. Thirty-three of the cookbooks included in *Recipes Worth Sharing* are winners of this prestigious award.

Beach Bites

8 ounces cream cheese, softened
2 tablespoons milk
1/2 teaspoon horseradish
1 tablespoon melted butter
1 tablespoon white wine (optional)
1/4 teaspoon salt
1/4 teaspoon pepper

1 cup flaked cooked crab meat, drained
2 scallions, chopped
1 cup cooked shrimp, cut into small pieces
40 frozen phyllo cups, thawed
Grated Parmesan cheese
Sliced almonds

Blend the cream cheese, milk, horseradish, butter, wine, salt and pepper in a mixing bowl. Fold in the crab meat, scallions and shrimp. Fill the phyllo cups with the seafood mixture. Place on a baking sheet. Sprinkle with the cheese and almonds. Bake at 400 degrees for 10 to 12 minutes or until heated through.

Toast of the Coast
The Junior League of Jacksonville, Jacksonville, Florida

Marna's Oysters Bienville

6 dozen oysters (save liquid)
1 bunch green onions, chopped
4 cloves garlic, minced
1/4 pound butter
8 tablespoons flour
1 1/2 cups liquid (Use oyster liquid, mushroom liquid and add heavy cream to make up the 1 1/2 cups)
Heavy cream
1/2 cup lemon juice

1/2 cup dry white wine
1/2 pound shrimp, chopped finely
One 5 3/4-ounce can chopped mushrooms
1/4 cup chopped parsley
Tabasco sauce to taste
White pepper and salt to taste
Rock salt
Parmesan cheese
Lemon wedges

Open oysters and reserve liquid. Sauté green onions and garlic in butter. Stir in flour and cook, over low heat, until bubbly. Add liquid, a little at a time, and simmer until smooth and creamy. Add remaining ingredients. Simmer this sauce about 15 minutes. Place oysters, in shells, on rock salt and bake until edges curl at 375 degrees. Drain excess liquid from shells and top with sauce. Sprinkle with grated Parmesan cheese and run under broiler until slightly brown on top. Serve with lemon wedges.

River Road Recipes II: Second Helping
The Junior League of Baton Rouge, Baton Rouge, Louisiana

Grilled Jumbo Atlantic Sea Scallops with Roasted Red Pepper Sauce

1 cup olive oil
Juice of 1/2 lemon
Juice of 1/2 lime
3 garlic cloves
2 scallions, chopped
1 sprig each of rosemary, dill weed and basil
1 teaspoon coarsely ground pepper

8 (2-ounce) sea scallops
1 red bell pepper
1 tablespoon chopped shallot
3 tablespoons dry white wine
1 cup heavy cream
Salt and freshly ground pepper to taste
4 ounces smoked salmon, cut into 8 slices

Mix the olive oil, lemon juice, lime juice, garlic, scallions, rosemary, dill weed, basil and pepper in a bowl. Place the scallops in the marinade and marinate in the refrigerator for 3 hours.

Grill the bell pepper over high heat until the skin is black, turning frequently. Remove the bell pepper from the grill and place in a brown paper bag. Lt stand for 10 minutes. Remove the blackened skin. Cut the bell pepper in half and remove the seeds. Purée the bell pepper in a food processor.

Combine the shallot with the wine in a skillet over medium heat. Cook until most of the liquid has evaporated, stirring frequently. Add the cream and cook until reduced by half, stirring frequently. Add the puréed bell pepper, salt and pepper to taste and mix well.

Drain the scallops, discarding the marinade. Wrap each scallop with a slice of salmon and secure with a wooden pick. Grill the prepared scallops over medium-high heat for 1 to 3 minutes per side. Serve over roasted red pepper sauce. Garnish with sour cream and caviar.

From Grouper to Grits
The Junior League of Clearwater-Dunedin, Clearwater, Florida

Community Cookbooks remind us of the importance of sitting down at the dinner table with family and friends. Eating should be an experience we share with those special people in our life.

Coconut Shrimp with Orange Dipping Sauce

Serves 6

2 pounds medium fresh shrimp
1 1/2 cups flour
1 (12-ounce) can beer
1/2 teaspoon baking powder
1/2 teaspoon paprika
1/2 teaspoon curry powder

1/2 teaspoon salt
1/4 teaspoon ground red pepper
1/2 cup flour
1 (14-ounce) package flaked coconut
Vegetable oil for frying
Orange Dipping Sauce

Peel and devein the shrimp, leaving the tails intact. Combine 1 1/2 cups flour, beer, baking powder, paprika, curry powder, salt and red pepper in a bowl and mix well. Dredge the shrimp in 1/2 cup flour. Dip in the batter and roll in the coconut. Preheat the vegetable oil to 350 degrees in a deep skillet. Add the shrimp. Fry until golden brown. Remove shrimp to a platter lined with paper towels to drain. Serve with Orange Dipping Sauce.

ORANGE DIPPING SAUCE
1 (10-ounce) jar orange marmalade
3 tablespoons prepared horseradish
3 tablespoons Creole mustard

Combine the orange marmalade, horseradish and mustard in a bowl and mix well.

A Sunsational Encore
Junior League of Greater Orlando, Orlando, Florida

Shrimp with Cajun Rémoulade Sauce

Serves 4 to 8

RÉMOULADE SAUCE
1/2 cup mayonnaise
1 tablespoon lemon juice
2 teaspoons minced garlic
2 teaspoons minced shallot
1 tablespoon minced cilantro

1 tablespoon minced parsley
1 tablespoon minced chives
1/2 hard-cooked egg, chopped
1 tablespoon chopped capers
1 to 2 teaspoons Cajun seasoning
Cayenne, salt and pepper to taste

SHRIMP
3 garlic cloves, chopped
2 shallots, chopped
2 teaspoons lime juice

2 tablespoons minced basil
Salt and pepper to taste
Vegetable oil
1 to 2 pounds large uncooked shrimp, peeled

For the sauce, combine the mayonnaise, lemon juice, garlic, shallot, cilantro, parsley, chives, egg, capers, Cajun seasoning, cayenne, salt and pepper in a bowl and mix well.

For the shrimp, combine the garlic, shallots, lime juice, basil, salt and pepper in a shallow dish. Add enough oil to coat the shrimp and mix well. Add the shrimp, stirring to coat well. Marinate in the refrigerator for 3 hours or longer; drain.

Grill the shrimp until opaque and pink. Serve with the sauce.

Savor the Moment
The Junior League of Boca Raton, Boca Raton, Florida

The Esther Department, a women's Sunday School class at Park Cities Baptist Church in Dallas, Texas, created *For Such A Time As This* cookbook as a way to continue the vision of their church and contribute to the Community Life Center building campaign.

Shrimp with Red Onions and Capers

Serves 20

2 pounds medium peeled cooked shrimp
2 cups sliced red onions
7 or 8 bay leaves
2 1/2 tablespoons capers with liquid

Dash of Tabasco sauce
1 1/2 cups vegetable oil
3/4 cup vinegar
1 1/2 teaspoons celery seeds

Layer the shrimp and onion slices in a large bowl. Combine the bay leaves, capers, Tabasco sauce, oil, vinegar and celery seeds in a bowl and stir. Pour the dressing over the shrimp. Marinate, covered, in the refrigerator for 24 hours. Discard the bay leaves before serving. Serve with party rye bread.

Between the Lakes
The Junior League of Saginaw Valley, Saginaw, Michigan

Tangy Shrimp

Serves 12

1/2 cup extra-virgin olive oil
1/4 cup Dijon mustard or spicy mustard
1/4 cup minced curly parsley
1/4 cup chopped shallots
1/4 cup tarragon vinegar

2 teaspoons salt
1 teaspoon red pepper flakes
1 teaspoon freshly ground black pepper
1 1/2 pounds large shrimp, peeled and deveined

Combine the olive oil, Dijon mustard, parsley, shallots, vinegar, salt, red pepper flakes and black pepper in a bowl and mix well. Boil the shrimp in enough water or beer to cover in a saucepan for 1 minute; drain. Place the shrimp in a large nonreactive bowl.

Pour the olive oil mixture over the shrimp and toss to coat. Marinate, covered, in the refrigerator for 1 to 10 hours, stirring occasionally; drain. To serve, thread the shrimp onto short wooden skewers. The flavor of the shrimp is enhanced if allowed to marinate overnight.

An Occasion to Gather
The Junior League of Milwaukee, Milwaukee, Wisconsin

Tequila-Marinated Shrimp

Serves 10 to 12

1/4 cup olive oil
3 tablespoons finely chopped onion
5 garlic cloves, chopped
2 pounds fresh peeled shrimp

1/4 cup tequila
1/4 cup lime juice
1/8 teaspoon salt
2 tablespoons chopped fresh cilantro

Heat the olive oil in a large skillet over medium heat. Add the onion and garlic and sauté for 3 minutes or until tender. Add the shrimp and tequila and bring to a boil. Simmer for 3 to 5 minutes or just until the shrimp turn pink, stirring occasionally. Remove the shrimp mixture to a bowl. Add the lime juice, salt and cilantro and toss well. Chill, covered, for 2 hours to 24 hours, stirring occasionally. Drain before serving.

Recipes of Note
Greensboro Symphony Guild, Greensboro, North Carolina

Hot Artichoke Parmesan Squares

Makes 32 squares

1/2 cup drained and mashed water-packed
   artichoke bottoms
1 teaspoon seeded and minced jalapeño chile
   (use more for a spicier taste)
1 1/2 cups grated Parmesan cheese

1/2 cup mayonnaise
1/2 cup sour cream
2 teaspoons grated onion
8 slices white bread, crusts trimmed
Paprika

Lightly grease a baking sheet. Preheat the oven to 400 degrees. Purée the artichokes and the jalapeño chile in a food processor. Combine the artichoke purée, cheese, mayonnaise, sour cream and onion in a small bowl and mix well. Adjust the seasoning to taste. Cut each slice of bread into 4 squares. Place a heaping tablespoonful of the artichoke mixture on each of the small squares, keeping the squares together. Spread the artichoke mounds evenly over the entire slice. Separate the squares and place them on the prepared baking sheet. Repeat with the remaining slices. Bake until the topping is bubbly but not browned. Sprinkle with paprika and serve hot.

Tastes, Tales and Traditions
Palo Alto Auxiliary for Children, Palo Alto, California

Brie and Apricot Phyllo Bites

Makes 30 appetizers

1 (8-ounce) wedge Brie cheese, rind removed
30 frozen phyllo shells
1/2 cup (1 stick) butter, melted

2/3 cup apricot preserves
2 cups fresh or dried apricots, finely chopped
1/4 to 1/2 cup sliced almonds, or to taste

Preheat the oven to 350 degrees. Cut the Brie into thirty 1/2-inch cubes. Arrange the phyllo shells on a baking sheet. Brush the phyllo shells with the butter. Bake for 5 minutes. Remove from the oven and let cool on the baking sheet. Spoon 1 teaspoon of the apricot preserves into each shell. Place a piece of Brie in each prepared shell. Top with a small amount of the apricots and sprinkle with the almonds. Bake for 5 to 10 minutes or until the Brie is melted and beginning to brown. Serve warm.

EveryDay Feasts
The Junior League of Tampa, Tampa, Florida

Bleu Cheese Puffs

Makes 50 to 60 puffs

16 ounces cream cheese, softened
1 cup mayonnaise or light mayonnaise
3 to 4 ounces bleu cheese, crumbled
1 tablespoon minced onion

1/4 cup minced fresh chives or green onion tops
1/2 teaspoon (scant) cayenne pepper
2 loaves thinly sliced firm white bread
Paprika

Combine the cream cheese and mayonnaise in a bowl and mix well. Stir in the bleu cheese, onion, chives and cayenne pepper. Cut the bread into 1 1/2- to 2-inch rounds using a round cutter. Spread 1 tablespoon of the cream cheese mixture on each round. Arrange the rounds in a single layer on a baking sheet and freeze, covered, until firm. Preheat the oven to 350 degrees. Bake for 15 to 25 minutes or until brown and bubbly. Sprinkle with paprika and serve immediately.

Compliments of
The Woman's Exchange of Memphis, Memphis, Tennessee

Bruschetta

Serves 10 to 12

6 Roma tomatoes, seeded, finely chopped
6 to 8 basil leaves, minced
1 small red onion, finely chopped
2 small garlic cloves, minced

1/2 cup balsamic vinegar
1/4 cup extra-virgin olive oil
1 baguette, sliced

Combine the tomatoes, basil, onion, garlic, balsamic vinegar and olive oil in a bowl and mix gently. Chill, covered, in the refrigerator for up to 2 hours, stirring occasionally.

Slice the baguette into 1/4-inch slices, discarding the ends. Arrange the slices in a single layer on a baking sheet. Spray lightly with nonstick cooking spray or olive oil nonstick cooking spray. Toast at 375 degrees for 8 to 10 minutes or until light brown. Remove to a wire rack to cool. Serve the tomato mixture with the bruschetta. May substitute toast points or crackers for the baguette slices.

Cooking by the Bootstraps
The Junior Welfare League of Enid, Enid, Oklahoma

Tarpon Springs Stuffed Mushrooms

Makes 24 appetizers

1 (10-ounce) package frozen chopped spinach
1/2 cup Parmesan cheese, freshly grated
4 ounces feta cheese, rinsed and crumbled
1/2 cup whole green onion, finely chopped

1/2 cup parsley, finely chopped, or
    2 tablespoons dried parsley
Salt to taste
24 large fresh mushrooms, cleaned and stemmed

Preheat oven to 350 degrees. Thaw spinach in colander. Squeeze all moisture from spinach. In mixing bowl, combine all ingredients except mushroom caps; mix well. Fill mushroom caps; bake 20 minutes. Serve warm.

Tampa Treasures
The Junior League of Tampa, Tampa, Florida

In 1997, the Dallas County Medical Society Alliance and Foundation published *A Thyme to Remember* in honor of our organization's 80th anniversary. Honored as the "Official Millennium Celebration Cookbook of Dallas" by the mayor, it has raised almost $60,000 for the DCMSA Edith Cavell Nursing Scholarship Fund. Through this scholarship fund, the DCMSA has provided financial aid for nearly 1,350 nursing students in North Texas, reflecting a continuing commitment to responding to the nationwide nursing shortage of more than 100,000 nursing vacancies.

Mushroom Tartlets

Makes 30 tartlets

3 shallots, chopped
3 garlic cloves, minced
3 tablespoons butter
1 cup white mushrooms, finely chopped
1 cup portobello mushrooms, finely chopped
1 cup white wine

1 cup fresh flat-leaf parsley
1/2 cup whipping cream
Juice of 1/2 lemon
Salt and pepper to taste
2 packages frozen phyllo tartlet shells
   (about 30 shells)

Sauté the shallots and garlic in the butter in a saucepan. Add the mushrooms and cook until all of the liquid has evaporated. Add the wine. Reduce the heat and simmer for 15 minutes or until almost all of the wine has evaporated. Stir in the parsley, whipping cream and lemon juice. Cook until heated through. Season with salt and pepper. Let frozen shells stand for 10 minutes. Spoon the mushroom mixture into the shells. Place on a baking sheet. Bake at 350 degrees for 3 to 5 minutes.

Life Is Delicious
Hinsdale Junior Woman's Club, Hinsdale, Illinois

Mushroom Toastwists

Makes 4 dozen

1 cup cream of mushroom soup
1/2 cup black olives, chopped
2 green onions, finely chopped

1/8 teaspoon Worcestershire sauce
2 loaves of bread
1/2 cup (1 stick) butter, melted

Combine the soup, black olives, green onions and Worcestershire sauce in a bowl and mix well. Trim the crusts from the bread. Roll each slice of bread thin with a rolling pin. Place 1 teaspoon of the soup mixture on each slice of bread and roll up tightly to enclose the filling. Dip in the butter and place on a baking sheet lined with waxed paper. Freeze until firm. To serve, place the roll-ups on a baking sheet and bake at 350 degrees for 10 minutes or until crisp and golden brown.

Now Serving
The Junior League of Wichita Falls, Wichita Falls, Texas

Potato Cakes with Portobellos

2 1/2 pounds russet potatoes (about 6 potatoes)
Salt to taste
1 1/2 teaspoons marjoram, crushed
1 1/2 teaspoon tarragon, crushed
1 1/2 teaspoons basil, crushed
4 to 5 ounces portobello mushrooms, thickly sliced
3 tablespoons olive oil
Pepper to taste
1/2 cup sliced shallots
1/2 cup sliced leek bulb
1/4 cup (1/2 stick) butter
5 ounces prosciutto, thinly sliced, chopped
1 1/2 cups shredded Emmentaler or Gruyère cheese

Combine the potatoes and salt with enough water to cover in a saucepan. Bring to a boil. Boil for 30 minutes or until tender; drain. Cool for 15 minutes. Peel the potatoes and mash in a bowl. Stir in the marjoram, tarragon and basil.

Brush the mushrooms with 2 tablespoons of the olive oil. Season with salt and pepper. Arrange on a broiler rack in a broiler pan. Broil in a preheated oven for 5 to 8 minutes or until tender. Chop coarsely.

Heat the remaining 1 tablespoon olive oil in a skillet over high heat. Add the shallots and leek. Sauté until tender. Stir in the potato mixture. Add the mushrooms and stir gently. Shape the mixture by 1/2 cupfuls into 3- to 4-inch cakes.

Heat 2 tablespoons of the butter in a large skillet over medium-high heat until melted. Add the cakes in batches. Cook for 4 minutes per side or until golden brown, adding the remaining butter as needed. Remove the cakes with a slotted spoon to a lightly oiled baking sheet. Top each cake with prosciutto and sprinkle with cheese. Bake at 400 degrees in a preheated oven for 10 minutes or until the cheese melts. Arrange on a serving platter or on individual plates. Garnish with sprigs of fresh parsley or basil. Serve immediately.

Beginnings: A Collection of Appetizers
The Junior League of Akron, Inc., Akron, Ohio

Crisp Potato Skins and Assorted Toppers

Serves 6

3 medium russet potatoes
(about 2 pounds), scrubbed
1/4 cup melted butter

1 teaspoon soy sauce
Coarse salt (optional)

Bake the potatoes at 425 degrees for 1 hour. Let cool. Cut into quarters lengthwise; then cut into halves crosswise to form 8 sections. Scoop the pulp from each skin, leaving a 1/4-inch shell; reserve the pulp for another use. Increase the oven temperature to 500 degrees. Brush both sides of each potato skin with a mixture of melted butter and soy sauce. Place on a baking sheet. Bake for 10 to 12 minutes or until crisp. Sprinkle with coarse salt. Serve alone or with the following dips.

TAPENADE
1 cup minced pitted black olives
6 anchovy fillets, rinsed
2 tablespoons capers, drained

2 cloves of garlic, minced
2 tablespoons lemon juice
1 tablespoon red wine vinegar
1/4 cup (or more) olive oil

Mash the olives, anchovies, capers and garlic together in a bowl or food processor. Stir in the lemon juice and vinegar. Beat in the olive oil gradually until the mixture is thick and smooth.

CHUTNEY YOGURT SAUCE
1 cup plain yogurt
1 tablespoon curry powder

1 teaspoon lemon juice
1/4 cup minced mango chutney

Mix the yogurt, curry powder, lemon juice and chutney in a bowl. Chill thoroughly.

Beyond Burlap
The Junior League of Boise, Boise, Idaho

Mango Quesadillas

1 bell pepper, julienned
1 onion, sliced in rings
Juice of 1 lime
Eight 10-inch flour tortillas

1 large mango, papaya, or 2 peaches,
  peeled and sliced
1 cup (4 ounces) reduced-fat Monterey Jack
  cheese, grated

Coat skillet with vegetable oil cooking spray and sauté bell pepper and onion until soft. Squeeze lime over mixture and stir to blend. Place tortilla in a coated skillet. Layer 1/4 of the vegetable mixture, fruit slices and grated cheese on tortilla and top with another tortilla. Cook 1 minute on each side. Cut into 8 wedges. Serve 4 wedges per serving. Top with mango chutney and light sour cream.

River Road Recipes III: A Healthy Collection
The Junior League of Baton Rouge, Baton Rouge, Louisiana

Side Door Quesadillas

Olive oil
8 large flour tortillas
2 cups cubed grilled chicken
1 cup chopped pecans

1 cup thinly sliced green onions
2 cups shredded sharp Cheddar cheese
1 cup cubed Gorgonzola cheese
2 ripe pears, cored and thinly sliced

Brush olive oil on 1 side of each tortilla. Lay 4 tortillas, oiled side down, on a work surface. Top each with the chicken, pecans, green onions, Cheddar cheese, Gorgonzola cheese and pears. Top each with a tortilla, oiled side up. Cook the quesadillas in a skillet over medium heat until golden brown on both sides and the cheese is slightly melted. Remove to a cutting board and cut each quesadilla into quarters.

A League of Our Own: From Blue Jeans to Ball Gowns
Rockwall Women's League, Rockwall, Texas

Ella's Cheese Straws

Makes 200

1 cup butter
2 ½ cups sifted flour
1 teaspoon salt

½ teaspoon cayenne
16 ounces grated sharp Cheddar cheese

Mix all ingredients as for pie dough. Squeeze through a pastry bag for straws or roll into small balls. Place on ungreased cookie sheets and bake at 400 degrees until they begin to brown, 10 to 15 minutes.

Little Rock Cooks
The Junior League of Little Rock, Little Rock, Arkansas

Chicken Nut Pâté

Makes 1 quart

1 cup pecan halves
1 cup walnut halves
1 pound boneless, skinless chicken breast
　halves, cooked
2 cloves garlic
1 cup mayonnaise

2 tablespoons crystallized ginger, minced
1 tablespoon soy sauce
2 teaspoons Worcestershire sauce
1 teaspoon white wine vinegar
½ cup green onions, minced

In a food processor bowl with chopping blade, combine pecans and walnuts. Process until coarsely ground. Set aside. Cut chicken into cubes. Chop chicken and garlic in food processor until very fine. Add mayonnaise, ginger, soy sauce, Worcestershire sauce, and vinegar. Process by cycling on and off until well-processed. Stir in green onions and nuts. Spoon mixture into crock. Chill thoroughly, preferably overnight.

Note: Serve with crackers or bread sticks. This will keep 2 to 3 weeks in refrigerator and freezes well.

The Bess Collection
Junior Service League of Independence, Independence, Missouri

Smoked Catfish Pâté

1/2 cup water
1/2 cup vermouth
1 pound catfish fillets
16 ounces cream cheese, softened
1 clove of garlic, minced

2 tablespoons lemon juice
2 teaspoons Creole seasoning
1/2 to 1 teaspoon liquid smoke
Salt and pepper to taste

Combine the water and vermouth in a skillet or shallow saucepan, stirring to blend. Bring to a simmer; add the catfish. Poach, covered, until the fish flakes easily when probed with a fork; drain. Let cool. Combine the catfish, cream cheese, garlic, lemon juice, Creole seasoning and liquid smoke in a food processor or blender container; process at medium speed until smooth and creamy. Season with salt and pepper. Chill, covered, in the refrigerator for 12 to 24 hours. Serve with assorted crackers or toast.

A Thyme to Remember
The Dallas County Medical Society Alliance, Dallas, Texas

Baked Caramel Cinnamon Brie

1/2 cup (1 stick) butter
1/2 cup packed brown sugar
1/3 cup sugar
1/2 cup heavy cream
1/4 teaspoon nutmeg

1/4 teaspoon cinnamon
1 (12-ounce) round Brie cheese
2 tablespoons sliced almonds, toasted
1 baguette French bread, thinly sliced

Combine the butter, brown sugar and sugar in a saucepan. Cook over low heat until the butter melts and the sugars dissolve, stirring frequently. Add the heavy cream gradually, stirring constantly. Stir in the nutmeg and cinnamon. Cook until thickened, stirring constantly.

Place the Brie in a round baking pan and drizzle with the brown sugar mixture. Bake at 225 degrees in a preheated oven for 10 minutes or until the Brie is heated through. Remove from oven. Sprinkle with the almonds. Let stand for 5 to 10 minutes before serving. Garnish with fresh strawberries and/or Golden Delicious or Granny Smith apple slices. Serve with the sliced bread.

Beginnings: A Collection of Appetizers
The Junior League of Akron, Inc., Akron, Ohio

Kahlúa Pecan Brie

Serves 8

1 (15-ounce) round Brie cheese
½ cup chopped pecans

2 tablespoons Kahlúa
1 ½ tablespoons brown sugar

Remove the top rind of the cheese and arrange the round on a serving platter. Heat the pecans, liqueur and brown sugar in a saucepan until the brown sugar dissolves, stirring occasionally. Pour the brown sugar mixture over the cheese. Serve with sliced Granny Smith apples, assorted party crackers and/or gingersnaps.

Simply Sarasota
Junior League of Sarasota, Sarasota, Florida

French Quarter Cheese

Serves 10 to 12

1 package (8 ounces) cream cheese, softened
1 garlic clove, minced
1 tablespoon grated onion
4 tablespoons butter

¼ cup dark brown sugar
1 teaspoon Worcestershire sauce
½ teaspoon prepared mustard
1 cup finely chopped pecans

Combine cream cheese, garlic, and onion with a fork. Shape into 6×1-inch disk, place on a serving plate, and refrigerate. Combine remaining ingredients in a saucepan, heating until butter melts. Cover chilled cheese with nut mixture. Wrap and chill. Serve at room temperature with crackers.

Very Virginia
The Junior League of
Hampton Roads,
Hampton Roads, Virginia

Many of the women who formed the *Simply Sarasota* cookbook committee did so not only because they love to cook or thought it would be fun, but also because they know that our community benefits directly from projects by the Junior League of Sarasota. We don't just give money; we also send trained volunteers to make things happen with the money that we give. Many needs can't be met with money alone, but when combined with our organized and resourceful volunteers, incredible things happen.

The enthusiastic members of the JLS volunteer thousands of hours each year and have raised more than a million dollars to support community projects. These projects include a commitment to literacy in Sarasota public schools, improving local parks, and providing a safe place for children to play, including developing the first handicapped accessible playground in Sarasota County. Our mission, like that of other Junior Leagues around the world, is to promote volunteerism, develop the potential of women, and improve the community through the effective action and leadership of trained volunteers. Sales of *Simply Sarasota* are part of the solution for making this happen.

The Junior League of Sarasota, Florida

Hot Pecan Spread

Serves 6 to 8

8 ounces cream cheese
2 tablespoons milk
1 (2 1/2-ounce) jar dried beef, shredded
2 tablespoons onion flakes
1/4 teaspoon pepper

1/4 cup bell pepper, finely chopped
1/8 teaspoon garlic powder
1/2 cup sour cream
1/2 cup pecans, chopped
2 tablespoons butter

Blend cream cheese with milk. Add beef, onion flakes, seasonings and bell pepper. Fold in sour cream. Spread in shallow ovenproof dish. Heat pecans in butter and sprinkle over cheese mixture. Bake at 350 degrees for 30 minutes. Serve with Melba rounds.

Savannah Style
Junior League of Savannah, Savannah, Georgia

Uptown Fromage

Serves 12 to 16

16 ounces cream cheese
8 ounces goat cheese
2 garlic cloves, minced
1 1/2 tablespoons chopped fresh oregano
1/4 cup basil pesto

1/2 cup oil-pack sun-dried tomatoes, drained and chopped
1/4 cup pine nuts
2 baguettes, thinly sliced

Line a loaf pan with plastic wrap; tape is helpful in keeping the plastic wrap in place. Combine the cream cheese, goat cheese, garlic and oregano in a food processor and process until blended. Spread one-third of the cheese mixture over the bottom of the prepared loaf pan. Top with the pesto and spread with half the remaining cheese mixture. Sprinkle with the tomatoes and spread with the remaining cheese mixture.

Chill, covered, for 8 hours or longer. Invert the pan onto a serving plate and discard the plastic wrap. Sprinkle the top of the cheese loaf with the pine nuts, pressing lightly to ensure the pine nuts adhere. Garnish with sprigs of oregano. Serve with the baguette slices. Do not substitute feta cheese for the goat cheese.

Worth Tasting
Junior League of the Palm Beaches, West Palm Beach, Florida

Mediterranean Cheese Torte

Serves 15

PESTO
4 cups firmly packed fresh basil
4 garlic cloves
1/4 cup pine nuts

2 (scant) teaspoons salt
2/3 to 1 cup olive oil
1 cup (4 ounces) grated Parmesan cheese

TORTE
1/4 cup extra-light olive oil
2 cups oil-pack sun-dried tomatoes

16 ounces cream cheese, softened
1/3 cup milk

For the pesto, pulse the basil, garlic, pine nuts, salt and olive oil in a food processor just until the basil, garlic and pine nuts are chopped. Add the cheese and process until incorporated. You may reduce the amount of olive oil and process 1/4 cup butter into the mixture until incorporated.

For the torte, coat a decorative mold with 1/4 cup olive oil. Rinse the sun-dried tomatoes with hot water; drain and pat dry. Chop the sun-dried tomatoes. Place the cream cheese in a mixing bowl.

Add the milk gradually, beating constantly until of a spreadable consistency. Spread half the sun-dried tomatoes over the bottom of the mold. Layer with half the pesto and half the cream cheese mixture, spreading to the edge. Repeat the layers with the remaining sun-dried tomatoes, pesto and cream cheese mixture. Chill, covered, for at least 2 hours. Dip the mold into warm water and loosen the side. Unmold onto a serving plate. Bring to room temperature before serving. Garnish with additional sun-dried tomatoes and serve with assorted crackers.

Hint: Spraying the mold with a light spray of oil, or lining it with plastic wrap can make for an easier torte removal. Any leftovers are delicious as a sauce with bow tie, or your favorite pasta.

Popovers to Panache
The Village Club, Bloomfield Hills, Michigan

Walnut Stilton Torta

Serves 10

2 1/2 tablespoons butter
1/2 cup chopped walnuts
1/4 cup packed light brown sugar
1/8 teaspoon salt
16 ounces cream cheese, softened
1/2 cup (1 stick) butter, softened

1/4 cup port (sweet, white wine)
1 1/2 cups (6 ounces) crumbled Stilton cheese
1 cup seedless raspberry jam, at room temperature
1 bunch seedless red grapes for garnish
1/4 cup thinly sliced green onions for garnish

Melt 2 1/2 tablespoons butter in a small skillet over medium heat. Stir in the walnuts, brown sugar and salt and cook for 5 minutes or until the brown sugar dissolves and the mixture is bubbly, stirring frequently. Spread the walnut mixture in an even layer on a sheet of baking parchment. Let stand until cool and break into pieces.

Combine the cream cheese and 1/2 cup butter in a mixing bowl and beat at medium speed until blended. Add the wine and beat until smooth. Line a small ring mold or small round bowl with plastic wrap.

Spread 1 cup of the cream cheese mixture in the prepared mold and sprinkle with 3/4 cup of the Stilton cheese. Spread with 1/2 cup of the jam and sprinkle with 1/3 of the candied walnuts. Layer with 1 cup of the remaining cream cheese mixture, the remaining Stilton cheese, the remaining jam and 1/2 of the remaining candied walnuts. Spread with the remaining cream cheese mixture.

Chill, tightly covered with plastic wrap, for 8 hours or until set. Invert the torta onto a serving platter and sprinkle with the remaining candied walnuts. Garnish with the grapes and green onions and serve with toasted French bread slices.

Tables of Content
Junior League of Birmingham, Inc., Birmingham, Alabama

Inspired by research supporting playgrounds as key to both physical and mental agility and concerned by the childhood obesity issues facing our community and nation, The Junior League of Birmingham, Alabama, Inc., developed a playground project in coordination with the Board of Education, school teachers, principals, and many community partners. Our League has since pledged to continue its campaign by building five more playgrounds—one every year for the next five years— creating paradise for the children, one playground at a time. Each cookbook sold contributes to projects like these.

Junior League of Birmingham, Alabama

Blue Cheese Logs

16 ounces cream cheese, softened
1 (8-ounce) package sliced sharp Cheddar cheese,
    cut into pieces
8 ounces blue cheese, crumbled
1/2 small onion, chopped
4 1/2 teaspoons Worcestershire sauce

1/2 teaspoon cayenne pepper
1 cup finely chopped toasted pecans
1/2 cup finely chopped fresh parsley
1/2 cup finely chopped toasted pecans
1 cup finely chopped fresh parsley

Combine the cream cheese, Cheddar cheese, blue cheese, onion, Worcestershire sauce and cayenne pepper in a food processor. Pulse for 1 to 2 minutes, stopping often to scrape down the sides. Remove to a bowl and stir in 1 cup pecans and 1/2 cup parsley. Cover and chill for 1 hour. Shape into 4 (7-inch-long) logs. Mix 1/2 cup pecans and 1 cup parsley on waxed paper. Roll the logs in the pecan mixture to coat. Cover and chill. Serve with crackers.

Note: The cheese logs may be frozen. Thaw overnight in the refrigerator before serving.

For Such A Time As This: A Cookbook
Park Cities Baptist Church, Dallas, Texas

Islander Cheese Ball

16 ounces cream cheese, softened
8 ounces crushed pineapple, drained
2 tablespoons green onions, including
    tops, chopped

1/4 to 1/2 cup green pepper, chopped
2 teaspoons seasoned salt
2 cups pecans, chopped

Mix cream cheese and pineapple with mixer. Stir in onions, green pepper, salt and 1/2 cup pecans. Roll into one large ball, 2 logs or fill a scooped-out fresh pineapple half. Roll or top with remaining pecans. Serve with bacon-flavored crackers.

Virginia Hospitality
The Junior League of Hampton Roads, Hampton Roads, Virginia

Beef Bread Bowl Dip

1 (2-ounce) jar dried beef, chopped
8 ounces cream cheese, softened
1 cup sour cream

1 (4-ounce) can chopped green chiles
2 cups (8 ounces) shredded sharp Cheddar cheese
1 round loaf of Hawaiian or sourdough bread

Combine beef, cream cheese, sour cream, green chiles and Cheddar cheese in a bowl and mix well. Cut the top off the bread and reserve. Hollow out the bread to make a bowl, reserving the bread chunks. Spoon the beef mixture into the bread bowl and replace the top. Place on a baking sheet and bake at 325 degrees for 1 hour. Serve the reserved bread with the dip.

Add Another Place Setting
Junior League of Northwest Arkansas, Springdale, Arkansas

Hot Reuben Dip

Makes 5 cups

1 (14-ounce) can sauerkraut, drained
4 ounces cooked corned beef
1 small onion, finely chopped
1 cup mayonnaise
1 cup sour cream

1 cup shredded Swiss cheese
2 tablespoons prepared horseradish
1 teaspoon Dijon mustard (optional)
Party rye bread

Squeeze the excess moisture from the sauerkraut. Process the sauerkraut, corned beef and onion in a blender or food processor fitted with a steel blade until finely chopped. Combine the corned beef mixture, mayonnaise, sour cream, cheese, horseradish and Dijon mustard in a bowl and mix well.

Spoon the corned beef mixture into a 1-quart baking dish sprayed with nonstick cooking spray. Bake at 350 degrees in a preheated oven for 30 to 40 minutes or until bubbly. Serve with party rye bread. May use reduced-fat mayonnaise and reduced-fat sour cream.

Beginnings: A Collection of Appetizers
The Junior League of Akron, Inc., Akron, Ohio

Hot Virginia Dip

2 teaspoons butter
1 cup pecans, chopped
16 ounces cream cheese, softened
4 tablespoons milk

5 ounces dried beef, minced
1 teaspoon garlic salt
1 cup sour cream
4 teaspoons onion, minced

Sauté pecans in butter. Reserve. Mix all remaining ingredients thoroughly. Place in 1 1/2-quart baking dish; top with pecans. Chill until serving time. Bake at 350 degrees for 20 minutes. Serve hot with crackers or small bread sticks.

Virginia Hospitality
The Junior League of Hampton Roads, Hampton Roads, Virginia

Ranch Chicken Dip

8 ounces cream cheese, softened
1 envelope ranch salad dressing mix
1 (5-ounce) can chicken, drained

Combine the cream cheese, salad dressing mix and chicken in a mixing bowl and beat well. Serve with assorted crackers.

Down Home: Treasured Recipes from Our House to Yours
West Point Junior Auxiliary, West Point, Mississippi

West Point Junior Auxiliary is dedicated to the health and welfare of the children of West Point and Clay County, Mississippi. Our members submitted their favorite recipes and we published *Down Home: Treasured Recipes from Our House to Yours* as a way to finance our many projects. With the proceeds from our cookbook, we are able to reach the children of our community and make their lives a little brighter each day.

Chile con Queso

¹/₃ cup vegetable oil
¹/₂ cup finely chopped onion, or
   3 green onions, chopped
1 garlic clove, finely minced
1 tablespoon flour
³/₄ cup evaporated milk

1 tomato, chopped
3 tablespoons finely minced jalapeño chiles
1 pound processed cheese, cut into 1-inch cubes
¹/₂ cup mixed shredded Monterey Jack cheese and
   Cheddar cheese

Heat the oil in a heavy saucepan. Add the onion and garlic. Sauté until onion is tender. Stir in the flour. Stir in the evaporated milk gradually. Cook until mixture thickens slightly, stirring constantly. Add the tomato, jalapeño chiles, processed cheese, Monterey Jack and Cheddar cheeses. Cook for 5 minutes or until thickened and smooth, stirring constantly. This may be kept warm in a chafing dish over hot, not boiling, water. Leftover Chile con Queso is excellent on hamburgers, used in omelets or spooned over crisp tortillas for instant nachos.

A Taste of Enchantment
The Junior League of Albuquerque, Albuquerque, New Mexico

Savannah Sin

2 cups shredded Cheddar cheese
8 ounces cream cheese, softened
1¹/₂ cups sour cream
¹/₂ cup chopped cooked ham

¹/₃ cup chopped green onions
¹/₃ cup chopped green chiles (optional)
¹/₈ teaspoon Worcestershire sauce
1 (1-pound) round loaf French bread

Combine the Cheddar cheese, cream cheese, sour cream, ham, green onions, green chiles and Worcestershire sauce in a bowl and mix well. Cut a thin slice from the top of the bread loaf; reserve. Remove the center carefully, leaving a shell. Cut the bread from the center into 1-inch cubes. Fill the bread shell with the dip; top with the reserved top. Wrap in foil. Bake at 350 degrees for 1 hour. Serve with the bread cubes, crackers or chips.

Downtown Savannah Style
The Junior League of Savannah, Savannah, Georgia

Savory Artichoke and Spinach Dip

Serves 8 to 12

1 (10-ounce) package frozen chopped spinach,
    thawed, drained
1 1/4 cups coarsely grated Parmesan cheese
1 cup mayonnaise

1 garlic clove, crushed
8 to 10 artichoke hearts, coarsely chopped
Chopped green onions (optional)
Butter crackers

Squeeze the excess moisture from the spinach. Combine the cheese, mayonnaise, garlic, artichokes and spinach in the order listed in a bowl, mixing well after each addition. Spoon into an ungreased quiche dish or baking dish and press lightly. Bake at 325 degrees in a preheated oven for 25 to 30 minutes or until brown and bubbly. Sprinkle with chopped green onions. Serve warm with butter crackers.

Beginnings: A Collection of Appetizers
The Junior League of Akron, Inc., Akron, Ohio

Corn Dip

Serves 12

2 cups shredded medium Cheddar cheese
1 (4-ounce) can chopped green chiles
2 tablespoons chopped jalapeños
2 tablespoons dried chopped cilantro
1/2 cup mayonnaise

1 cup sour cream
1/2 teaspoon Tabasco sauce
2 (11-ounce) cans whole kernel corn, drained
Salt to taste

Combine the cheese, green chiles, jalapeños, cilantro, mayonnaise, sour cream and Tabasco sauce in a large bowl and mix well. Stir in the corn and salt. Chill for 8 hours or longer. Serve with corn chips.

Apron Strings
The Junior League of Little Rock, Little Rock, Arkansas

Roasted Corn Guacamole

6 tablespoons corn oil
2 cups frozen corn kernels, thawed
6 avocados, chopped
4 tomatoes, chopped
1/4 cup minced red onion
1/2 cup chopped cilantro

1/4 cup lime juice
2 teaspoons minced jalapeño pepper
2 teaspoons minced garlic
2 teaspoons apple cider vinegar
1/4 teaspoon cumin
1 tablespoon kosher salt

Spread 2 tablespoons of the corn oil on a baking sheet and add the corn. Roast at 450 degrees for 8 minutes. Transfer to a mixing bowl. Add the remaining 4 tablespoons corn oil, avocados, tomatoes, onion, cilantro, lime juice, jalapeño pepper, garlic, vinegar, cumin and kosher salt to the corn in the order listed and mix well. Chill until serving time. Serve with round tortilla chips.

Lone Star to Five Star
The Junior League of Plano, Plano, Texas

Vidalia Onion Dip

1 cup coarsely chopped Vidalia onions
1 cup mayonnaise
1 cup grated sharp Cheddar cheese

Paprika
Corn chips, tortilla chips or crackers

Combine onions, mayonnaise and cheese; pour into a 1-quart baking dish. Sprinkle with paprika and bake, uncovered, in a preheated oven at 350 degrees for 25 minutes. Serve with corn chips, tortilla chips or crackers.

A Southern Collection Then and Now
The Junior League of Columbus, Columbus, Georgia

A Southern Collection Then and Now benefits programs within our organization's focus of parenting and children's welfare.

Black Bean Salsa

2 cups canned black beans, cooked, drained
1/2 cup canned corn
1 avocado, chopped
1/2 cup chopped red bell pepper
1/2 cup chopped red onion
1 or 2 jalapeño chiles, seeded, chopped

2 to 3 tablespoons extra-virgin olive oil
1/2 cup finely chopped fresh cilantro
3 to 4 tablespoons lime juice, or to taste
Salt and pepper to taste
Blue tortilla chips or toasted pita wedges

Combine the beans, corn, avocado, red pepper, onion, jalapeños, olive oil and cilantro in a bowl and mix well. Stir in the lime juice. Season with salt and pepper. Serve with tortilla chips or pita wedges.

Beginnings: A Collection of Appetizers
The Junior League of Akron, Inc., Akron, Ohio

First-Prize Bean Salsa

1 (15-ounce) can black beans
1 (15-ounce) can white Northern beans
1 (15-ounce) can pinto beans
1 (15-ounce) can garbanzo beans or chickpeas
1 (15-ounce) can black-eyed peas
1 (15-ounce) can white hominy
1 (15-ounce) can yellow hominy or whole kernel
    yellow corn
2 tomatoes, chopped and drained
2 avocados, cut into small pieces

1 red onion, chopped
1/2 green bell pepper, chopped
1/2 red or yellow bell pepper, chopped
1 cup chopped celery
1 (16-ounce) bottle Italian salad dressing
3/4 cup honey, at room temperature
2 tablespoons yellow mustard
Salt and coarsely ground pepper to taste
1 avocado, sliced

Rinse and drain the beans, peas and hominy and place in a large bowl. Add the tomatoes, two avocados, the onion, bell peppers and celery and mix gently. Combine the salad dressing, honey, mustard, salt and pepper in a bowl and blend until smooth. Pour over the vegetable mixture and mix gently. Cover and chill in the refrigerator until ready to serve. To serve, garnish with one sliced avocado and serve with tortilla chips.

Note: The salsa may be stored in the refrigerator for up to one week, but is best served the same day.

A Thyme to Entertain
Junior League of Annapolis, Inc., Annapolis, Maryland

Caribbean Salsa

Makes 18 (1/4-cup) servings

1 (15-ounce) can black beans, drained and rinsed
1 each ripe papaya and mango, peeled and
  finely chopped (1/2 cup each)
1 cup finely chopped pineapple
3/4 cup pineapple juice
1/2 cup fresh lime juice (about 4 limes)
1/2 cup finely chopped red bell pepper

1/2 cup finely chopped green bell pepper
1/2 cup finely chopped red onion
1/2 cup cilantro, chopped
1 1/2 teaspoons ground cumin
1/4 teaspoon kosher salt
1/4 teaspoon pepper

Combine the beans, papaya, mango, pineapple, pineapple juice, lime juice, bell peppers, onion and cilantro in a bowl and mix well. Stir in the cumin, salt and pepper. Chill, covered, in the refrigerator.

Tables of Content
Junior League of Birmingham, Inc., Birmingham, Alabama

Jackson County Caviar

Serves 12

2 (4-ounce) cans chopped black olives
2 (4-ounce) cans chopped green chiles
2 tomatoes, peeled, chopped
3 green onions, chopped
1 tablespoon olive oil

2 cloves of garlic, minced
2 teaspoons red wine vinegar
1 teaspoon pepper
1/8 teaspoon seasoned salt

Combine the olives, chiles, tomatoes, green onions, olive oil, garlic, vinegar, pepper and seasoned salt in a bowl and mix well. Chill, covered, for several hours. Serve with chips.

If You Can't Stand the Heat, Get Out of the Kitchen
Junior Service League of Independence, Independence, Missouri

Roasted Red Pepper, Corn and Black Bean Salsa

Makes 6 cups

2 (15-ounce) cans black beans,
   drained and rinsed
1 (15-ounce) can corn, drained and rinsed
1 1/2 cups hot thick salsa
3 green onions, sliced

1 large red bell pepper
6 to 8 ounces canned tomato juice
1/2 cup minced fresh cilantro
Salt to taste

Combine the beans, corn, salsa and green onions in a bowl and mix well. Place the bell pepper on a baking sheet and broil until the skin is blistered and charred, turning frequently. Remove the bell pepper to a glass bowl and let stand, covered, until cool. Peel and seed the bell pepper. Chop into 1/2-inch pieces. Add the roasted bell pepper and tomato juice to the bean mixture and mix well. Stir in the cilantro. Chill, covered, for 1 hour or for up to 2 days. Stir and season with salt. Serve with tortilla chips.

Worth Tasting
Junior League of the Palm Beaches, West Palm Beach, Florida

Cranberry Salsa

Makes 2 cups

1 (12-ounce) package fresh cranberries
4 or 5 green onions, chopped
1 jalapeño chile, seeded and chopped

1/2 cup sugar
Grated zest and juice of 2 limes
1/4 teaspoon salt

Place the cranberries in a food processor and pulse until coarsely chopped. Add the green onions and jalapeño chile and pulse several more times. Add the sugar, lime zest, lime juice and salt and pulse until combined. Chill, covered, for 24 hours to enhance the flavor. Serve with tortilla chips.

Mardi Gras to Mistletoe
Junior League of Shreveport-Bossier, Shreveport, Louisiana

Fruit Salsa

1 cup strawberries, finely chopped
1 orange, peeled and finely chopped
2 large kiwifruit, peeled and finely chopped
1/2 cup chopped fresh pineapple, or
    1 (8-ounce) can crushed
    pineapple, drained

1/4 cup thinly sliced green onions
1/4 cup finely chopped yellow bell pepper or
    green bell pepper
1 fresh jalapeño chile, seeded and chopped
    (optional)
1 tablespoon lime juice or lemon juice

Combine the strawberries, orange, kiwifruit, pineapple, green onions, bell pepper, jalapeño chile and lime juice in a bowl and stir to mix. Chill, covered, for 6 to 24 hours. Serve with Cinnamon Crisps (below). Note: If you plan to chill the salsa for more than 6 hours, stir in the strawberries just before serving.

Cinnamon Crisps

Makes 32 triangles

Cut each of four 8-inch flour tortillas into eight triangles. Lightly coat both sides of each triangle with nonstick cooking spray. Lightly brush each side with a mixture of 1 tablespoon water and 1/2 teaspoon vanilla extract. Sprinkle each side with a mixture of 1/4 cup sugar and 1 teaspoon ground cinnamon. Place on a baking sheet and bake at 400 degrees for 8 to 10 minutes or until light brown.

Now Serving
The Junior League of Wichita Falls, Wichita Falls, Texas

When we decided to tackle a third cookbook to coincide with our 50th anniversary celebration for the Junior League of Wichita Falls, we knew we had big shoes to fill. The two previous books, published in 1961 and 1977, were tremendously successful. However, we had no idea just how successful until we began the search for a copy of the first book, *Discoveries in Dining*. Several people were quick to respond that they had a copy of the coveted cookbook, but no one was willing to part with it—except one woman who said she would leave it to the League in her will! She was serious! We only hope that in 45 years someone will be saying the same thing about *Now Serving*.

Grape Salsa

Serves a crowd

1 bunch seedless green grapes, cut into halves
1 bunch seedless red grapes, cut into halves
1 pint grape tomatoes
1/2 to 1 purple onion, chopped
1/2 green bell pepper, chopped
1/2 red, yellow or orange bell pepper, chopped

1 bunch cilantro, stems removed and chopped
3 garlic cloves, finely chopped
1 jalapeño chile, seeded and chopped
Juice of 3 limes
Olive oil to taste

Combine the grapes, tomatoes, onion, bell peppers, cilantro, garlic and jalapeño chile in a bowl and mix well. Add the lime juice and olive oil and toss to coat. Let stand at room temperature for 1 hour. Serve as an appetizer with corn chips or as a side salad.

River Road Recipes IV: Warm Welcomes
Junior League of Baton Rouge, Baton Rouge, Louisiana

Bunco Jumble

Makes handfuls of fun

1 box mini Ritz peanut butter sandwich crackers
1 cup dry roasted peanuts
1 (12-ounce) bag mini pretzel sticks or twists
1 cup sugar
1/2 cup (1 stick) butter

1/2 cup light corn syrup
2 tablespoons vanilla extract
1 teaspoon baking soda
1 (10-ounce) package mini or regular "M&M's" chocolate candies

Combine the sandwich crackers, peanuts and pretzels in a large roasting pan. Heat the sugar, butter and corn syrup in a saucepan over medium-high heat. Bring to a boil and cook for 5 minutes, stirring frequently. Stir in the vanilla and baking soda. Pour over the cracker mixture, stirring to coat well. Bake at 250 degrees for 45 minutes, stirring the mixture every 15 minutes. Remove to waxed paper to let cool completely. Add the chocolate candies. Break up the mixture into small pieces as necessary.

The Life of the Party
The Junior League of Tampa, Tampa, Florida

Portage Trail Mix

1 (12-ounce) package Crispix cereal
1 (16-ounce) jar dry-roasted peanuts
1 (16-ounce) package small pretzels

2 cups packed brown sugar
1 cup (2 sticks) margarine
1/2 cup light corn syrup

Combine the cereal, peanuts and pretzels in a roasting pan and toss to mix well. Combine the brown sugar, margarine and corn syrup in a saucepan. Bring to a boil, stirring occasionally. Boil for 1 1/2 minutes, stirring occasionally. Pour over the cereal mixture, stirring until coated. Bake at 350 degrees in a preheated oven for 15 minutes, stirring 3 or 4 times. Spread the cereal mixture in a thin layer on a sheet of waxed paper. Let stand until cool.

Beginnings: A Collection of Appetizers
The Junior League of Akron, Inc., Akron, Ohio

Pecans with a Punch

1/2 cup sugar
1/4 cup Jack Daniel's Old No. 7 sour mash whiskey
1 teaspoon chili powder

1 teaspoon salt
3/4 teaspoon cayenne pepper
2 cups pecan halves

Combine the sugar, whiskey, chili powder, salt and cayenne pepper in a saucepan. Cook over medium heat until the sugar dissolves, stirring frequently. Bring to a boil and boil gently for 3 minutes, stirring occasionally. Add the pecans, stirring to coat well. Spread in a single layer on a baking sheet lined with buttered foil. Bake at 250 degrees for 15 to 20 minutes or until toasted and glazed. Let stand until cool.

Oh My Stars!
The Junior League of Roanoke Valley, Roanoke, Virginia

Best Tea Punch

Makes 1 gallon

2 cups water
2 cups sugar
8 tea bags, or 2 family-size tea bags
2 cups orange juice

⅔ cup lemon juice
2 quarts cold water
Sprigs of mint

Combine 2 cups water and the sugar in a saucepan and bring to a boil. Boil for 5 minutes. Remove from the heat and add the tea bags to the sugar syrup. Steep for 5 to 10 minutes. Pour the tea mixture into a 1-gallon pitcher and squeeze the tea bags to remove any remaining tea. Discard the tea bags. Add the orange juice, lemon juice and 2 quarts cold water and mix well. Add enough ice to fill the pitcher. Pour into glasses and garnish each serving with a sprig of mint.

Mardi Gras to Mistletoe
Junior League of Shreveport-Bossier, Shreveport, Louisiana

Southern Citrus Punch

Serves 10 to 12

6 lemons
4 navel orange
2 (6-ounce) cans frozen lemonade concentrate
1 (6-ounce) can frozen orange juice concentrate
2 liters lemon-lime soda
1 liter sweet bourbon
1 star fruit, thinly sliced

Slice the lemons very thin and layer to fit the size of the punch bowl opening. Place on a baking sheet lined with plastic wrap. Slice the oranges very thin and also layer to fit the punch bowl on a second baking sheet lined with plastic wrap. Freeze for 2 to 2½ hours or until firm.

Combine the frozen lemonade concentrate and frozen orange juice concentrate in a large punch bowl. Add the lemon-lime soda, bourbon and several handfuls of ice and stir until the concentrates are well mixed. Arrange the frozen fruit over the top of the punch. Add the thinly sliced star fruit. Ladle into punch cups to serve.

Savor the Moment
The Junior League of Boca Raton, Boca Raton, Florida

Milk Punch

Serves 1

²/₃ glass sweet milk
1 large tablespoon brandy or whiskey

Crushed ice
Nutmeg

Fill large glass ²/₃ full of sweet milk. Add brandy or whiskey. Fill remainder of glass with crushed ice and pour into shaker, shaking until foamy. Sprinkle a pinch of grated nutmeg on top.

River Road Recipes: The Textbook of Louisiana Cuisine
The Junior League of Baton Rouge, Baton Rouge, Louisiana

Bay Point Milk Punch

Serves 4

Vanilla ice cream
6 ounces brandy
2 ounces light crème de cacao

Ice
Nutmeg

Fill blender 3/4 full with ice cream. Add brandy and crème de cacao and fill blender to the top with ice. Blend. Pour into glasses and sprinkle each with nutmeg.

A Southern Collection Then and Now
The Junior League of Columbus, Columbus, Georgia

Pirate's Milk Punch

Makes 1 gallon (16 servings)

1 cup sugar
1 cup high-quality bourbon (do not use
    sour mash bourbon)
1 cup French brandy (such as Cognac)
1 cup high-quality vodka

2 ounces pure vanilla extract (do not use
    imitation vanilla)
1 teaspoon freshly grated nutmeg
Whole milk

Combine the sugar, bourbon, brandy and vodka in a gallon container with a lid. An empty gallon milk jug will work. Secure the lid and shake vigorously until the sugar is dissolved. Add the vanilla and nutmeg; shake well. Add the milk, 2 cups at a time, until the jug is full; shaking well after each addition. Chill for 8 to 24 hours before serving. Serve very cold or over ice in old-fashioned glasses. Sprinkle freshly grated nutmeg over the top before serving.

The Life of the Party
The Junior League of Tampa, Tampa, Florida

Orange Sangria

Makes 6 cups

1 orange
1/2 cup sugar
Juice of 2 limes

2 cups fresh orange juice
1 (750-milliliter) bottle dry red wine
1/2 cup Cointreau or Triple Sec

Cut the orange into halves. Cut several thin slices from one half and reserve for the garnish. Remove a thin layer of the outer peel of the other orange half with a vegetable peeler. Combine the peel with the sugar in a bowl and bruise with the back of a spoon to release the oils. Add the lime juice, orange juice, wine and orange liqueur. Pour into a pitcher and chill, covered, in the refrigerator, removing the orange peel after 15 minutes. Garnish with the orange slices and serve over ice, if desired.

The Bells are Ringing: A Call to Table
Mission San Juan Capistrano Women's Guild, San Juan Capistrano, California

Ultimate Sangria

Makes about 4 1/2 quarts

3 liters red wine (cabernet sauvignon)
2 cups sugar
6 to 8 ounces plain brandy
2 large lemons, thinly sliced

2 large oranges, thinly sliced
2 large apples, sliced
1 to 2 liters citrus-flavor bubbly water (orange or
    lemon preferred)

Mix the wine, sugar, brandy, lemons, oranges and apples in a large container. Chill, covered, for 18 to 24 hours, stirring occasionally. Just before serving, stir again and taste, adding additional sugar or brandy if desired. It should have a fairly strong flavor and be fairly sweet, almost syrupy. Add 1 liter of the bubbly water, stirring until the sangria has a thinner, more wine-like consistency and adding additional bubbly water as needed. Pour into glasses.

California Sol Food
Junior League of San Diego, Inc., San Diego, California

Sparkling White Sangria

Serves 6

1 small lemon
1 small orange
1 bottle (750 ml) dry white wine
$1/2$ cup canned pineapple chunks, drained
1 fresh peach, sliced, or $1/2$ cup canned sliced
    peaches, drained

$1/2$ cup Cognac
$1/4$ cup sugar
7 ounces club soda
Small ice cubes or ice ring

At least one hour before serving: Cut lemon and orange in half. Squeeze half of each into a pitcher; thinly slice the other halves. Add fruit slices, wine, pineapple, peaches, Cognac and sugar to pitcher. Stir gently to dissolve sugar. Cover pitcher; refrigerate 1 hour.

When ready to serve: Add club soda and ice. Serve very cold with pieces of fruit in each glass. Note: More fruit can be added, such as strawberries, seedless red grapes or unpeeled red apple slices.

Tampa Treasures
The Junior League of Tampa, Tampa, Florida

Wedding Punch

Serves 100

1 (16-ounce) can frozen orange juice concentrate
1 (12-ounce) can frozen lemonade concentrate
1 (6-ounce) can frozen limeade concentrate

2 (46-ounce) cans unsweetened pineapple juice
$2 1/2$ quarts water
2 quarts ginger ale

Combine all juices. Ginger ale should be added just before serving. An ice ring may be made with the juices (all except ginger ale) several days before serving. Slices of fruit and mint leaves may be frozen in ring. Use a ring mold or a bundt pan.

Stir Ups
The Junior Welfare League of Enid, Enid, Oklahoma

Jo Vincent's Wedding Punch

Makes 2 gallons

1/2 gallon bourbon (or vodka)
1/2 gallon white port
2 large cans frozen lemonade (undiluted)
5 bottles soda water ice ring—optional

Combine first 3 ingredients and chill. Add chilled soda water just before serving. May serve from punch bowl with floating ice ring or from a pitcher.

Charleston Receipts Repeats
The Junior League of Charleston, Charleston, South Carolina

Dr. Scott's Postpartum Cosmos

Makes a variable amount

Cracked ice
2 parts vodka
1 part cointreau or Grand Marnier
1 part cranberry juice
Juice of 1 lime wedge

Place cracked ice in a cocktail shaker. Pour the vodka, Cointreau, cranberry juice and lime juice over the ice. Place the lid on the cocktail shaker. Wrap in a bar towel and shake vigorously for 30 seconds. Strain into chilled glasses. Serve immediately to chase away those postpartum blues.

Roux To Do
Junior League of Greater Covington, Covington, Louisiana

Mint Julep

Rinds of 12 lemons, juice removed
4 quarts water
2 handfuls fresh mint
Juice from the 12 lemons
2 1/2 to 3 cups sugar
Bourbon

Syrup: Simmer the first 3 ingredients for 15 minutes, but do not boil. Strain and discard the mint and rinds. To the remaining syrup add the juice from 12 lemons and 2 1/2 to 3 cups sugar. Add a small amount of bourbon to syrup and pour into chilled julep cups packed with ice.

A Taste of Georgia
Newnan Junior Service League, Newnan, Georgia

Kentucky's Hard Lemonade

1 (12-ounce) can frozen lemonade concentrate or
    pink lemonade concentrate, thawed
2 (12-ounce) cans beer
1 1/2 cups vodka

Mix the lemonade concentrate and beer in a large container. Add the vodka and mix well. Chill until serving time. Pour over ice in glasses.

Home Again, Home Again
The Junior League of Owensboro, Owensboro, Kentucky

After twenty-five years, *A Taste of Georgia* is considered a timeless classic among community cookbooks and continues to provide its readers with a unique insight into the delights and traditions that make Georgia a place of gracious hospitality and fine cooking.

Cranberry Margaritas

3/4 cup tequila
1/4 cup Triple Sec
1 cup frozen cranberry juice concentrate
3 cups crushed ice

Lime wedges
Kosher salt
Lime slices
Cranberries

Process the tequila, Triple Sec, cranberry juice concentrate and crushed ice in a blender until smooth. Rub the rims of margarita glasses with lime wedges and dip in kosher salt. Pour the mixture into the prepared glasses. Garnish with lime slices and cranberries.

Roux To Do
Junior League of Greater Covington, Covington, Louisiana

Killer Margaritas

2 cups tequila
1/2 cup fresh lime juice
1 cup water
1/4 cup Grand Marnier

1 1/2 cups sweet-and-sour mix
1 1/2 cups margarita mix
8 to 10 lime wedges

GARNISH
8 to 10 lime wedges or slices

Combine the tequila, lime juice, water, Grand Marnier, sweet-and-sour mix and margarita mix in a pitcher and mix well. Pour over ice in glasses. Squeeze the juice of 1 lime wedge into each glass and garnish with additional lime.

Notably Nashville
Junior League of Nashville, Nashville, Tennessee

Frozen Lemon Drop Martini

Serves 4

1 cup water
3/4 cup sugar
1/2 cup fresh lemon juice
1 large sprig of mint, finely chopped

1 cup lemon-flavored vodka
1/4 cup sparkling water
Sprigs of mint for garnish
1 tablespoon grated lemon zest for garnish

Bring the water and sugar to a boil in a small saucepan and boil for 3 minutes to make a simple syrup, stirring occasionally. Let stand until cool. Combine the simple syrup, lemon juice and chopped mint in a bowl and mix well. Pour the lemon mixture into sealable freezer bags and freeze for 1 hour or longer. Process the frozen mixture, vodka and sparkling water in a blender until blended and pour evenly into 4 sugar-rimmed martini or margarita glasses. Garnish with additional sprigs of mint and the lemon zest.

Tables of Content
Junior League of Birmingham, Inc., Birmingham, Alabama

Louisiana Mint Mojitos

Serves 8

32 sprigs of mint, stems removed (about 1 bunch)
2 cups fresh lime juice
1 cup sugar

2 cups light rum
2 cups club soda

Combine the mint, lime juice and sugar in a large pitcher. Crush the mint mixture with a wooden spoon or pestle. Add the rum and club soda and mix well. Immediately pour over crushed ice in glasses. Garnish with sugar cane stalks.

River Road Recipes IV: Warm Welcomes
The Junior League of Baton Rouge, Baton Rouge, Louisiana

Vodka Sipper

1 to 2 cups sugar
9 cups water
1 can (12 ounces) frozen orange juice concentrate
1 can (12 ounces) frozen lemonade concentrate

3 cups vodka
2 bottles (2 liters each) lemon-lime
  carbonated beverage
Fresh mint sprigs for garnish

Boil sugar and water together until sugar is dissolved. Cool slightly, then add frozen orange juice and lemonade concentrates and vodka, mixing well. Put in covered container and store in freezer. To serve, fill each glass halfway with frozen mixture, and continue filling with carbonated beverage. Garnish each glass with a mint sprig.

Very Virginia
The Junior League of Hampton Roads, Hampton Roads, Virginia

Café Finale

1 cup Cognac
1 cup brandy
1 cup coffee liqueur
1 cup extra-strong coffee
1 lemon, cut into halves

1/4 cup superfine sugar
1 cup whipping cream, whipped
1/8 teaspoon cinnamon
1 tablespoon grated dark chocolate

Combine the Cognac, brandy, coffee liqueur and coffee in a pitcher and stir gently. Let stand at room temperature for 8 hours or longer. Rub the rims of 6 microwave-safe burgundy wine goblets with the lemon. Dip the moist rims into the sugar and gently shake out any excess sugar that has fallen into the goblets. Stir the Cognac mixture gently and pour into the goblets. Microwave on High just until the coffee begins to boil. Top each with whipped cream. Sprinkle with the cinnamon and chocolate. Serve immediately.

Art Fare
Toledo Museum of Art Aides, Toledo, Ohio

Whispers

1 quart coffee ice cream
1/2 ounce brandy
1/2 ounce crème de cocoa

Pack enough of the ice cream into a blender to fill three-fourths full. Add the brandy and liqueur and process until of a liquid consistency. Pour the ice cream mixture into a freezer container and freeze until firm. Serve in small goblets.

Simply Sarasota
Junior League of Sarasota, Sarasota, Florida

Fireside Coffee

Makes 35 (3-tablespoon) servings

2 cups fat-free coffee creamer
1 1/2 cups hot cocoa mix
1 1/2 cups instant coffee granules
1 1/2 cups sugar
1 teaspoon cinnamon
1/2 teaspoon nutmeg

Combine the creamer, cocoa mix, coffee granules, sugar, cinnamon and nutmeg in a bowl and mix well. Store in an airtight container. Combine 3 tablespoons of the coffee mix with 1 cup boiling water in a mug for each serving.

A Taste of the Good Life: From the Heart of Tennessee
Saint Thomas Hospital, Nashville, Tennessee

Breads and Brunch

"'Helping Others to Help Themselves.' For nearly three-quarters of a century, this motto has been invisibly emblazoned on every Christening gown, every gooseneck bib, and every Tea Room treat sold at The Woman's Exchange of Memphis. Through the years, wherever the location, whatever the period in history, the goal of the membership of The Woman's Exchange, originally known as The Craft's Exchange, has been to provide a suitable outlet for men and women to display and sell their crafts, and thus enrich life for themselves and their families.

The consignors, the seamstresses, and the customers who benefit from the one-of-a kind treasures sold at The Exchange are as different as roses in a summer garden. Bama Watts sewed for The Woman's Exchange for more than a half century. For her 100th birthday, she gave The Woman's Exchange a gift of an exquisite Christening gown, made of batiste with French Val lace and over seventy handmade tucks. The glory of this gift was not only its beauty and that it was hand sewn with her aged fingers, but that she was blind. This gown is now framed and proudly displayed in our shop. Bama's daughter and granddaughter carry on her legacy today as seamstress consignors with The Exchange.

Our membership roster also includes daughters and granddaughters of the founding women. Dedication and commitment to the founders' vision are at the very roots of this organization and its volunteer members.

Providing a venue for local and national artisans is costly at the very least. Self-published cookbooks have been a valuable source of revenue for us and many other charitable groups. Compiling, testing, and selecting recipes becomes a community effort, encouraging the participation of the membership. New friendships are forged, old acquaintances are renewed, and lasting bonds are cemented.

All proceeds from the sales of our four cookbooks have allowed us to continue to extend help to those in need and to better the lives of the deserving. With the passing of time, we live and work by our motto 'Helping Others to Help Themselves.'"

Mary Ann Stevens
Woman's Exchange of Memphis, Tennessee

Apple Cheddar Corn Bread

Serves 9

1 cup cornmeal
1 cup flour
1/2 cup sugar
1 tablespoon baking powder
1 egg

1/4 cup melted butter
1 cup milk
2 small tart red apples, chopped
1/2 cup shredded Cheddar cheese

Preheat the oven to 425 degrees; grease a 9-inch square baking pan, iron muffin pan or iron skillet. Combine the cornmeal, flour, sugar and baking powder in a large bowl, whisking to mix well. Beat the egg, butter and milk in the large mixer bowl of an electric mixer at medium speed until well blended. Add the flour mixture; stir just until moistened. Stir in the apples and cheese. Pour into the pan. Bake for 20 to 25 minutes or until a cake tester inserted in the center comes out clean. Cool in the pan on a wire rack.

A Thyme to Remember
The Dallas County Medical Society Alliance, Dallas, Texas

Gougère

Serves 7

1 cup milk
1/4 cup (1/2 stick) butter
1/2 teaspoon salt
Dash of cayenne pepper

1 cup all-purpose flour
4 eggs
1 cup (4 ounces) shredded Swiss or Gruyére cheese

Combine the milk, butter, salt and cayenne pepper in a saucepan. Bring to a boil over medium heat. Add the flour all at once. Cook for 2 minutes or until the mixture pulls away from the side of the saucepan, stirring constantly with a vigorous motion. Remove from the heat and cool slightly. Beat in the eggs one at a time. Beat by hand until the mixture is smooth and shiny. Beat in half the cheese. Let cool to room temperature. Reserve one-fourth of the dough. Spoon seven equal portions of the remaining dough in a connected circle on a greased baking sheet.

Make seven equal-size balls from the reserved dough and place one ball on top of each mound. Sprinkle the mounds with the remaining cheese. Bake at 375 degrees on the middle rack of the oven for 45 to 55 minutes or until crisp and golden brown. Do not open the oven door while baking. Serve hot with butter.

Note: The baked gougère can be stored in an airtight container. Crisp in a 300-degree oven just before serving.

Popovers to Panache
The Village Club, Bloomfield Hills, Michigan

Grilled Bread with Rosemary Butter

Serves 6 to 8

2 tablespoons butter, softened
2 tablespoons chopped fresh rosemary
6 tablespoons extra-virgin olive oil

1 cup grated Parmesan cheese
5 garlic cloves, minced
1 baguette

Process the butter and rosemary in a food processor until mixed. Add the olive oil gradually, processing until well mixed. Add the cheese and garlic and process until well mixed. Cut the bread in half lengthwise. Slice each half diagonally at 1 1/2-inch intervals, cutting 3/4 of the way through the bread. Spread the butter mixture between the slices and on top of the bread. Wrap the bread in foil and grill for 8 minutes, or place unwrapped, cut side up, on a baking sheet and bake at 400 degrees for 8 to 10 minutes or until the edges are crisp.

Par 3: Tea-Time at the Masters
The Junior League of Augusta, Augusta, Georgia

Rainbow Cheese Toasts

Makes 2 dozen toasts

3 hoagie rolls, cut lengthwise into eighths
1/2 cup (1 stick) butter, melted
4 ounces sharp Cheddar cheese, shredded
4 ounces Monterey Jack cheese, shredded

1 tablespoon garlic powder
1/2 teaspoon dill weed
1/2 cup (2 ounces) grated Parmesan cheese or
    Romano cheese

Preheat the oven to 350 degrees. Dip the hoagie slices in the butter and arrange in a single layer in a 9×13-inch baking pan. Sprinkle with the Cheddar cheese, Monterey Jack cheese, garlic powder and dill weed. Top with the Parmesan cheese. Bake for 20 to 25 minutes or until the cheese is light brown and bubbly. Serve with soups, salads or stews. You may substitute Dubliner Irish cheese and asiago cheese for the Cheddar cheese and Monterey Jack cheese for a different twist.

Compliments of
The Woman's Exchange of Memphis, Memphis, Tennessee

So Good It's Sinful Bread

Serves 16 to 20

1 loaf Italian bread
Olive oil
Finely chopped garlic
4 ounces bleu cheese, crumbled
1/2 red onion, cut into paper-thin slices

Freshly ground pepper to taste
16 to 20 kalamata olives, pitted and cut into halves
1 teaspoon finely chopped fresh rosemary
Sprigs of rosemary

Preheat the oven to 400 degrees. Cut the loaf horizontally into halves. Cut a thin slice from the top half to form a flat base. Arrange the halves cut side up on a baking sheet lined with foil.

Brush the cut sides of the bread halves with olive oil and sprinkle with garlic and the cheese. Layer evenly with the onion slices, pepper and olives and sprinkle with chopped rosemary. Bake for 8 to 10 minutes or until the cheese melts. Cool for 2 minutes and cut into 1 1/2-inch slices.

Arrange the slices on a serving platter and garnish with sprigs of fresh rosemary. Serve warm. You may prepare up to 2 hours in advance and store, wrapped in plastic wrap, in the refrigerator. Bake as directed above just before serving.

Compliments of
The Woman's Exchange of Memphis, Memphis, Tennessee

Jazz Fest Crawfish Braided Bread

Serves 10

1 pound crawfish tails or shrimp, coarsely chopped
1 (4-ounce) jar pimentos, drained and chopped
3/4 cup chopped green onions
1/2 cup (2 ounces) shredded Pepper Jack cheese
1/2 cup (2 ounces) shredded Cheddar cheese
Salt, pepper and Creole seasoning to taste

2 (8-count) cans refrigerator crescent roll dough
1/2 teaspoon thyme, chopped (optional)
1/2 teaspoon oregano, chopped (optional)
1/2 teaspoon sweet basil, chopped (optional)
1 egg white, lightly beaten
Sesame seeds (optional)

Combine the crawfish, pimentos, green onions, Pepper Jack cheese and Cheddar cheese in a large bowl and mix well. Season with salt, pepper and Creole seasoning. Unroll the crescent roll dough. Place in a large bowl. Add the thyme, oregano and basil. Knead until the herbs are combined with the dough. Roll into a 10×14-inch rectangle on a floured surface. Spoon the crawfish mixture lengthwise down the center. Cut the dough into 1- to 1 1/2-inch strips from the edge to the filling on each side with a sharp paring knife. Fold the strips alternately across the filling to form a braid. (You may cover the bread at this point and refrigerate until ready to bake.) Brush the braid with the egg white. Sprinkle with sesame seeds. Bake at 400 degrees for 30 to 35 minutes or until golden brown. Cut into slices before serving.

Roux To Do
Junior League of Greater Covington, Covington, Louisiana

Applesauce Nut Bread

PECAN TOPPING
1/2 cup packed brown sugar
1/2 teaspoon ground cinnamon
1/4 cup chopped pecans

BREAD
1 cup applesauce
1 cup sugar
1/2 cup vegetable oil
2 eggs
2 tablespoons milk
2 cups sifted all-purpose flour

1 teaspoon baking soda
1/2 teaspoon baking powder
1/2 teaspoon ground cinnamon
1/3 teaspoon grated nutmeg
1/4 teaspoon salt
1/4 cup chopped pecans

For the topping, mix the brown sugar, cinnamon and pecans in a bowl and set aside.

For the bread, preheat the oven to 350 degrees. Mix the applesauce, sugar, oil, eggs and milk in a bowl. Add the flour, baking soda, baking powder, cinnamon, nutmeg and salt and mix well. Stir in the pecans. Spread in one large or two small greased and floured loaf pans. Sprinkle the topping over the batter. Bake for 30 minutes and cover loosely with foil to prevent overbrowning. Bake for 15 to 30 minutes longer or until the bread tests done. Cool in the pan for several minutes and remove to a wire rack to cool completely.

The Bells are Ringing: A Call To Table
Mission San Juan Capistrano Women's Guild, San Juan Capistrano, California

Since the premier of *Bells Are Ringing* for the Mission of San Juan Capistrano in November 2006, we have sold the first 5,000 copies and helped fund the preservation of the South Wing, an original 18th-century building. We're now on to our second printing and continuing to create a long-lasting source of funds for the preservation of our "Jewel of the Missions."

Banana Bread

Makes 2 loaves

1 cup butter
1 ½ cups sugar
2 eggs
4 ripe bananas, mashed
1 teaspoon vanilla extract

4 tablespoons buttermilk
2 cups all-purpose flour
1 ½ teaspoons baking soda
1 teaspoon salt

TOPPING:
6 tablespoons butter
10 tablespoons brown sugar

5 tablespoons milk
Chopped pecans, optional

Preheat oven to 350 degrees. Cream butter and sugar in a bowl. Beat eggs and add to sugar mixture. Add bananas, vanilla and buttermilk. Sift together flour, soda and salt. Add to banana mixture. Beat well. Pour into 2 greased and floured 9 by 5 by 3-inch loaf pans. Bake 45 to 50 minutes or until bread pulls away from sides of pan. Cool. To prepare topping, melt butter in saucepan. Add sugar and milk. Cook until syrupy. Remove from heat and add chopped pecans. Pour over bread and place under broiler 5 minutes.

Necessities and Temptations
The Junior League of Austin, Austin, Texas

Ponte Vedra Innlet Banana Bread

Makes 2 loaves

2 cups sugar
1 cup oil
4 eggs, beaten
1 pound very ripe bananas (weighed after peeling), mashed

2 cups all-purpose flour
1 ½ teaspoons salt
1 tablespoon soda
1 cup buttermilk
1 cup chopped pecans, optional

Beat sugar and oil together in a bowl. Add eggs and bananas and mix well. Sift together flour, salt and soda and add to banana mixture, alternating with buttermilk. Stir in pecans. Pour into 2 greased regular loaf pans or 4 small ones and bake in a preheated oven at 300 degrees for 30 minutes, then at 350 degrees for 30 minutes longer. Check to see if they are done. The large loaves may need a few more minutes.

A Southern Collection Then and Now
Junior League of Columbus, Columbus, Georgia

Blueberry Bread

Makes 2 loaves

3 cups flour
1 teaspoon salt
1 teaspoon soda
1 tablespoon ground cinnamon
2 cups sugar

3 eggs, well beaten
1 1/4 cups salad oil
2 pints blueberries
1 1/4 cups chopped pecans

Preheat oven to 350 degrees. Combine flour, salt, soda, cinnamon, and sugar in a bowl. Make a well in center of dry ingredients. Add eggs and oil, stir only until dry ingredients are moistened. Stir in blueberries and pecans. Spoon batter into 2 lightly greased 8×4-inch loaf pans. Bake for 1 hour. Let stand overnight before slicing.

Magic
The Junior League of Birmingham, Inc., Birmingham, Alabama

Chocolate Cherry Banana Bread

Serves 10

2 cups all-purpose flour
1 teaspoon baking soda
1/4 teaspoon salt
1/2 cup (1 stick) butter, softened
1 cup packed brown sugar
2 eggs

2 teaspoons vanilla extract
2 cups mashed bananas (2 or 3 bananas)
1 teaspoon ground cinnamon
1/2 teaspoon freshly grated or ground nutmeg
1/4 cup sour cream
3/4 cup each chocolate chips and dried cherries

Preheat the oven to 350 degrees. Mix the flour, baking soda and salt together. Beat the butter and brown sugar in a mixing bowl until creamy, scraping the bowl occasionally. Add the eggs one at a time, beating well after each addition. Stir in the vanilla. Add the bananas, cinnamon and nutmeg and beat until blended. Add the flour mixture and sour cream alternately, beating well after each addition. Fold in the chocolate chips and cherries. Spoon the batter into a buttered 4×8-inch loaf pan and bake for 1 hour or until a wooden pick inserted in the center comes out clean. Cool in the pan for 10 minutes. Remove to a wire rack to cool completely.

Simply Sarasota
Junior League of Sarasota, Sarasota, Florida

Cranberry Orange Nut Bread

Makes 1 loaf

2 cups flour
1 cup sugar
1 1/2 teaspoons baking powder
1 teaspoon salt
1/2 teaspoon baking soda
1/4 cup margarine

2/3 cup orange juice
1 egg, beaten
1 tablespoon grated orange peel
1 cup coarsely chopped cranberries
1/2 cup chopped nuts

Sift the flour, sugar, baking powder, salt and baking soda into a bowl and mix well. Cut in the margarine until crumbly. Whisk the orange juice, egg and orange peel in a bowl. Add to the flour mixture, stirring just until moistened. Fold in the cranberries and nuts. Spoon into a greased loaf pan. Bake at 350 degrees for 1 hour or until the loaf tests done.

Made in the Shade
The Junior League of Greater Fort Lauderdale, Fort Lauderdale, Florida

Christmas Cranberry Bread

Makes 1 loaf

2 cups flour
3/4 cup sugar
1 1/2 teaspoons baking powder
1 teaspoon salt
1/2 teaspoon soda

1/2 cup nuts, chopped
1 cup fresh or frozen cranberries, chopped
1 egg, beaten
3/4 cup orange juice
2 tablespoons salad oil

Preheat oven to 350. Sift dry ingredients together in a bowl. Stir in nuts and cranberries. Add remaining ingredients and blend until thoroughly moistened. Bake in greased, floured loaf pan 50 minutes or until golden brown.

Virginia Hospitality
The Junior League of Hampton Roads, Hampton Roads, Virginia

Macadamia Nut Bread

Makes 2 loaves

1/2 cup sour cream
2 teaspoons baking soda
3 to 4 ripe bananas, mashed
4 medium eggs, beaten
1 cup (2 sticks) butter, softened
2 teaspoons vanilla extract

3 cups sifted flour
2 cups sugar
2 pinches salt
1/2 cup coarsely chopped macadamia nuts
1/2 cup coarsely chopped fresh cranberries
   (optional)

Combine the sour cream and baking soda in a bowl and mix well. Combine the bananas, eggs, butter and vanilla in a large mixing bowl and beat until blended. Add the flour, sugar, salt and sour cream mixture and mix well. Stir in the macadamia nuts and cranberries. Spoon into 2 greased and floured loaf pans. Bake at 350 degrees for 35 to 40 minutes or until a wooden pick inserted in the center comes out clean.

Hint: Save one of the loaves to eat later by freezing it. When freezing bread, double-wrap tightly in plastic wrap and place in a sealable freezer bag with the description and date marked on the bag. The bread will keep for up to two months.

From Grouper to Grits
The Junior League of Clearwater-Dunedin, Clearwater, Florida

Pumpkin Bread

Makes 1 bundt pan plus 1 small loaf pan

3 1/3 cups all-purpose flour
3 cups sugar
1 1/2 teaspoons salt
2 teaspoons soda
1 teaspoon nutmeg

2 teaspoons cinnamon
2 cups canned pumpkin
2/3 cup water
1 cup vegetable oil
4 eggs, beaten

Sift dry ingredients together. In another bowl mix pumpkin, water, oil, and eggs. Pour dry mixture into liquid mixture and mix well. Fill greased and floured bundt pan and 1 small loaf pan (greased and floured). Bake at 350 degrees for 1 hour and 15 minutes. Remove the small loaf pan after approximately 45 minutes.

Cookbook Committee Suggestion: Small round loaves may be made by using well greased 10-ounce soup cans. To remove loaf, invert can, open bottom with can opener and push loaf out. Makes great little round tea sandwiches with cream cheese filling. Chilled loaves slice better for this purpose.

Stir Ups
The Junior Welfare League of Enid, Enid, Oklahoma

Buttery Biscuit Rolls

Makes 2 dozen rolls

- 2 sticks butter (no substitute)
- 1 (8-ounce) carton sour cream
- 2 cups self-rising flour, unsifted

Preheat oven to 350 degrees. Melt butter in large saucepan. Add sour cream and flour to butter and mix. Drop batter into miniature, ungreased muffin tins. Fill to top. Bake for 25 minutes. May be prepared ahead and frozen.

Magic

Junior League of Birmingham, Inc., Birmingham, Alabama

Cream Cheese Biscuits

Makes 40 biscuits

- 1 (3-ounce) package cream cheese
- 1 cup all-purpose flour
- 1 stick butter
- 1/2 teaspoon salt

Soften cream cheese and butter. Mix all ingredients together in a bowl. Shape into a log (1 1/2 inch diameter) and refrigerate for 1 hour. When dough is hardened, slice into 1/4-inch wafers. Bake on ungreased baking sheet for 20 minutes at 350 degrees or for 10 minutes at 400 degrees. Biscuits will be light brown around the edges.

Charleston Receipts Repeats

Junior League of Charleston, Charleston, South Carolina

Cornmeal Sage Biscuits with Sausage Gravy

Serves 6

SAUSAGE GRAVY
1 pound bulk pork sausage
1/4 cup all-purpose flour

2 1/4 cups milk
Salt and pepper to taste

CORNMEAL SAGE BISCUITS
1 3/4 cups baking mix
1/2 cup yellow cornmeal

1 teaspoon dried sage leaves, crumbled
2/3 cup milk

GRAVY

Brown the sausage in a skillet until cooked through. Remove to paper towels to drain and break the sausage into small pieces. Remove the drippings from the skillet and add the flour. Cook for 1 minute, stirring constantly. Add the milk and season with salt and pepper. Cook for 5 minutes or until thickened, stirring constantly. Stir in the sausage and keep warm.

BISCUITS

Combine the baking mix, cornmeal and sage in a bowl. Add the milk and stir until a soft dough forms. Beat for 30 seconds. Drop by twelve spoonfuls onto a greased baking sheet. Bake in a preheated 450-degree oven for 8 to 10 minutes or until golden brown. Serve the gravy over the biscuits.

Marshes to Mansions
Junior League of Lake Charles, LA, Lake Charles, Louisiana

Many people read cookbooks the way other people read novels; they may not ever actually make the recipes, but it's fun to read them, and to speculate what kind of people do cook them and how they would taste. A cookbook allows us to create our own imagined view of the world.

Three-Cheese Drop Biscuits

Makes 2 dozen biscuits

1 1/4 cups all-purpose flour
1 1/2 tablespoons sugar
1 teaspoon baking powder
1/4 teaspoon baking soda
1/4 teaspoon salt

3 tablespoons chilled butter, chopped
1/2 cup packed shredded sharp Cheddar cheese
1/2 cup packed shredded Monterey Jack cheese
1/2 cup grated Parmesan cheese
2/3 cup buttermilk

Whisk the flour, sugar, baking powder, baking soda and salt together in a bowl. Cut in the butter until crumbly. Add the Cheddar cheese, Monterey Jack cheese and Parmesan cheese and mix well. Stir in the buttermilk gradually. Drop dough by 1/4 cups 2 inches apart onto a lightly buttered baking sheet. Bake at 400 degrees for 16 minutes or until golden on top. Serve warm.

Life is Delicious
Hinsdale Junior Woman's Club, Hinsdale, Illinois

Cinnamon Flip

Makes 15 large servings

1 heaping cup of sugar
1 rounded mixing spoon of shortening
1 cup of milk

1 egg
2 teaspoons baking powder

Cream sugar and shortening in a bowl; add milk, egg, flour, and baking powder. Grease 9 by 12-inch baking pan; add mixture, smooth even with spatula. Sift a sprinkling of flour lightly over top, dot generously with brown sugar, butter and cinnamon. Bake 40 minutes in moderate oven. Serve hot or cold.

Charleston Receipts
The Junior League of Charleston, Charleston, South Carolina

Piña Colada Muffins

1 (2-layer) package yellow cake mix
1 teaspoon coconut extract
1 teaspoon rum flavoring
1 cup flaked coconut

1 cup chopped nuts (preferably macadamia
   or pecans)
1 cup drained crushed pineapple

Prepare the cake mix according to the package directions. Stir in the coconut extract, rum flavoring, coconut, nuts and pineapple; do not overmix. Fill greased or paper-lined muffin cups 3/4 full. Bake at 350 degrees for 15 to 20 minutes or until a wooden pick inserted in the center comes out clean. You may also bake in mini muffin pans. Bake at 350 degrees for 12 minutes.

The Life of the Party
The Junior League of Tampa, Tampa, Florida

Sunrise Muffins

1 pound bacon
1 cup milk
1 cup pancake syrup
2 eggs
3/4 cup wheat flour
3/4 cup all-purpose flour

1/2 cup firmly packed brown sugar
1/2 teaspoon salt
2 teaspoons baking powder
1 teaspoon baking soda
1 cup rolled oats

Cook the bacon in a skillet until crisp; drain. Crumble into small pieces. Combine the milk, syrup, and eggs in a large bowl and mix well. Combine the wheat flour, all-purpose flour, brown sugar, salt, baking powder, baking soda and oats in a bowl and mix well. Add to the milk mixture and mix well. Stir in the crumbled bacon. Fill 18 greased muffin cups 2/3 full. Bake at 350 degrees for 15 to 18 minutes or until a wooden pick inserted in the center of the muffins comes out clean.

Variation: May substitute miniature muffin pans for regular muffin pans and adjust the cooking time to 13 to 15 minutes, or use large muffin pans and bake for 20 to 25 minutes.

If You Can't Stand the Heat, Get Out of the Kitchen
Junior Service League of Independence, Independence, Missouri

Blueberry Lemon Scones

Makes 6 scones

SCONES
1 3/4 cups all-purpose flour
1 cup fresh blueberries
1/4 cup sugar
1 tablespoon freshly grated lemon zest
1 1/2 teaspoons baking powder
1/2 teaspoon baking soda

1/4 teaspoon salt
1/4 cup (1/2 stick) unsalted butter, chilled
1/4 cup sour cream
1 egg, lightly beaten
3 tablespoons lemon juice
1 teaspoon almond flavoring

CONFECTIONERS' SUGAR GLAZE
1/2 cup confectioners' sugar
1 teaspoon unsalted butter, softened

1/8 teaspoon almond flavoring
2 to 3 teaspoons milk

To prepare the scones, mix the flour, blueberries, sugar, lemon zest, baking powder, baking soda and salt in a large bowl. Cut in the butter with a pastry blender or fork until coarse crumbs form. Combine the sour cream, egg, lemon juice and flavoring in a small bowl and mix well. Add the sour cream mixture to the blueberry mixture and stir for 1 minute or just until moistened.

Knead the dough on a lightly floured surface five to eight times or until smooth. Pat into a 7-inch round on a greased baking sheet. Score into six wedges; do not separate. Bake at 375 degrees for 18 to 25 minutes or until light brown. Cool on the baking sheet for 10 minutes. Remove to a platter and cut into six wedges.

To prepare the glaze, mix the confectioners' sugar, butter, flavoring and desired amount of milk in a bowl until of a glaze consistency. Drizzle the glaze over the warm scones.

Starfish Café: Changing Lives One Recipe at a Time…
Union Mission/Starfish Café, Savannah, Georgia

We operate a restaurant as part of our culinary arts program, so a cookbook seemed a natural fundraiser and marketing piece for our school and learning tool for our students. To ensure that our recipes passed the cooking and tasting tests of mere mortals (and not just our talented chefs in training), the staff took recipes home to cook with their families and serve at a recipe tasting potluck. As with most community cookbooks, our testing forms asked the testers to rate the clarity, accuracy, and difficulty of each recipe and asked tasters to rate the overall taste of the dish. The party exceeded our expectations—we had hundreds of dishes to sample and received completed testing forms for each one, and to top it off, the local press covered the event. We knew immediately from the rave reviews of the testers and guests that the Starfish Café cookbook was well on its way to being a huge success.

Pumpkin Scones with Cranberry Butter

CRANBERRY BUTTER
2 tablespoons dried cranberries
1/2 cup boiling water

1/2 cup (1 stick) butter or margarine, softened
3 tablespoons confectioners' sugar

PUMPKIN SCONES
2 1/4 cups all-purpose flour
1/4 cup packed brown sugar
2 teaspoons baking powder
1 tablespoon pumpkin pie spice
1/4 teaspoon baking soda

1/4 teaspoon salt
1/2 cup (1 stick) butter or margarine, chilled
1/2 cup canned pumpkin
1/3 cup milk
1 egg, beaten

To prepare the butter, combine the cranberries and boiling water in a heatproof bowl. Let stand for 10 minutes. Drain and finely chop the cranberries. Mix the butter and confectioners' sugar in a bowl until combined. Fold in the cranberries. Chill, covered, for 1 hour or longer to allow the flavors to blend. You may substitute dried blueberries for the cranberries, if desired.

To prepare the scones, mix the flour, brown sugar, baking powder, pumpkin pie spice, baking soda and salt in a bowl and mix well. Cut in the butter using a pastry blender until the mixture resembles coarse crumbs. Make a well in the center of the crumb mixture.

Combine the pumpkin, milk and egg in a bowl and mix well. Add the pumpkin mixture all at once to the well and stir just until moistened. Turn the dough onto a lightly floured surface. Knead the dough by folding and pressing gently for ten to twelve strokes or until almost smooth. Pat the dough into an 8-inch round and cut the round into twelve wedges. Arrange the wedges one inch apart on an ungreased baking sheet. Brush the tops with additional milk, if desired.

Bake at 400 degrees for 12 to 15 minutes or until golden brown. Remove the scones to a wire rack and cool for 5 minutes. Serve warm with the cranberry butter.

Worth Tasting
Junior League of the Palm Beaches, West Palm Beach, Florida

The Village Club Popovers

Serves 12

5 eggs
4 cups milk
5 1/2 cups all-purpose flour

1/4 teaspoon salt
1/4 teaspoon sugar
3 teaspoons vegetable oil

Beat the eggs and milk in a bowl. Stir in the flour, salt and sugar. Chill, covered, for 24 hours. Place 1/4 teaspoon of the oil in each of twelve popover tins or cups. Fill the popover tins three-quarters full with batter. Bake at 325 degrees for 1 hour and 15 minutes.

Note: If baking a smaller batch of popovers, keep the batter chilled until ready to bake. Nonstick popover tins may be filled with batter and chilled overnight before baking.

Popovers to Panache
The Village Club, Bloomfield Hills, Michigan

Cinnamon Streusel Coffee Cake

Serves 12

2 cups flour
1 teaspoon baking powder
1 teaspoon baking soda
1/2 teaspoon salt
3/4 cup granulated sugar

1/2 cup brown sugar
1 1/2 sticks butter, softened
1 cup buttermilk
2 eggs, lightly beaten
1 teaspoon cinnamon

TOPPING:
1/2 cup brown sugar

1 teaspoon cinnamon
1/2 cup chopped pecans (optional)

Combine flour, baking powder, baking soda, salt, sugars, butter, buttermilk, eggs and cinnamon in a bowl and mix well. Pour into a greased 9×13 baking pan. Cover with plastic wrap and refrigerate overnight or at least 8 hours. The next morning mix topping and sprinkle on top of batter. Bake for 30 to 35 minutes or until tester comes out clean.

Topping: Mix brown sugar, cinnamon and pecans, if desired. Sprinkle on top of batter before baking.

Add Another Place Setting
Junior League of Northwest Arkansas, Springdale, Arkansas

Blueberry Sausage Breakfast Cake

Serves 15

BREAKFAST CAKE
2 cups all-purpose flour
1 teaspoon baking powder
1/2 teaspoon baking soda
1/2 cup (1 stick) butter or margarine
3/4 cup granulated sugar
1/4 cup packed brown sugar
2 eggs
1 cup sour cream
1 pound sausage, cooked and drained
1 cup blueberries
1/2 cup chopped pecans

BLUEBERRY SAUCE
1/2 cup sugar
2 tablespoons cornstarch
2 cups fresh or frozen blueberries
1/2 cup water
1/2 teaspoon lemon juice

CAKE

Mix the flour, baking powder and baking soda together. Beat the butter in a mixing bowl at medium to high speed until light and fluffy. Add the granulated sugar and brown sugar and beat until smooth. Add the eggs one at a time, beating for 1 minute after each addition. Add the flour mixture alternately with the sour cream, beating just until combined after each addition. Fold in the sausage and blueberries.

Spoon the batter into an ungreased 9×13-inch baking pan and sprinkle with the pecans. You may cover and chill at this point for 8 to 10 hours, if desired. Bake at 350 degrees for 35 to 40 minutes or until a wooden pick inserted in the center comes out clean. Store leftovers in the refrigerator.

SAUCE

Mix the sugar and cornstarch in a saucepan. Stir in the blueberries and water and cook over medium heat until thickened, stirring constantly. Cook for 2 minutes longer, stirring constantly. Stir in the lemon juice and cool slightly. Serve with the warm cake. Store leftovers in the refrigerator.

Mardi Gras to Mistletoe
Junior League of Shreveport-Bossier, Shreveport, Louisiana

Sweet Potato Coffee Cake

2 teaspoons cinnamon

2 1/4 cups flour

1 1/2 teaspoons baking powder

1 teaspoon baking soda

1/2 teaspoon salt

1/2 cup tub margarine

1/2 cup brown sugar

1/2 cup sugar

2 egg whites plus 1 whole egg

1/2 cup light sour cream

2/3 cup cooked and mashed sweet potato

3/4 cup nonfat yogurt

2 teaspoons vanilla

Nut topping

1 tablespoon melted tub margarine

Nut Topping

1/3 cup brown sugar

2 tablespoons sugar

2 tablespoons wheat germ

1 teaspoon cinnamon

1/2 teaspoon nutmeg

1/2 cup chopped nuts

Combine first 5 dry ingredients. In a mixer, beat 1/2 cup margarine and sugars until well blended, adding eggs 1 at a time. Add sour cream, sweet potato, yogurt and vanilla. Gradually add dry ingredients. Prepare a 10-inch tube or bundt pan with vegetable oil cooking spray and dust with flour. Combine nut topping ingredients. Spread 1/2 of batter into pan, covering with 1/2 of nut topping. Spread remaining batter over topping. Stir 1 tablespoon margarine into remaining nut topping. Sprinkle over batter. Bake at 350 degrees for 50 to 60 minutes or until toothpick comes out clean. Cool 10 minutes.

River Road Recipes III: A Healthy Collection
Junior League of Baton Rouge, Baton Rouge, Louisiana

River Road Recipes, quite possibly the most famous Junior League cookbook, has printed 75 times between 1959 and 2008, bringing the total to 1,340,000 books in print.

As of May 2005, the combined sales of *River Road Recipes; River Road Recipes II, A Second Helping; River Road Recipes III, A Healthy Collection;* and *River Road Recipes IV, Warm Welcomes* have earned more than $3,000,000 for the Junior League of Baton Rouge to fund projects in their community.

Community cookbooks do more than just fill the family dinner table with delicious food. The income from their sales improves the quality of life of the community in visible, tangible ways.

The Closet Coffee Cake

1 (18-ounce) box deluxe yellow cake mix
1 (3-ounce) package vanilla instant pudding mix
1 cup vegetable oil
4 eggs
1 teaspoon vanilla extract
1 cup sour cream

1/2 cup sugar
1/2 cup packed brown sugar
1/2 cup (1 stick) margarine, melted
6 tablespoons flour
2 teaspoons cinnamon

Combine the cake mix, pudding mix, oil, eggs, vanilla and sour cream in a bowl. Beat with an electric mixer at medium speed for 2 minutes. Pour half the batter into a greased and floured 9×13-inch baking pan. Mix the sugar, brown sugar, melted margarine, flour and cinnamon in a bowl. Sprinkle half over the batter in the pan. Top with the remaining batter and sprinkle with the remaining sugar mixture. Bake at 350 degrees for 45 minutes or until a wooden pick inserted in the center comes out clean. Remove to a wire rack to cool.

For Such A Time As This: A Cookbook
Park Cities Baptist Church, Dallas, Texas

Orange Blossom French Toast

12 eggs
1/2 cup cream
2 tablespoon orange juice

Grated zest of 1 orange
1/2 teaspoon vanilla extract
1 loaf French bread

Combine the eggs, cream, orange juice, orange zest and vanilla in a bowl and mix well. Pour into a shallow baking dish. Cut the bread into 1-inch slices and arrange in the dish, turning to coat well. Chill, covered, for 8 hours or longer. Remove the bread slices to a greased baking sheet. Bake at 375 degrees for 20 to 25 minutes or until golden brown. Serve with maple syrup or fruit.

Oh My Stars!
The Junior League of Roanoke Valley, Roanoke, Virginia

Baked French Toast with Berry Sauce

FRENCH TOAST
1 cup packed brown sugar
1/2 cup (1 stick) butter
2 tablespoons corn syrup
1 loaf (about) French bread, sliced

1 3/4 cups half-and-half
1/2 cup Triple Sec
6 eggs
1/2 teaspoon vanilla extract
1/8 teaspoon salt

BERRY SAUCE
2 cups raspberries
2 cups strawberries

1/2 cup sugar
1/2 cup orange juice
2 to 3 tablespoons lemon juice

For the toast, heat the brown sugar, butter and corn syrup in a saucepan over medium heat until blended, stirring frequently. Pour the brown sugar mixture into a greased 9×13-inch baking pan. Arrange the bread slices in a single layer over the prepared layer. Whisk the half-and-half, liqueur, eggs, vanilla and salt in a bowl until blended. Pour the egg mixture over the bread. Chill, covered with greased foil, for 8 to 10 hours. Bake, covered, at 350 degrees for 35 to 45 minutes, removing the foil after the first 15 minutes of baking.

For the sauce, combine the raspberries, strawberries, sugar, orange juice and lemon juice in a saucepan and mix well. Cook over medium heat for 5 minutes, stirring frequently. Process the raspberry mixture in a blender until puréed. Return the purée to the saucepan. Cook just until heated through, stirring frequently. Serve warm with the French toast.

An Occasion to Gather
Junior League of Milwaukee, Milwaukee, Wisconsin

"I am not a cook. This small fact made the prospect of working on our Junior League's new cookbook feel daunting. With trepidation, I put together a budget and attended meetings. But with no cooking required thus far and the tremendous support of our members, our committee was well on the way to publishing a cookbook.

I eventually worked up the courage to become a recipe tester. As it happened, I was the perfect tester! Who knew?! Because I lacked cooking skills (though not eating skills!), no step in the cooking process could be assumed; it had to be spelled out. My lack of knowledge ensured that every recipe was edited and written for the most novice of cooks, improving our cookbook in the process. It was fun—my family enjoyed all the testing and tasting, and I now love to cook and enjoy sharing recipes from our wonderful cookbook."

Jane Kueppers Bartlett
The Junior League of Milwaukee, Wisconsin

The Bridgewater House French Toast

Serves 8

CREAM CHEESE FILLING
8 ounces cream cheese, softened
1 teaspoon milk or cream
1 cup chopped fresh strawberries or
   fresh raspberries

1/2 cup chopped toasted pecans or walnuts
1/4 cup strawberry or raspberry preserves
2 tablespoons Chambord

FRENCH TOAST
1 loaf French bread
2 cups milk or half-and-half
4 eggs
1 teaspoon ground cinnamon

3/4 teaspoon ground nutmeg
3/4 teaspoon vanilla extract
Vegetable oil
Butter

For the filling, beat the cream cheese and milk in a mixing bowl until light and fluffy. Stir in the strawberries, pecans, preserves and liqueur.

For the French toast, cut the loaf diagonally into 1 1/2-inch slices using a serrated knife. Make a slit in the top of each bread slice cutting to form a pocket. Fill each pocket with 1 1/2 tablespoons of the filling. The stuffed bread slices may be frozen at this point for future use.

Whisk the milk, eggs, cinnamon, nutmeg and vanilla in a bowl until blended. Soak the bread slices in the milk mixture until moderately saturated; drain. If the bread slices are frozen, partially thaw in the refrigerator before soaking in the milk mixture.

Coat a grill pan or skillet with oil and a small amount of butter and preheat. Sauté the coated bread slices on the hot grill pan until brown on both sides. Serve warm with confectioners' sugar, fresh strawberries, fresh raspberries and/or toasted pecans.

Compliments of
The Woman's Exchange of Memphis, Memphis, Tennessee

French Toast Baked in Honey Pecan Sauce

HONEY BUTTER
1/2 cup (1 stick) butter, softened

2/3 cup honey
1/3 cup packed brown sugar

FRENCH TOAST
4 eggs, beaten
3/4 cup half-and-half
1 1/2 teaspoons brown sugar
1 teaspoon vanilla extract
4 thick slices French bread

1/4 cup (1/2 stick) butter
1/4 cup packed brown sugar
1/4 cup honey
1/4 cup maple syrup
1/4 cup chopped pecans

For the honey butter, combine the butter, honey and brown sugar in a mixing bowl and beat until light and fluffy. Spoon into a crock and chill until firm.

For the French toast, mix the eggs, half-and-half, 1 1/2 teaspoons brown sugar and vanilla in a small bowl. Pour half of the mixture into a shallow dish. Arrange the bread in the dish and top with the remaining egg mixture. Chill, covered, for 8 hours or longer.

Melt 1/4 cup butter in a 9×13-inch baking pan. Stir in 1/4 cup brown sugar, honey, maple syrup and pecans. Arrange the bread slices on top. Bake at 350 degrees for 30 to 35 minutes or until puffed and golden brown. Serve immediately with the honey butter.

Note: Before measuring honey, coat the cup or spoon with vegetable cooking spray. The honey will slide off easily. Try the same technique with peanut butter, syrup, and molasses.

Savor the Moment
Junior League of Boca Raton, Boca Raton, Florida

Whoever started the Junior League joke that a Leaguer's dream home wouldn't have a kitchen has obviously never been through the cookbook recipe testing process. Leave it to a Junior Leaguer to find a way to use a daily task like cooking as a way to raise funds to benefit the community.

Puffed Apple Pancake

1 cup milk
4 eggs
2/3 cup all-purpose flour
3 tablespoons granulated sugar
1 teaspoon vanilla extract
1/2 teaspoon salt

1/4 teaspoon cinnamon
1/4 cup (1/2 stick) unsalted butter
12 ounces Golden Delicious apples, peeled, cored
 and thinly sliced (about 2)
3 tablespoons brown sugar
Confectioners' sugar

Whisk the milk, eggs, flour, granulated sugar, vanilla, salt and cinnamon in a bowl until the batter is smooth. Place the butter in a 9×13-inch glass baking dish and bake at 425 degrees for 5 minutes or until melted. Remove from the oven and cover the bottom of the baking dish with the apples. Bake for 10 minutes or until the apples begin to soften and the butter is bubbly. Pour the batter over the apples and sprinkle with the brown sugar. Bake for 20 minutes or until puffed and brown. Sprinkle with confectioners' sugar. Serve warm with syrup, if desired.

Great Women, Great Food
Junior League of Kankakee County, Kankakee, Illinois

Lemon Waffles with Lemon Cream

Serves 4 to 5

5 egg yolks
1/2 cup sugar
1 cup scalded milk
5 tablespoons fresh lemon juice
4 egg yolks
3 tablespoons sugar
1/2 teaspoon salt

1 cup milk
2 teaspoons fresh lemon juice
2 tablespoons grated lemon peel
1/4 cup cooled melted butter
1 cup flour
4 egg whites, stiffly beaten but not dry
1/2 cup whipping cream, whipped

Combine 5 egg yolks and 1/2 cup sugar in a double boiler and beat until thick and pale yellow. Blend in the scalded milk. Cook over simmering water for 8 minutes or until the mixture thickens and coats a spoon, stirring constantly. Remove to a medium glass or porcelain bowl. Stir in 5 tablespoons lemon juice. Chill, covered, for 3 hours or longer. Beat 4 egg yolks, 3 tablespoons sugar and salt in a medium bowl. Blend in the milk, 2 teaspoons lemon juice, lemon peel and melted butter. Sift in the flour. Fold in the egg whites. Spoon onto a hot greased waffle iron. Bake until golden brown. Fold the whipped cream into the chilled mixture. Serve immediately with the waffles.

Note: To scald milk, heat milk almost to the boiling point—just until tiny bubbles begin to form around the edge of the pan. Watch closely so as not to burn.

A Sunsational Encore
Junior League of Greater Orlando, Orlando, Florida

Bananas Foster Waffles

BROWN SUGAR BUTTER
1/2 cup (1 stick) unsalted butter, browned

1/2 cup plus 3 tablespoons packed brown sugar
1 to 2 teaspoons heavy cream

WAFFLES
1 1/2 cups all-purpose flour
1/4 cup granulated sugar
1 1/2 teaspoons baking soda
1 teaspoon salt
1 1/2 cups buttermilk
6 tablespoons butter, melted

2 eggs, beaten
4 bananas, sliced
1/8 teaspoon ground cinnamon
1 tablespoon banana liqueur
1 ounce brandy
Confectioners' sugar to taste

For the brown sugar butter, mix the browned butter, brown sugar and heavy cream in a bowl.

For the waffles, preheat the oven to 200 degrees. Sift the flour, granulated sugar, baking soda and salt into a bowl and mix well. Whisk in the buttermilk, butter and eggs. Preheat a waffle iron coated with nonstick cooking spray. Pour 1 cup of the batter per waffle onto the hot waffle iron and bake until brown using the manufacturer's directions. Arrange the waffles on a baking sheet and keep warm in the oven.

Combine 3 tablespoons of the Brown Sugar Butter, the bananas and cinnamon in a skillet and cook for 2 to 3 minutes, stirring frequently. Remove from the heat. Stir in the liqueur and brandy and ignite with a long match. Allow the flames to subside. Spoon the banana mixture evenly over the waffles on serving plates and sprinkle with confectioners' sugar. Serve immediately with crisp-cooked bacon, Canadian bacon or browned sausage links.

Compliments of
The Woman's Exchange of Memphis, Memphis, Tennessee

Charleston Receipts, first published November 1, 1950, is the oldest Junior League cookbook still in print.

Orange Sticky Buns

1/4 cup (1/2 stick) margarine or butter
1/4 cup packed brown sugar
1/2 cup flaked coconut
1/4 cup sliced or slivered almonds

1/2 cup orange marmalade
1/4 to 1/2 teaspoon grated gingerroot
1 (10-ounce) can refrigerated flaky biscuits

Combine the margarine, brown sugar, coconut and almonds in a mixing bowl. Spoon into a 5×9-inch loaf pan. Bake at 375 degrees until the margarine melts. Remove from the oven. Spread the coconut mixture evenly on the bottom of the pan. Combine the marmalade and gingerroot in a small bowl and set aside. Separate the dough into 10 biscuits. Spread about 2 teaspoons marmalade mixture on 1 side of each biscuit. Stand the biscuits on edge slightly overlapping in 2 rows of 5 biscuits each in the pan. Bake at 375 degrees for 25 to 30 minutes or until deep golden brown, covering the pan with foil during the last 15 minutes of baking to prevent overbaking. Cool for 4 minutes. Run a knife around the edges to loosen. Invert onto a serving plate.

Between the Lakes
The Junior League of Saginaw Valley, Saginaw, Michigan

Pull-Aparts

2 (16-ounce) loaves frozen bread dough
1 cup packed brown sugar
1 (6-ounce) package vanilla pudding and
   pie filling mix
1/2 cup (1 stick) butter, melted
2 tablespoons milk

2 teaspoons cinnamon
1/2 (1-pound) package confectioners' sugar
1/4 cup milk
2 to 3 tablespoons butter, melted
1 teaspoon vanilla extract

Spray 2 glass dishes with nonstick cooking spray. Place 1 bread loaf in each dish. Spray plastic wrap with nonstick cooking spray and loosely cover each loaf. Let rise for 8 to 10 hours. Pinch 1 loaf of dough into small pieces and arrange in the bottom of a greased 9×13-inch baking pan. Combine the brown sugar, pudding mix, 1/2 cup butter, 2 tablespoons milk and cinnamon in a bowl and mix well. Drizzle the brown sugar mixture over the bread pieces. Pinch the remaining bread loaf into small pieces and place over the prepared layers. Bake at 350 degrees for 25 minutes. Combine the confectioners' sugar, 1/4 cup milk and 2 to 3 tablespoons butter in a bowl and mix until of a spreading consistency. Stir in the vanilla. Spread over the baked layer.

Cooking by the Boot Straps
Junior Welfare League of Enid, Enid, Oklahoma

Bruncheon Eggs

6 eggs
2 cups milk
1 teaspoon salt
1 teaspoon dry mustard

1 pound sausage, mild or hot
3 or 4 slices French bread, cubed and sautéed in
  melted butter
1 to 1 1/2 cups sharp cheese, grated

Beat eggs, milk, salt and mustard in a bowl. Sauté and drain sausage. Layer bread, cheese and sausage in greased 9×13-inch dish. Pour milk and egg mixture over all. Refrigerate overnight. Bake at 350 degrees for 45 to 50 minutes.

Savannah Style
Junior League of Savannah, Savannah, Georgia

Breakfast Bread

1 can flaky Grands biscuits
8 eggs, beaten
1 pound bacon, crisp-cooked
  and crumbled

1 (4-ounce) can chopped green chiles
2 cups shredded Cheddar cheese

Cut the biscuits into eighths. Combine the biscuit pieces, eggs, bacon, green chiles and Cheddar cheese in a bowl and mix gently. Spoon the biscuit mixture into a well greased tube or bundt pan. Bake at 350 degrees for 40 minutes. Run a knife around the outer edge of the pan and invert onto a serving platter. Slice and serve plain or topped with syrup.

Cooking by the Boot Straps
Junior Welfare League of Enid, Enid, Oklahoma

Breakfast Casserole

Serves 6 to 8

1 pound bulk pork sausage
1 (8-count) can crescent rolls
1 1/2 cups (6 ounces) shredded Monterey
    Jack cheese

1 1/2 cups (6 ounce) shredded sharp Cheddar cheese
6 eggs, beaten
3/4 cup milk

Brown the sausage in a skillet, stirring until crumbly; drain. Unroll the crescent roll dough. Place in a 9×13-inch baking dish, stretching the dough to cover the bottom of the dish. Layer the sausage over the dough. Sprinkle with the Monterey Jack cheese and Cheddar cheese. Beat the eggs and milk in a bowl. Pour over the layers. Bake at 350 degrees for 40 minutes or until set.

Down Home: Treasured Recipes from our House to Yours
West Point Junior Auxiliary, West Point, Mississippi

Chile and Cheese Breakfast

Serves 8

3 English muffins, split
2 tablespoons butter, softened
1 pound hot pork sausage
1 (4-ounce) can green chiles, drained, chopped

3 cups shredded Cheddar cheese
1 1/2 cups sour cream
12 eggs, beaten

Spread the cut side of each muffin with 1 teaspoon butter. Arrange cut side down in a buttered 9×13-inch baking pan. Brown the sausage in a skillet, stirring until crumbly; drain. Rinse with hot water; drain. Layer 1/2 of the sausage, 1/2 of the chiles and 1/2 of the cheese over the muffins. Spread with a mixture of the sour cream and eggs. Layer with the remaining sausage, remaining chiles and remaining cheese. Chill, covered, for 8 to 10 hours. Let stand at room temperature for 30 minutes. Bake, uncovered, at 350 degrees for 30 to 45 minutes or until brown and bubbly.

Texas Ties
Junior League of North Harris and South Montgomery Counties, Inc., Spring, Texas

Ham and Asparagus Breakfast Casserole

Serves 12

8 ounces fresh asparagus, trimmed
1 bell pepper, chopped
1 onion, chopped
1/4 cup (1/2 stick) margarine
1 loaf French bread, cut into cubes
1 cup chopped ham

2 cups (8 ounces) shredded Cheddar cheese
8 eggs
2 1/2 cups milk
1/3 cup honey
1/2 tablespoon salt
1/2 tablespoon pepper

Sauté the asparagus, bell pepper and onion in the margarine in a skillet for 3 to 5 minutes or until tender. Layer the bread, ham, 1 cup of the Cheddar cheese and the sautéed vegetables in a greased 9×13-inch baking dish. Beat the eggs, milk, honey, salt and pepper in a bowl until smooth. Pour over the layers and sprinkle with the remaining 1 cup Cheddar cheese. Chill, covered, for 8 to 10 hours. Uncover and bake at 350 degrees for 40 to 45 minutes or until set.

Now Serving
Junior League of Wichita Falls, Wichita Falls, Texas

Ham and Eggs Brunch Bake

Serves 6 to 8

1/2 cup onion, chopped
1 tablespoon margarine
1 cup ham, chopped
1 cup tomato, chopped
2 cups biscuit mix
1/2 cup cold water
1 cup Cheddar or Swiss cheese, shredded

1/4 cup milk
2 eggs
1/4 teaspoon salt
1/4 teaspoon pepper
3/4 teaspoon dried dill weed
2 tablespoons green onions, chopped

In a small pan, sauté onion in margarine until translucent. Remove from heat; stir in ham and tomato. Combine biscuit mix and water. With floured hands, pat dough into a greased 9×13-inch baking dish, pressing evenly over bottom and 1/2 inch up the sides of dish. Spread ham mixture over dough. Sprinkle with shredded cheese. Beat milk, eggs, salt, pepper, and dill weed until foamy. Pour egg mixture over cheese layer and sprinkle with green onions. Bake, uncovered, at 350 degrees for 30 minutes.

The Bess Collection
Junior Service League of Indendence, Independence, Missouri

Eggs "Bama"-dict

EGGS
6 English muffins, split into halves
Butter to taste
12 slices Canadian bacon

15 eggs
1 cup (4 ounces) shredded sharp Cheddar cheese
Salt and pepper to taste

HOLLANDAISE SAUCE
4 egg yolks
1 tablespoon lemon juice

1/2 teaspoon salt
Dash of Tabasco sauce
1/2 cup (1 stick) butter

To prepare the eggs, toast the English muffin halves and spread with butter. Brown the Canadian bacon in a skillet; drain. Whisk the eggs in a bowl until light and frothy. Add the cheese, salt and pepper and mix well. Arrange the muffin halves in the bottom of a baking dish, split side up. Top each muffin half with a slice of Canadian bacon. Pour the egg mixture evenly over the Canadian bacon. Bake at 350 degrees for 20 to 25 minutes or until the eggs are set. Let stand for 5 minutes before serving. Slice into squares around the muffin halves.

To prepare the sauce, combine the egg yolks, lemon juice, salt and Tabasco sauce in a blender and process until smooth. Bring the butter to a simmer in a saucepan. Remove from the heat and immediately add to the egg yolk mixture in a fine stream, processing constantly at high speed until combined.

To serve, top each serving with a spoonful of Hollandaise Sauce.

Note: The Hollandaise Sauce can be kept warm in a baking dish placed in a pan of hot water.

Shall We Gather
Trinity Episcopal Church, Wetumpka, Alabama

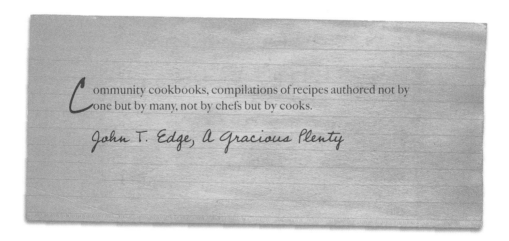

Community cookbooks, compilations of recipes authored not by one but by many, not by chefs but by cooks.

John T. Edge, A Gracious Plenty

Italian Frittata with Goat Cheese

Serves 4 to 6

2 1/2 tablespoons unsalted butter
1/3 cup minced onion
1/3 cup minced green bell pepper
5 eggs
3 egg whites
5 or 6 slices prosciutto, cut into bite-size pieces
1 (7-ounce) can artichoke hearts, drained and
  coarsely chopped

1/2 cup chopped fresh basil
1/2 cup chopped cooked potatoes
  (2 or 3 small red bliss potatoes or
  1 Yukon Gold potato)
1/2 teaspoon salt
Ground pepper to taste
2 ounces goat cheese, crumbled

Heat the butter in a large cast-iron skillet over medium heat. Add the onion and bell pepper and mix well. Cook for 8 minutes or until the vegetables are tender but not brown, stirring frequently. Preheat the broiler. Whisk the eggs and egg whites in a bowl until blended. Stir in the prosciutto, artichokes, basil, potatoes, salt and pepper. Pour the egg mixture over the onion mixture, tilting the skillet to ensure even coverage. Sprinkle the cheese over the top. Cook over medium-low heat for 10 to 15 minutes or until the center is almost set; do not stir. Broil for 5 minutes or until brown. Cut into wedges and serve immediately.

California Sol Food
Junior League of San Diego, Inc., San Diego, California

The first Junior League cookbook was published by the Junior League of Minneapolis in 1943–1944.

Vegetable Brunch Frittata

3 tablespoons olive oil
1 large onion, thinly sliced
3 garlic cloves, minced
3 summer squash, sliced 1/4 inch thick
3 zucchini, sliced 1/4 inch thick
1 red bell pepper, cut into 1/4-inch strips
1 yellow bell pepper, cut into 1/4-inch strips
1 green bell pepper, cut into 1/4-inch strips

8 ounces fresh mushrooms, sliced
6 eggs
1/4 cup heavy cream or half-and-half
2 teaspoons salt
2 teaspoons freshly ground pepper
2 cups (1/2-inch cubes) stale French bread
8 ounces cream cheese, cut into small pieces
2 cups shredded Swiss cheese

Heat the olive oil in a large saucepan. Add the onion, garlic, summer squash, zucchini, red bell pepper, yellow bell pepper, green bell pepper and mushrooms. Sauté for 15 minutes or until the vegetables are tender-crisp. Remove from the heat. Whisk the eggs, cream, salt and pepper in a large bowl. Stir in the bread, cream cheese and Swiss cheese. Add the sautéed vegetables and stir to mix well. Pour into a greased 10-inch springform pan and press down to pack tightly. Place on a foil-lined baking sheet. Bake at 350 degrees for 1 hour or until puffed, golden brown and firm to the touch. Cover the top of the frittata with foil while baking if becoming too brown. Remove to a wire rack. Loosen from the side of the pan with a sharp knife and remove the side. Serve hot, cold or at room temperature.

A League of Our Own: From Blue Jeans to Ball Gowns
Rockwall Women's League, Rockwall, Texas

Creole Eggs

CREOLE SAUCE

1 bell pepper, chopped
1 rib celery, chopped
1 onion, chopped

2 tablespoons butter
1 (28-ounce) can tomatoes, chopped
1 tablespoon sugar
Salt and pepper to taste

WHITE SAUCE AND ASSEMBLY

2 tablespoon butter
2 tablespoons all-purpose flour

1 cup milk
4 eggs, hard-cooked and sliced
Cracker crumbs

For the Creole sauce, sauté the bell pepper, celery and onion in the butter in a saucepan until the onion is tender. Stir in the undrained tomatoes and sugar and cook over low heat until thickened. Season to taste with salt and pepper.

For the white sauce, preheat the oven to 350 degrees. Heat the butter in a saucepan and stir in the flour. Cook until blended and bubbly, stirring constantly. Add the milk gradually and cook over low heat until thickened, stirring constantly.

Layer the eggs, white sauce, Creole sauce and cracker crumbs in a baking dish. Bake for 20 to 30 minutes or until heated through. Serve with ham and/or grits.

Compliments of
The Woman's Exchange of Memphis, Memphis, Tennessee

The best cookbooks are storybooks, their purpose as much to document the communal draw of the meal table as to show the curious cook how to bake a gravity-defying biscuit or stir up a tasty kettle of Brunswick stew. When all the dishes have been cleared from the table, these recipes remain, a tangible link to a time, a place, a people.

John T. Edge, A Gracious Plenty

Chunky Potato Omelet

Serves 1

½ small onion, chopped
1 tablespoon butter
⅔ cup cubed potato, cooked
2 eggs, beaten

Salt and pepper to taste
2 slices bacon, crisp-fried, crumbled
1 teaspoon finely chopped chives

Sauté the onion in the butter in a skillet. Stir in the potato and set aside. Beat the eggs, salt and pepper in a bowl. Place a skillet coated with nonstick cooking spray over medium heat. Pour in the egg mixture; reduce the heat to low. Cook for 1 minute. Sprinkle the potato mixture over the egg mixture and mix well. Cook until set. Sprinkle the bacon and chives over the top. Fold the omelet in half. Slide from the skillet onto a serving plate.

Beyond Burlap
The Junior League of Boise, Boise, Idaho

Spinach Cheddar Squares

Makes 16 (2-inch) squares

1½ cups cholesterol-free egg substitute
¾ cup skim milk
1 tablespoon onion flakes
1 tablespoon grated low-fat Parmesan cheese
⅛ teaspoon garlic powder
⅛ teaspoon ground black pepper

¼ cup dry bread crumbs
¾ cup shredded reduced-fat Cheddar cheese
1 (10-ounce) package frozen chopped spinach, thawed and well drained
¼ cup fresh roasted sweet red bell pepper (optional)

In medium bowl, combine egg substitute, milk, onion flakes, Parmesan cheese, garlic powder, pepper and red pepper, if desired; set aside. Sprinkle bread crumbs evenly onto bottom of lightly greased (canola oil) 8×8×2-inch baking dish. Top with ½ cup Cheddar cheese and spinach. Pour egg mixture evenly over spinach; top with remaining Cheddar cheese. Bake at 350 degrees for 35 to 40 minutes. Let stand 10 minutes. Cut into 2-inch squares. Serve hot.

A Taste of the Good Life: From the Heart of Tennessee
Saint Thomas Hospital, Nashville, Tennessee

Sweet Mustard Bacon

Serves 4

8 thick slices bacon
2 teaspoon Dijon mustard
4 teaspoons packed light brown sugar

Preheat the oven to 350 degrees. Line a baking sheet with foil. Place a rack over the foil. Arrange the bacon on the rack. Spread with the Dijon mustard and sprinkle with the brown sugar. Bake for 45 minutes; drain.

Art Fare
Toledo Museum of Art Aides, Toledo, Ohio

Baked Pineapple

Serves 6

1 (16-ounce) can crushed pineapple, drained
3 eggs, beaten
3/4 cup sugar

4 tablespoons cornstarch
Butter
Cinnamon

Combine pineapple with 3 well-beaten eggs. Mix the sugar and cornstarch together and add to the egg and pineapple mixture. Mix well. Pour into 1-quart baking dish. Dot with butter and sprinkle with cinnamon. Bake at 350 degrees for 45 to 60 minutes or until firm and brown.

A Taste of Georgia
Newnan Junior Service League, Newnan, Georgia

Fig and Gruyère Palmiers

Makes 56 pieces

1 (17-ounce) package frozen puff pastry
   sheets, thawed

2 cups (8 ounces) shredded Gruyère cheese
1/2 cup fig preserves, melted

Roll one puff pastry sheet into a 10×14-inch rectangle on a work surface. Sprinkle with 1 cup of the cheese. Roll as for a jelly roll, starting from each short side to meet in the center. Repeat with the remaining pastry sheet and the remaining 1 cup of cheese. Wrap separately in plastic wrap and chill for at least 1 hour or up to 10 hours. Cut each roll into 1/4-inch slices. Place slices on parchment-lined baking sheet. Brush with fig preserves. Bake at 400 degrees for 8 to 10 minutes or until golden brown. Serve warm.

Be Present At Our Table
Germantown United Methodist Women, Germantown, Tennessee

Curried Fruit

Serves 6 to 8

1 (24-ounce) jar mixed salad fruit
1/4 cup (1/2 stick) butter
1/4 cup chutney

1 tablespoon curry powder
2 cups fresh or frozen cantaloupe or honeydew
   melon balls

Drain the salad fruit, reserving 3/4 cup syrup. Combine the butter, chutney, curry powder and reserved syrup in a saucepan and bring to a boil. Cook for 10 minutes or until thickened. Stir in the salad fruit and melon balls. Chill, covered, until serving time. Let stand for 30 minutes before serving.

Note: Be sure to use the jars of salad fruit found in the produce section of your market—not canned fruit cocktail.

Tastes, Tales and Traditions
Palo Alto Auxiliary for Children, Palo Alto, California

Saturday Morning Chocolate Gravy

Serves 4 to 6

4 tablespoons cocoa
4 tablespoons sugar
4 tablespoons flour
2 cups milk
1 egg, beaten
1 teaspoon vanilla extract

Mix cocoa, sugar and flour in a bowl and set aside. Slowly bring milk and egg just below boil in a saucepan, stirring. Whisk in dry ingredients, stirring almost constantly until gravy thickens. Serve over biscuits.

Add Another Place Setting
Junior League of Northwest Arkansas, Springdale, Arkansas

Fancy Butters

Variable servings

PRALINE BUTTER
1/2 cup sugar
1/3 cup water
1/2 cup chopped pecans
3/4 cup (1 1/2 sticks) butter, softened

ORANGE HONEY BUTTER
1/2 cup (1 stick) unsalted butter,
    at room temperature
2 tablespoons honey
1 tablespoon grated orange zest

RASPBERRY BUTTER
1/2 cup (1 stick) butter, softened

1/2 cup crushed raspberries
1 tablespoon sugar, or 1/4 cup raspberry jam

For the praline butter, combine the sugar and water in a saucepan over medium heat and stir until the sugar dissolves. Cook for 8 to 10 minutes or until the mixture reaches 300 degrees on a candy thermometer and is amber-colored. Do not stir. Remove from the heat and stir in the pecans. Pour onto a buttered baking sheet. Let stand for 10 to 15 minutes or until cool. Break the praline into pieces and place in a food processor. Process until a coarse powder consistency. Combine with the butter in a small bowl and mix well. This may be prepared several days in advance and stored in the refrigerator. Bring to room temperature before serving.

For the orange honey butter, beat the butter in a small bowl until light and fluffy. Add the honey and orange zest and beat until blended.

For the raspberry butter, combine the butter, raspberries and sugar in a small bowl and beat until blended. You may substitute strawberries and strawberry jam for the raspberries and raspberry jam if preferred.

From Grouper to Grits
The Junior League of Clearwater-Dunedin, Clearwater, Florida

Soups, Salads and Sandwiches

"After managing and staffing a tearoom and luncheon restaurant for more than seventy-five years, our organization decided to publish its first cookbook and I was appointed recipe chair. I diligently led a team of ladies who had the formidable task of sorting through hundreds of recipes used in the restaurant dating back to the early 1930s. Week after week, our team met at my house reviewing, sorting, and choosing possible recipes for inclusion. Next came the testing, tasting, and rewriting phase. Throughout the whole project, I handled the computerized database, making every edit to every recipe. My recipe team knew that I had looked at one too many recipes when I emailed directions to my house, and instead of writing 'Exit at Foothill Expressway,' I wrote, 'Exit at Foothill Expressway!'

Since 1931, the members of our organization have raised funds to help pay for uncompensated medical expenses so that every child at Lucile Packard Children's Hospital receives the care needed. Fundraising activities by our volunteers have included operating and staffing the Allied Arts Guild Restaurant in Menlo Park, California, for seventy-five years, hosting and catering bridal, wedding, and other receptions, special lunches and fashion shows, holiday teas, and the American Girl Event. Each year, volunteers sew tote bags and fill them with goodies to bring a little cheer to children who must spend the holidays in the hospital. Most recently we created our award-winning cookbook, *Tastes, Tales and Traditions*, to raise money and bring hope to the children of Lucile Packard Children's Hospital."

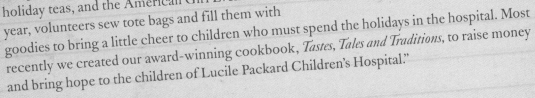

Mary Hicks
Palo Alto Auxiliary for Children
Menlo Park, California

Minestrone

2 large beef shanks
4 to 5 carrots, sliced
3 to 4 ribs celery, sliced
2 to 3 potatoes, sliced
1/2 head cabbage, shredded
1 (6-ounce) can tomato paste
1 tablespoon salt, or to taste

1 tablespoon dried parsley
Pepper to taste
2 to 3 tablespoons olive oil
2 large onions, sliced
6 garlic cloves, minced
1 (15-ounce) can cannellini beans (optional)

Combine the shanks and enough water to cover in a large stockpot. Stir in the carrots, celery, potatoes, cabbage, tomato paste, 1 tablespoon salt, the parsley and pepper. Heat the olive oil in a large skillet. Add the onions and garlic. Sauté until tender. Add to the stockpot. Bring to a boil. Reduce the heat to low. Simmer for 1 1/2 to 2 hours or until the meat is tender. Remove the bones from the pot. Shred the meat and return the meat to the pot. Stir in the beans and cook until heated through. Season with salt and pepper to taste.

Note: Slice and shred the vegetables in a food processor for easy preparation.

Boston Uncommon
The Junior League of Boston, Boston, Massachusetts

Chili Queen's Chili

2 pounds lean chili meat
1/2 pound lean ground chuck
1 onion, chopped
1/4 cup green pepper, chopped
2 cloves garlic, minced
1 tablespoon chili powder
1 tablespoon cumin
3/4 teaspoon oregano
1/2 teaspoon sage

2 tablespoons cornmeal
2 tablespoons chili seasoning
1 teaspoon salt
1/4 teaspoon black pepper
1 tablespoon Worcestershire sauce
1/4 to 1/2 cup chili sauce
1 (6-ounce) can tomato paste
1 (16-ounce) can whole tomatoes

Sauté ground meats, onion, green pepper, and garlic in 6-quart roasting pan. Add remaining ingredients, blending well. Bring to a boiling point. Reduce heat and simmer, covered, two hours. Beans may be added, if desired.

Stir Ups
Junior Welfare League of Enid, Enid, Oklahoma

Meatball Tortellini Soup

Serves 6 to 8

8 ounces ground beef
1 small onion, chopped
2 slices bread
3/4 cup (3 ounces) shredded Parmesan cheese
2 large cans chicken broth
1 1/2 cups chopped onions
1 1/2 cups chopped carrots

1 teaspoon basil
1/4 teaspoon hot pepper flakes
2 cups fresh tortellini
1 small zucchini, sliced
3 to 5 ounces spinach, chopped
Freshly grated Parmesan cheese

Process the ground beef, 1 onion, the bread and shredded Parmesan cheese in a food processor until combined. Shape into meatballs and set aside. Bring the broth, onions, carrots, basil and hot pepper flakes to a boil in a large stockpot. Add the meatballs and simmer for 15 to 20 minutes or until cooked through. Add the pasta and cook until al dente. Stir in the zucchini and spinach. Cook for 3 minutes. Ladle into soup bowls and sprinkle with freshly grated Parmesan cheese.

Note: For the meatballs, add 2 to 3 tablespoons milk and salt and pepper to taste while processing.

Great Women, Great Food
Junior League of Kankakee County, Kankakee, Illinois

Santa Fe Soup

Makes 4 quarts

2 pounds ground turkey or beef
1 onion, chopped
2 (.5-ounce) packages ranch-style dressing mix
2 (1 1/4-ounce) packages taco seasoning mix
1 (16-ounce) can black beans, undrained
1 (16-ounce) can kidney beans, undrained
1 (16-ounce) can pinto beans, undrained

1 (16-ounce) can diced tomatoes with chilies, undrained
1 (16-ounce) can tomato wedges, undrained
2 (16-ounce) cans white corn, undrained
2 cups water
GARNISH: sour cream, shredded Cheddar cheese, sliced green onions

Cook meat and onion together in a stockpot until meat is browned. Stir ranch-style dressing mix and taco seasoning mix into meat. Add remaining ingredients with juices from all. Add water. Simmer for 2 hours. (If mixture is too thick, add additional water.) Garnish each serving with sour cream, shredded Cheddar cheese, and sliced green onions, if desired. Serve with tortilla chips.

Food for Thought
Junior League of Birmingham, Inc., Birmingham, Alabama

Father Art's Pozole

Serves 6

1 tablespoon vegetable oil
1 (2-pound) pork shoulder, trimmed and
    cut into 1 1/2-inch cubes
1 large onion, minced
4 garlic cloves, minced
5 cups chicken broth

10 tomatillos, husked, cored and
    cut into quarters
1 bunch cilantro, stems removed
1 (15-ounce) can hominy, drained and rinsed
2 whole dried red chiles, stems removed
Salt and pepper to taste

Heat the oil in a large heavy skillet over high heat. Add the pork and sauté until brown on all sides. Reduce the heat to medium and add the onion. Cook for 10 minutes or until the onion is tender, stirring occasionally. Add the garlic and cook for 1 minute. Combine the pork mixture with 3 cups of the chicken broth in a large saucepan. Simmer for 1 1/2 hours or until the pork is very tender. Combine the remaining 2 cups chicken broth with the tomatillos and cilantro in a blender and process until puréed. Add the purée, hominy and red chiles to the pork mixture and simmer for 15 minutes. Remove and discard the chiles and season with salt and pepper. Ladle into bowls and serve with chopped onion, shredded lettuce, thinly sliced radishes, cheese, cilantro and lime wedges.

Note: Pozole can be prepared a day or two in advance and chilled, covered, until needed. Reheat over low heat to serve.

The Bells are Ringing: A Call to Table
Mission San Juan Capistrano Women's Guild, San Juan Capistrano, California

Potato Soup

Serves 8

1 pound bacon or bulk sausage
1 cup chopped onion
1 cup chopped celery
4 large russet potatoes, peeled, cubed
1 tablespoon mustard seeds

2 tablespoons salt
1 cup light cream
2 cups milk
2 (10 1/2 ounces each) cans any flavor cream soup
    (optional)

GARNISH
Chopped parsley

Cook the bacon in a saucepan over low heat until crisp. Remove to a warm plate with a slotted spoon and drain the saucepan, reserving 1 tablespoon drippings. Add the onion and celery to the reserved drippings in the saucepan and sauté until tender. Add the potatoes, mustard seeds and salt. Add just enough water to cover the potatoes. Simmer for 15 minutes or until the potatoes are tender but still firm; reduce the heat. Stir in the cream and milk. Add the canned soup if a thicker soup is desired. Cook just until heated through; do not boil. Pour into large mugs and top with the crumbled bacon. Garnish with parsley. Add corn bread, apple salad, gingerbread cookies and cider for a complete autumn supper. Then find a cozy blanket and a good book.

Beyond Burlap
Junior League of Boise, Boise, Idaho

Chicken Stew

3 pounds skinless chicken pieces
1/2 teaspoon salt
1/4 teaspoon black pepper
1/4 teaspoon red pepper
One 10-ounce bag frozen seasoning
    vegetables, or 1 cup chopped onion
2 stalks celery, chopped

1/2 red bell pepper, chopped
1/2 green bell pepper, chopped
2 tablespoons chopped parsley
1 to 2 cups water
1 tablespoon bottled browning sauce
2 tablespoons gravy flour

Season chicken pieces with salt and both peppers. Place frozen vegetables or chopped fresh vegetables in large skillet or Dutch oven. Add 1/4 cup water and boil until vegetables are softened. Place chicken pieces into pan. Add 1 cup water and browning sauce. Reduce heat to simmer and cover pan. Let cook one hour, turning pieces occasionally. Dissolve flour in 1/2 cup water. Add to pan juices and cook on high heat until gravy is thickened. Add water as needed. Correct seasonings. Serve over rice.

River Road Recipes III: A Healthy Collection
Junior League of Baton Rouge, Baton Rouge, Louisiana

Wild Duck Gumbo

2 dressed ducks
1/2 cup butter
1 cup sifted flour
1 heaping soup plate chopped onion (about 3 cups)
1 heaping soup plate chopped celery (about 3 cups)
3 cloves garlic, finely chopped
1 (6-ounce) can tomato paste
1 (20-ounce) can tomatoes, undrained
2 teaspoons Accent
1 heaping soup plate chopped green peppers
    (about 3 cups)

1 bunch green onions, chopped
1 bunch parsley, finely chopped
    (remove 1/2 cup for garnish)
1 teaspoon oregano
1 teaspoon thyme
1 tablespoon salt
1 tablespoon pepper
1/2 tablespoon red pepper
2 pounds shrimp, cooked and peeled
Wild and white rice, cooked

Boil dressed ducks until tender (2 hours or so) in slightly salted water to cover. Drain, reserving stock. Melt butter in a heavy iron pot and add flour to make roux the color of an Indian squaw. Stir constantly over medium heat. When roux is ready, add onions and celery. Cook with reduced heat until onions and celery brown. Add garlic, tomato paste, tomatoes, Accent, green peppers, green onions, parsley and seasonings. Add 2 quarts of reserved duck stock and boil rapidly for 1/2 hour. Remove meat from duck carcasses and cut into bite-sized pieces. Add meat to pot. More stock may be added to make a rich gumbo. Add cooked and peeled shrimp. To serve, pour gumbo over cooked rice in soup plates. Sprinkle parsley on top.

Traditions: A Taste of the Good Life
Junior League of Little Rock, Little Rock, Arkansas

Curried Pumpkin Crab Bisque

Serves 8 to 10

1 small onion, finely chopped
4 garlic gloves, minced
2 tablespoons curry powder
2 teaspoons ground ginger or
    2 tablespoons grated fresh ginger
1 teaspoon ground nutmeg
1/2 teaspoon Tabasco sauce
1/2 cup (1 stick) butter, melted

1 tablespoon cornstarch
1 (16-ounce) can pumpkin purée
4 cups chicken broth
2 cups heavy cream
2 cups fresh lump back-fin crab meat, flaked
Salt and pepper to taste
Cognac (optional)
Fresh or dried parsley

Cook the onion, garlic, curry powder, ginger, nutmeg and Tabasco sauce in the butter in a stockpot until the onion is tender, stirring frequently. Stir in the cornstarch and cook until thickened. Add the pumpkin and broth and bring the mixture to a boil. Reduce the heat and simmer for 15 minutes, stirring occasionally. Stir in the cream and crab meat. Cook until thickened and bubbly, stirring constantly. Season with salt and pepper. Ladle into soup bowls. Pour a splash of cognac over each serving. Sprinkle with parsley.

Savor the Seasons
The Junior League of Tampa, Tampa, Florida

She Crab Soup

Serves 6

2 tablespoons tub margarine
3 tablespoons flour
One 12-ounce can evaporated skim milk
2 1/2 cups skim milk

2 cups defatted turkey or chicken stock, less salt
5 shallots, chopped
1 pound crabmeat
1/4 cup white wine

In double boiler, melt margarine. Stir in flour and slowly add milks. Cook until it thickens. Heat 1/2 cup chicken stock in a separate saucepan and sauté the shallots until soft. Add this mixture to the sauce and stir well. Then gradually stir in remaining stock. Add crabmeat and wine. Heat thoroughly and serve.

River Road Recipes III: A Healthy Collection
Junior League of Baton Rouge, Baton Rouge, Louisiana

Crawfish and Corn Soup

Serves 4

1/2 cup (1 stick) butter
1 bunch green onions, trimmed and chopped
4 to 8 ounces fresh mushrooms, sliced
2 garlic cloves, minced
8 ounces cream cheese, cubed

2 (10-ounce) cans niblet corn, drained
2 (10-ounce) cans cream of potato soup
2 cups half-and-half
1 pound crawfish tails

Melt the butter in a saucepan and add the green onions, mushrooms and garlic. Sauté until the green onions and mushrooms are tender. Add the cream cheese and stir until combined. Stir in the soup, corn, half-and-half and crawfish. Cook until heated through, stirring occasionally; do not boil. Ladle into soup bowls and serve immediately.

Mardi Gras to Mistletoe
Junior League of Shreveport-Bossier, Shreveport, Louisiana

Oyster Artichoke Soup

Serves 6

1 large onion, chopped
1 bunch green onions, chopped
1/2 cup (1 stick) butter, melted
2 garlic cloves, crushed or minced
2 tablespoons chopped parsley
2 (16-ounce) cans artichoke hearts, drained and
    cut into quarters

2 (10-ounce) cans cream of mushroom soup
1 cup oyster liquor or water
1 bay leaf
2 dozen (or more) shucked oysters
Salt and pepper to taste

Sauté the onions in the butter in a large heavy saucepan until transparent. Add the garlic and parsley and sauté for 2 to 3 minutes. Add the artichoke hearts and sauté for 3 to 4 minutes. Add the soup, oyster liquor and bay leaf. Cook for 20 minutes, stirring occasionally. Add the oysters and cook for 5 minutes. Simmer for up to 30 minutes to allow the flavors to meld. Discard the bay leaf.

Shall We Gather
Trinity Episcopal Church, Wetumpka, Alabama

Grand Central Station Oyster Bar Stew

Serves 2

Celery salt to taste
Salt to taste
Pepper to taste
Paprika to taste
1/2 teaspoon Worcestershire sauce

2 tablespoons butter
1 pint oysters, drained, liquid reserved
1 pint half-and-half
2 pats of butter
Cayenne pepper

In a double boiler combine celery salt, salt, pepper, paprika, Worcestershire, butter, and oyster liquid. Allow to simmer a few minutes over boiling water. Add half-and-half. Let soup become very hot and then add oysters. Remove from heat as soon as oysters are heated because you want them to remain plump and juicy. Top each serving with a pat of butter and a dash of cayenne pepper.

Magic
Junior League of Birmingham, Inc., Birmingham, Alabama

Seafood Gumbo

Serves 10 to 12

1 cup flour
1 cup vegetable oil
3 medium white or yellow onions, chopped
5 ribs celery, chopped
2 tablespoons oil
2 quarts chicken broth

1 (24-ounce) jar hot picante sauce
1 (14.5-ounce) can chopped tomatoes (do not drain)
1 (16-ounce) bag frozen okra
2 (12.5-ounce) cans chunk chicken
2 or 3 (6-ounce) cans crab meat
2 pounds medium peeled, deveined, tail-off shrimp

Mix flour and oil in iron skillet and bake for 1 to 1 1/2 hours at 350 degrees or until a golden copper color. You can also prepare roux on top of the stove, stirring continuously until a golden copper color. Sauté onions and celery in oil in stockpot. Add roux, chicken broth, picante sauce, tomatoes, okra, chicken and crab meat to onions and celery in stockpot. Simmer for 1 hour. Add shrimp and simmer for 20 to 30 minutes more. Serve over a scoop of rice.

Add Another Place Setting
Junior League of Northwest Arkansas, Springdale, Arkansas

Northshore Seafood Gumbo

Serves 8 to 10

SHRIMP STOCK
3 pounds uncooked medium shrimp
12 cups (3 quarts) water
1 tablespoon shrimp boil
2 onions, sliced
10 peppercorns
1 lemon, sliced
4 garlic cloves, crushed
3 ribs celery, cut into quarters

GUMBO
8 ounces okra, thinly sliced
2 tablespoons vegetable oil
1 1/2 cups flour
1 cup vegetable oil
2 onions, finely chopped
1/2 cup thinly sliced celery
1 cup chopped red bell pepper
6 garlic cloves, minced
4 ounces ham, cut into cubes
Salt to taste
3 bay leaves
1/2 teaspoon white pepper
1/2 teaspoon black pepper
1/4 teaspoon cayenne pepper
1/2 teaspoon oregano
1/2 teaspoon thyme
1 (16-ounce) can tomatoes, crushed
1 (8-ounce) can tomato paste
3 tablespoons Worcestershire sauce
4 gumbo crabs
1 pound lump crabmeat, shells removed
1 pint oysters
Hot cooked rice

For the shrimp stock, peel and devein the shrimp, reserving the shells. Chill the shrimp in a bowl in the refrigerator until ready to add to the gumbo. Combine the reserved shrimp shells, water, liquid shrimp boil, onions, peppercorns, lemon, garlic and celery in a large stockpot and mix well. Bring to boil over high heat and reduce the heat. Simmer for 30 to 45 minutes. Drain the stock, discarding the solid ingredients. Return the strained stock to the stockpot. Simmer over medium-low heat.

For the gumbo, sauté the okra in 2 tablespoons oil in a skillet for 10 to 15 minutes or until tender. Cook the flour and 1 cup oil in a skillet to make a dark rich roux, stirring constantly. Add the onions, celery and bell pepper. Sauté for 4 minutes. Add the sautéed okra, garlic, ham, salt, bay leaves, white pepper, black pepper, cayenne pepper, oregano and thyme. Sauté for 2 minutes. Spoon gradually into the heated stock and stir to mix well. Add the undrained crushed tomatoes, tomato paste, and Worcestershire sauce. Bring to a boil over medium heat and reduce the heat, stirring constantly. Simmer for 30 minutes, stirring occasionally. Add the gumbo crabs and crab meat. Cook for 15 minutes.

Drain the oysters, reserving 2 tablespoons liquor. Add the oysters, reserved liquor and chilled shrimp to the gumbo. Cook for 5 to 10 minutes or until the shrimp turn pink and the oysters curl. Discard the bay leaves. Serve over hot fluffy rice.

Roux To Do
Junior League of Greater Covington, Covington, Louisiana

Cooter Soup

1 large or 2 small "yellow belly" cooters
    (preferably female)
1 large onion, chopped
Salt to taste
2 teaspoons allspice
Red pepper to taste

3 tablespoons dry sherry
4 quarts of water
1 small Irish potato, diced
12 whole cloves
2 tablespoons Worcestershire
Flour to thicken

Kill cooter by chopping off head. Let it stand inverted until thoroughly drained, then plunge into boiling water for five minutes. Crack the shell all around very carefully, so as not to cut the eggs which are lodged near surface. The edible parts are the front and hind quarters and a strip of white meat adhering to the back of the shell, the liver and the eggs. Remove all outer skin which peels very easily if water is hot enough. Wash thoroughly and allow to stand in cold water a short while, or place in refrigerator overnight.

Boil cooter meat, onion and potato in the water, and cook until meat drops from bones—about 2 hours. Remove all bones and skin and cut meat up with scissors. Return meat to stock, add spices and simmer. Brown flour in skillet, mix with 1 cup of stock to smooth paste and thicken soup. Twenty minutes before serving add cooter eggs. Add sherry and garnish with thin slices of lemon.

Note: A cooter is a large river turtle of the Southern United States.

Charleston Receipts
Junior League of Charleston, Charleston, South Carolina

Turtle Soup

3 pounds turtle meat, cut into 1-inch cubes
1 cup oil
1 cup flour
1 cup diced onions
1 cup diced celery
6 cloves chopped garlic
One 8-ounce can tomato sauce
2 quarts water

1/4 cup beef extract
2 teaspoons celery salt
4 bay leaves
2 lemons, halved
1 teaspoon thyme
1/2 cup chopped parsley
Salt and lemon-pepper to taste
Garnish: sliced lemon, chopped egg, sherry

Sauté turtle meat in oil until brown. Set aside. Brown flour, and add onion, celery and garlic. Cook 10 minutes. Add remaining ingredients and turtle meat. Simmer about 2 hours until meat is very tender. Garnish with sliced lemon, chopped egg and sherry before serving.

River Road Recipes II: Second Helping
Junior League of Baton Rouge, Baton Rouge, Louisiana

Creamy Broccoli Soup

3 tablespoons butter
1 onion, chopped
1 (14-ounce) package frozen broccoli florets,
    cooked and drained
1/4 cup chopped fresh parsley
1/4 cup all-purpose flour
2 cups low-sodium chicken broth,
    at room temperature
1 cup half-and-half

1 cup 2% milk
2 tablespoons lemon juice
1/2 teaspoon kosher salt
1/2 teaspoon garlic powder
1/2 teaspoon cayenne pepper
1/4 teaspoon black pepper
1/8 teaspoon ground nutmeg
2 pounds Velveeta cheese, cubed

Melt the butter in a large saucepan and add the onion. Sauté until tender. Stir in the broccoli and parsley and simmer for 3 minutes, stirring occasionally. Sprinkle the flour over the broccoli mixture and cook over medium heat for 2 minutes or until the flour is absorbed, stirring constantly. Cool slightly and spoon the broccoli mixture into a blender.

Add enough of the broth to fill the blender 3/4 full and process until puréed. Return the purée to the saucepan and stir in the half-and-half, milk, lemon juice, salt, garlic powder, cayenne pepper, black pepper and nutmeg.

Microwave the cheese in a microwave-safe dish on Low until melted or melt in a double boiler. Stir the melted cheese into the soup and simmer for 20 to 30 minutes or to the desired consistency, stirring occasionally. Ladle into soup bowls. You may substitute 2 cups chopped cooked fresh broccoli florets for the frozen broccoli.

Tables of Content
Junior League of Birmingham, Inc., Birmingham, Alabama

Being involved in a community cookbook project not only inspired me to pursue a new career in the publishing industry, but it helped me network with the people to make it possible. Throughout the development process, I worked with incredibly talented individuals both on the cookbook committee and in the publishing industry. Once the cookbook was complete, I moved to a new city and landed my dream job as a cookbook editor and project leader with a leading publishing company.

It was the contacts I made while working on *Tables of Content* combined with perseverance that made this possible. In my new hometown, I continue to volunteer with the Junior League and have become involved with other nonprofit organizations. After all, it was the love and desire to give back to the community that got me involved with my first cookbook in the first place. I wish to thank all of the talented people I met while working on that cookbook, and I want to extend my appreciation and gratitude for the friendship and support that they have given me.

Mary Spotswood Underwood
Junior League of Birmingham, Inc., Birmingham, Alabama

Walla Walla Onion Soup

5 cans (14 ounces each) beef broth
3 cups apple cider or apple juice
2 bay leaves
6 sprigs fresh thyme or 1 teaspoon dried thyme
2 teaspoons freshly ground black pepper
Salt
4 tablespoons unsalted butter
3 pounds Walla Walla sweet onions, thinly sliced

1 teaspoon sugar
2/3 cup dry sherry
8 baguette slices (1 inch thick)
1 cup freshly grated Parmesan cheese
Sliced Gruyère cheese
2/3 cup finely diced red apple, such as Red Delicious, chilled

Combine the beef broth, apple cider, bay leaves, thyme, pepper, and a good pinch of salt in a large stockpot. Bring to a boil over high heat, reduce the heat to medium-low, and simmer, covered, for 1 hour.

While the broth is simmering, melt the butter in a large skillet over medium heat. Add the onions and sauté until beginning to soften, about 8 minutes. Add the sugar and cook, covered, but stirring occasionally, until the onions are very tender and nicely browned, about 40 to 45 minutes. You may have to add 1 to 2 tablespoons of water if the pan gets dry. When the onions are soft and brown, stir the sherry into the pan, scraping up any cooked bits from the bottom.

Add the onions and sherry to the broth. Cover and simmer for 1 hour. Remove the bay leaves and thyme sprigs and taste the soup for seasoning, adding more salt to taste

Preheat the broiler. Ladle the soup into ovenproof bowls, top with a slice of baguette, sprinkle with Parmesan and top with 1 or 2 slices of Gruyère. Broil until the cheese is melted and bubbly, about 1 to 2 minutes. Top with the diced apple and serve.

Celebrate the Rain
The Junior League of Seattle, Seattle, Washington

Coordinating the ten-person cookbook committee for The Village Club of Bloomfield Hills, Michigan, was an exercise in leadership, diplomacy, enthusiasm, and restraint. Our committee was made up of all variety of individuals with various interests and experiences, from gourmet chefs to fix-it-fast-and-easy cooks. Combining all of our personal interests and visions made for a slow process, but one that evolved into an elegant final result in *Popovers to Panache*. Knowing that the proceeds from the sale of our cookbook would provide continued support for local charitable organizations motivated us all the more.

The Village Woman's Club Foundation is the philanthropic arm of The Village Club and distributes grants to charitable organizations in the tri-county area of Detroit. In 2006, after twenty-four years in existence, the Foundation surpassed the $1 million mark for giving back to the community. Our outreach only continues to grow, and many of our efforts are funded by proceeds from the sales of *Popovers to Panache*.

Red Pepper Brie Soup

2 tablespoons olive oil
1 rib celery, chopped
1 carrot, chopped
1/2 cup chopped onion
1 garlic clove, chopped
2 cups water
1 ounce chicken base
3 large red bell peppers, roasted
4 1/2 ounces Brie cheese, rind removed and chopped

4 1/2 ounces cream cheese, chopped
2 sprigs fresh basil
1 sprig fresh thyme
1/2 sprig fresh rosemary
2 bay leaves
Cornstarch
1 cup heavy cream, heated
Salt and pepper to taste

Heat the olive oil in a saucepan. Add the celery, carrot and onion and sauté for 5 minutes. Add the garlic and cook until the garlic is light brown. Stir in the water, chicken base, bell peppers, Brie cheese, cream cheese, basil, thyme, rosemary and bay leaves. Bring to a boil and reduce the heat. Simmer for 30 minutes. Blend enough cornstarch to thicken the soup with a small amount of water. Add to the soup and cook until thickened, stirring constantly. Process in a blender or food processor until smooth. Strain back into the saucepan and add the heated cream. Season with salt and pepper and ladle into soup bowls.

From Grouper to Grits
The Junior League of Clearwater-Dunedin, Clearwater, Florida

Low-Fat Potato Soup

4 cups chopped potatoes
1 (10-ounce) can chicken broth
1 cup thinly sliced celery
1/2 cup chopped carrot
1/2 cup chopped onion
1 1/2 teaspoons salt

1/8 teaspoon pepper
1/8 teaspoon dillweed
4 cups skim or whole milk
3 1/2 tablespoons flour
2 tablespoons butter
Shredded Cheddar cheese

Combine the potatoes, broth, celery, carrot, onion, salt, pepper and dillweed in a 3-quart saucepan and mix well. Bring to a boil; reduce heat. Simmer, covered, for 15 to 20 minutes or until the vegetables are tender, stirring occasionally. Stir 3 cups of the skim milk into the potato mixture. Cook until heated through, stirring occasionally. Whisk the flour into the remaining 1 cup skim milk. Add the flour mixture to the soup, stirring constantly. Cook until thickened and heated through, stirring frequently. Stir in the butter. Ladle into soup bowls. Sprinkle with cheese.

Cooking By the Bootstraps
Junior Welfare League of Enid, Enid, Oklahoma

Potato and Green Chile Chowder

6 slices bacon
1 tablespoon butter
2 tablespoons olive oil
1 large red bell pepper, finely chopped, or
  1 (4-ounce) jar chopped pimentos, drained
1 large onion, finely chopped
1 small jalapeño chile, seeded and finely chopped
1/3 cup all-purpose flour
6 cups chicken broth, heated

5 or 6 large thin-skinned potatoes, peeled and
  cubed (preferably Yukon Gold)
1 (4-ounce) can diced mild green chiles, drained
1 teaspoon dry mustard
1 teaspoon salt, or to taste
1/2 teaspoon pepper
2 cups half-and-half
1 cup milk

Cook the bacon in a skillet until crisp; drain, reserving 1 tablespoon drippings. Crumble the bacon. Combine the reserved bacon drippings, butter and olive oil in a 6-quart soup pot over medium-low heat. Add the bell pepper, onion and jalapeño chile and sauté until the vegetables are tender crisp. Reduce the heat to low and sprinkle the flour over the vegetables. Cook for 1 to 2 minutes, stirring constantly. Whisk in the chicken broth. Add the potatoes, chiles, dry mustard, salt and pepper. Bring to a boil. Reduce the heat and simmer, covered, for 10 to 15 minutes or just until the potatoes are tender. Stir in the half-and-half and milk. Simmer gently, covered, over very low heat for 20 to 30 minutes or up to 1 hour to concentrate the flavors. Add the crumbled bacon just before serving. Adjust the seasonings. Garnish each serving with chopped cilantro, pats of herb butter, shredded Monterey Jack cheese or shredded Cheddar cheese.

CHILE PEPPER TIPS

When working with hot chiles, wear plastic gloves and avoid touching your face and eyes. The heat, located mainly in the seeds and ribs, can irritate the skin and cause burning. When finished, wash your hands, the cutting board, and the knife.

When purchasing, look for chiles with shiny, smooth, unblemished skins. Generally, larger chiles are milder, while smaller ones are hotter. Store fresh for 7 to 10 days in the refrigerator, after first wrapping in paper towels and sealing in a plastic bag. Red chiles are fully ripe and will not keep as long as green chiles.

Tastes, Tales and Traditions
Palo Alto Auxiliary for Children, Palo Alto, California

West African Sweet Potato Soup

2 medium onions, chopped
1 tablespoon vegetable oil or olive oil
2 or 3 carrots, chopped
2 teaspoons grated gingerroot
1/8 to 1/4 teaspoon cayenne pepper
2 medium sweet potatoes, peeled and
    sliced 1/2 inch thick

3 to 4 cups water or stock
2 cups tomato juice or vegetable juice cocktail
1 tablespoon peanut butter
1 tablespoon sugar (optional)

GARNISH
chopped green onions and/or peanuts

Sauté the onions in the oil in a large saucepan. Add the carrots, ginger and cayenne pepper. Sauté for 5 minutes. Add the sweet potatoes and water and cook for 20 minutes or until the sweet potatoes are tender. Stir in the tomato juice. Process the soup in batches in a food processor or blender until smooth. Combine the batches in the saucepan and whisk in the peanut butter and sugar. Garnish the servings with green onions and/or peanuts.

Notably Nashville
Junior League of Nashville, Nashville, Tennessee

Pumpkin Soup

1/4 cup (1/2 stick) butter
1 cup chopped onion
1 garlic clove, crushed
1 teaspoon curry powder
1/2 teaspoon salt
1/4 teaspoon ground coriander
1/8 teaspoon crushed red pepper

3 cups chicken broth
1 (29-ounce) can pumpkin, or 3 1/2 cups mashed
    cooked fresh pumpkin
1 (12-ounce) can evaporated milk
1/4 cup packed light brown sugar (optional)
Sour cream for garnish
Chopped fresh chives for garnish

Melt the butter in a large saucepan and add the onion and garlic. Sauté for 3 to 4 minutes or until the onion is tender. Stir in the curry powder, salt, coriander and red pepper. Cook for 1 minute, stirring frequently. Add the broth and bring to a gentle boil. Boil gently for 15 to 20 minutes, stirring occasionally. Stir in the pumpkin and evaporated milk. Mix in the brown sugar for a sweeter flavor and cook for 5 minutes. Cool slightly; pour into a blender and process until creamy. Ladle the warm soup into soup bowls and garnish with sour cream and chives.

Tables of Content
Junior League of Birmingham, Inc., Birmingham, Alabama

Butternut Squash Soup

2 1/2 to 3 pounds butternut squash
2 cups chopped onions
3 garlic cloves, chopped
1 (3-inch) piece gingerroot
2 tablespoons olive oil

1 teaspoon curry powder
1/4 teaspoon cinnamon
2 teaspoons salt
1/4 teaspoon pepper
4 cups chicken stock or water

GARNISH
Chopped fresh cilantro

Cut the squash into halves lengthwise, discarding the seeds. Place cut side down on a foil-lined baking sheet. Bake at 425 degrees for 1 hour or until tender. Cool slightly. Sauté the onions, garlic and gingerroot in the heated olive oil in a large saucepan for 10 minutes or until tender but not brown. Stir in the curry powder, cinnamon, salt and pepper. Cook over low heat for 10 minutes, stirring constantly. Stir in the chicken stock. Bring to a boil and reduce the heat. Scoop the squash pulp from the shells and add to the soup. Simmer for 20 minutes; discard the gingerroot. Purée the soup in batches in a blender. Combine in the saucepan and simmer until heated through. Ladle into soup bowls and garnish with cilantro. You may prepare the soup several days in advance and store in the refrigerator; reheat to serve.

Oh My Stars!
Junior League of Roanoke Valley, Roanoke, Virginia

Tomato Basil Soup

1 1/2 onions, coarsely chopped
3 ribs celery, coarsely chopped
3 garlic cloves, coarsely chopped
1/2 bunch basil, coarsely chopped
2 tablespoons olive oil
3/4 cup white wine
3 cups rich chicken stock

6 cups tomato sauce
Salt to taste
1 teaspoon white pepper
6 tablespoons butter
6 tablespoons all-purpose flour
1 1/2 cups heavy cream
Chopped fresh basil

Sauté the onions, celery, garlic and basil in the olive oil in a large saucepan over medium heat until the vegetables are tender. Stir in the wine. Cook until the wine is reduced by half. Stir in the stock and bring to a boil. Stir in the tomato sauce and return to a boil. Reduce the heat and stir in the salt and white pepper. Simmer over low heat for 1 hour.

Melt the butter in a small skillet over medium-low heat. Stir in the flour. Cook until golden brown, stirring constantly. Whisk enough of the flour mixture into the soup to reach the desired thickness. Simmer for 30 minutes. Strain the soup into a saucepan and discard the vegetables. Bring to a simmer. Stir in the cream and basil and cook gently until heated through.

Popovers to Panache
The Village Club, Bloomfield Hills, Michigan

Cold Squash Soup

1 pound yellow squash, thinly sliced
1 onion, chopped
1 1/2 cups chicken stock or broth, divided
1/2 cup sour cream

Salt to taste
White pepper to taste
Chopped fresh dill weed

Combine squash, onion and 1 cup chicken stock in saucepan and bring to a boil. Cook 30 minutes or until vegetables are tender. Purée squash mixture in blender and pour into mixing bowl. Stir in remaining 1/2 cup stock, sour cream, salt and white pepper to taste. Chill. Garnish with chopped dill weed.

A Southern Collection Then and Now
Junior League of Columbus, Columbus, Georgia

Sweet Potato Vichyssoise

Serves 8

1 pound sweet potatoes
2 cups (1/4-inch) sliced leeks (see Note)
1/4 teaspoon grated fresh ginger
1/4 teaspoon grated fresh nutmeg
3 tablespoons butter
1 1/2 to 3 cups chicken stock

1 1/2 cups coconut milk
1 cup heavy cream
Salt and freshly ground pepper to taste
Crème fraîche or sour cream
1/4 cup chopped macadamia nuts, toasted

Peel the sweet potatoes and cut into uniform pieces. Sauté the leeks with the ginger and nutmeg in the butter in a saucepan until the leeks are wilted but not brown. Stir in the sweet potatoes and add just enough stock to cover. Simmer until the sweet potatoes are tender, stirring occasionally. Combine the sweet potato mixture, coconut milk and cream in a blender and process until puréed. Season with salt and pepper. Pour the soup into a bowl and chill, covered, for 8 to 10 hours. Ladle into chilled soup bowls and top with crème fraîche and macadamia nuts.

Note: Trim roots and tough green leaves from leeks. Split leeks lengthwise approximately 1 inch from root ends and spread layers under cold running water, washing out any grit. Pat dry with paper towels. Cut the bulb into slices.

The Cook's Canvas 2
Cameron Art Museum, Wilmington, North Carolina

Gazpacho

1 garlic clove
1/2 teaspoon salt
1 1/2 cucumbers, peeled, seeded and chopped
1 1/2 large tomatoes, peeled and chopped
1 mild onion, finely chopped
3/4 cup finely chopped celery
1 red bell pepper, finely chopped
1/2 green bell pepper, finely chopped
1 (4-ounce) can chopped green chiles, drained
2 jalapeño chiles, seeded and minced

2 tablespoons chopped fresh cilantro, or to taste
2 (14-ounce) cans fat-free chicken broth, or
   3 3/4 cups defatted homemade chicken broth
1 (48-ounce) can tomato juice
3 tablespoons fresh lemon juice
1 tablespoon fresh lime juice
1/4 cup virgin olive oil
1 1/2 teaspoons sugar
2 teaspoons cumin
Seasoned salt to taste

Mash the garlic with the salt. Combine the garlic, cucumbers, tomatoes, onion, celery, red bell pepper, green bell pepper, green chiles, jalapeño chiles and cilantro in a large bowl. Add the broth, tomato juice, lemon juice, lime juice, olive oil, sugar, cumin and seasoned salt; mix well. Chill for several hours to develop the flavors. Serve plain or add toppings such as sour cream crushed tortilla chips, shredded Cheddar cheese, garlic croutons, chopped avocado and/or chopped cooked bacon.

The Bells are Ringing: A Call to Table
Mission San Juan Capistrano Women's Guild, San Juan Capistrano, California

White Spanish Gazpacho

3 cucumbers, peeled and cubed
1 small garlic clove
3 (14-ounce) cans chicken broth
3 cups sour cream
3 tablespoons white vinegar
2 teaspoons salt, or to taste

4 tomatoes, chopped
1/2 cup chopped fresh parsley
1/2 cup sliced green onions
3/4 cup sliced almonds, toasted and salted
Croutons

Purée the cucumbers and garlic in a blender. Pour into a bowl. Whisk in a small amount of chicken broth until smooth. Whisk in the remaining chicken broth gradually. Whisk the cucumber mixture gradually into the sour cream in a bowl. Stir in the vinegar and salt. Chill, covered, until cold. Ladle into 6 chilled soup bowls. Top each with equal portions of the tomatoes, parsley, green onions, almonds and croutons.

Recipes of Note
Greensboro Symphony Guild, Greensboro, North Carolina

Autumn Salad

APPLE CIDER VINAIGRETTE
1/2 cup vegetable oil
1/4 cup sugar

3 tablespoons apple cider vinegar
1/4 teaspoon salt

SALAD
4 cups spring mix
1 pear, sliced or chopped

4 ounces blue cheese, crumbled
1/2 cup dried cranberries
1/4 cup pecans, toasted

For the vinaigrette, combine the oil, sugar, vinegar and salt in a jar with a tight-fitting lid and shake to mix. For the salad, toss the spring mix, pear, cheese, cranberries and pecans in a salad bowl. Add the vinaigrette and toss to coat. Serve immediately.

Simply Sarasota
Junior League of Sarasota, Sarasota, Florida

Caribbean Spinach Salad

Serves 4 to 6

FOR THE DRESSING:
1 teaspoon Dijon mustard
2 cloves garlic, crushed

3 tablespoons white wine vinegar
1/3 cup extra-virgin olive oil
Salt and freshly ground pepper to taste

FOR THE SALAD:
3/4 pound fresh spinach
6 slices bacon, cooked and crumbled
1 cup cashews, toasted

2 ripe mangoes, peeled, pitted, quartered,
    and thinly sliced
1/4 red onion, thinly sliced

DRESSING
Combine mustard and garlic in mixing bowl. Stir in vinegar. Gradually beat in oil, salt and pepper.

SALAD
Rinse spinach under cold water; dry thoroughly. Pull leaves from stems and discard stems. Place leaves in salad bowl; add bacon, cashews, mangoes and onion. Toss with dressing and serve immediately.

The Bess Collection
Junior Service League of Independence, Independence, Missouri

Celestial Salad

Serves 8

1 head romaine lettuce
1 (11-ounce) can mandarin oranges (drained)
1 cup seedless grapes (halved)

½ cup chopped green onions
½ cup sliced fresh mushrooms
¼ cup sliced toasted almonds (optional)

SALAD DRESSING:
2 tablespoons olive or canola oil
¼ cup sugar
1 teaspoon celery seeds

2 tablespoons chopped fresh parsley
2 tablespoons red wine vinegar
¼ cup orange juice
½ teaspoon dry mustard

Wash lettuce and tear into bite-size pieces in a bowl. Add remaining salad ingredients and ½ of the almonds, if desired.

To make dressing, combine all ingredients in a jar with a tight-fitting lid. Shake well. Just before serving, pour over greens. Toss lightly. Sprinkle the remaining almonds over top, if desired.

A Taste of the Good Life: From the Heart of Tennessee
Saint Thomas Hospital, Nashville, Tennessee

Dried Cherry and Toasted Pecan Salad with Maple Dressing

Serves 6

MAPLE DRESSING
¼ cup mayonnaise
¼ cup pure maple syrup
3 tablespoons Champagne vinegar or
   white wine vinegar

2 teaspoons sugar
½ cup vegetable oil
Salt and pepper to taste

SALAD
1 bunch Bibb lettuce, torn into
   bite-size pieces
1 bunch red leaf lettuce,
   torn into bite-size pieces

¼ cup toasted chopped pecans
½ cup dried tart cherries
¼ cup toasted chopped pecans
1 red onion, thinly sliced

For the dressing, whisk the mayonnaise, maple syrup, vinegar and sugar in a bowl. Add the oil gradually, whisking constantly until the mixture is slightly thickened. Season with salt and pepper.

For the salad, combine the Bibb lettuce, red leaf lettuce, ¼ cup pecans and the dried cherries in a bowl and toss to mix well. Add the desired amount of the dressing and toss to coat. Divide the salad evenly among six salad plates. Sprinkle with ¼ cup pecans and top with the sliced onion.

Popovers to Panache
The Village Club, Bloomfield Hills, Michigan

Spinach-Orange Salad with Honey Vinaigrette Dressing

Serves 4

4 cups spinach leaves
1 (11-ounce) can mandarin orange sections, drained
1/2 cup red onion, sliced

1 (2-ounce) package slivered almonds, toasted to light brown

DRESSING:
3 tablespoons distilled white vinegar
3 tablespoons vegetable oil
1 tablespoon honey

1/2 teaspoon salt
Dash pepper
Dash poppy seeds
Dash celery seeds

In large bowl, mix spinach, oranges, onion and almonds. Pour in dressing mixture and toss. (Dressing mixture can be made ahead and kept in refrigerator for weeks. Also good on fresh fruit salad.)

A Taste of Georgia, Another Serving
Newnan Junior Service League, Newnan, Georgia

Spring Greens and Pome Fruit

Serves 10 to 12

1/2 cup lemon juice
1/2 cup (or more) vegetable oil
1/4 cup sugar
2 teaspoons chopped green onions
1 teaspoon poppy seeds
3/4 teaspoon salt

6 cups spring mix or other mixed greens or chopped Romaine
1 red apple, chopped
1 green pear, chopped
1 cup toasted pecans, chopped
Crumbled blue cheese

Combine the lemon juice, oil, sugar, green onions, poppy seeds and salt in a jar with a tight-fitting lid and seal tightly. Shake to mix. Toss mixed greens, apple, pear and pecans with the dressing in a large salad bowl. Sprinkle with blue cheese.

Be Present At Our Table
Germantown United Methodist Women, Germantown, Tennessee

Spring Sensation Salad with Sweet Spicy Pecans

Serves 10 to 12

BALSAMIC VINAIGRETTE
1/2 cup balsamic vinegar
3 tablespoons Dijon mustard
3 tablespoons honey
3 garlic cloves, pressed

3 green onions, minced
1/4 teaspoon salt
1/4 teaspoon pepper
Extra-virgin olive oil

SWEET SPICY PECANS
1 cup water
1/4 cup sugar
1 cup pecan halves

3 tablespoons sugar
1 tablespoon chili powder
1/4 teaspoon ground red pepper

SALAD
8 ounces spring mix greens
1 head red leaf lettuce, rinsed and torn into
   bite-size pieces

4 ounces feta cheese, crumbled
2 (11-ounce) cans mandarin oranges, drained
1 pint strawberries, sliced

For the vinaigrette, whisk the balsamic vinegar, Dijon mustard, honey, garlic, green onions, salt and pepper in a 2-cup measure until blended. Whisk in enough olive oil gradually to make 2 cups. Chill, covered, until ready to serve.

For the pecans, microwave the water in a small microwave-safe glass bowl until the water boils. Add 1/4 cup sugar and stir until dissolved. Add the pecans. Soak for 15 minutes; drain. Combine 3 tablespoons sugar, the chili powder and red pepper in a sealable plastic bag. Add the pecans and shake to coat. Arrange in a single layer on a lightly greased baking sheet. Bake at 350 degrees for 15 minutes, stirring once.

For the salad, toss the spring mix greens, red leaf lettuce, cheese and balsamic vinaigrette in a large salad bowl. Add the mandarin oranges and strawberries and toss gently. Sprinkle with the sweet spicy pecans just before serving.

Roux To Do
Junior League of Greater Covington, Covington, Louisiana

Strawberry and Onion Salad with Poppyseed Dressing

Serves 8

1 head romaine lettuce
1 pint fresh strawberries, or 1 package whole frozen strawberries
1 Bermuda onion, sliced

Wash romaine lettuce. Pat dry. Refrigerate until serving time. Place greens on individual salad plates, or in large salad bowl. Slice strawberries. If using frozen strawberries, let partially thaw before slicing. Put berries and onions on top of greens. Drizzle poppyseed dressing over salad. Toss, if using large salad bowl.

DRESSING
½ cup mayonnaise
2 tablespoons vinegar

⅓ cup sugar
¼ cup whole milk
2 tablespoons poppyseeds

Place all ingredients in a jar. Cover and shake until blended. Dressing keeps several days in refrigerator.

Applehood & Motherpie
Junior League of Rochester, Inc., Rochester, New York

Sweet Tart Salad

Serves 8

POPPY SEED DRESSING
½ cup sugar
½ cup vegetable oil
¼ cup apple cider vinegar

1 tablespoon poppy seeds
¼ teaspoon paprika
¼ teaspoon Worcestershire sauce

SALAD
10 ounces salad greens, or 16 cups torn lettuce
4 cups chopped Granny Smith apples
2 cups garlic bagel chips, crushed

4 ounces blue cheese, crumbled
¼ cup chopped pecans
1 tablespoon pepper

For the dressing, combine the sugar, oil, vinegar, poppy seeds, paprika and Worcestershire sauce in a jar with a tight-fitting lid and seal tightly. Shake to mix. Chill, covered, in the refrigerator until serving time. The flavor is enhanced if made in advance and chilled.

For the salad, mix the salad greens, apples, bagel chips, cheese, pecans and pepper in a salad bowl. Add the dressing and toss to coat. Serve immediately.

Tables of Content
Junior League of Birmingham, Inc., Birmingham, Alabama

Town and Country Salad

Serves 8

POPPY SEED DRESSING
1/4 onion, grated
1/2 cup sugar
1/2 cup salad oil

1/3 cup apple cider vinegar
1 teaspoon dry mustard
1 1/2 teaspoons poppy seeds

CARAMELIZED ALMONDS
1/2 cup slivered almonds

1/4 cup sugar

SALAD
Romaine, Bibb or red leaf lettuce, torn

Strawberries, sliced
Brie cheese, cubed

For the dressing, combine the onion, sugar, half the oil and a small amount of the vinegar in a bowl and mix well. Add the remaining oil and vinegar gradually, mixing well. Stir in the dry mustard and poppy seeds. Chill until serving time.

For the almonds, combine the almonds with the sugar in a skillet. Cook over medium heat until the sugar melts and browns, stirring constantly. Spread on foil to cool.

For the salad, combine the lettuce, strawberries and cheese in a serving bowl. Add the dressing and toss to coat. Top with the almonds. Note: Do not use double-cream Brie for this recipe.

Tip: To keep strawberries fresh, arrange them in a single layer on a paper towel-lined plate and place them in the refrigerator. Wash and trim them just before serving.

Savor the Moment
Junior League of Boca Raton, Boca Raton, Florida

Minted Melon Salad

Serves 6

1/4 cup crème de cassis, berry liqueur, or
   currant nectar
1/4 cup freshly squeezed lemon juice, more to taste
2 tablespoons honey, more to taste
4 cups cubed, seeded watermelon

1/2 cantaloupe, cut into melon balls
1/2 honeydew, cut into melon balls
2/3 cup chopped fresh mint, more or less to taste,
   plus additional sprigs for garnish

Stir together the crème de cassis, lemon juice, and honey in a small bowl until the honey has dissolved. Adjust the sweetness to taste by adding either more lemon juice or more honey. Gently toss together the melons with the mint in a large bowl, then stir in the cassis dressing. Serve either chilled or at room temperature.

Celebrate the Rain
The Junior League of Seattle, Seattle, Washington

Cool Watermelon Salad

8 cups (3/4-inch cubes) seeded watermelon, chilled
1 cup crumbled feta cheese
1/3 cup chopped mint leaves

1/4 cup extra-virgin olive oil
Juice of 2 limes
Freshly ground pepper to taste

Combine the watermelon, feta cheese, mint, olive oil, lime juice and pepper in a bowl, tossing to mix. Serve immediately.

Texas Ties
Junior League of North Harris and South Montgomery Counties, Inc., Spring, Texas

Avocado and Tomato Salad

Serves 4

DIJON BALSAMIC VINAIGRETTE
6 tablespoons olive oil
2 tablespoons balsamic vinegar
1 teaspoon mild Dijon mustard

1 garlic clove, finely chopped
1/2 teaspoon salt
Freshly ground pepper to taste

SALAD
1 small Haas avocado, chopped
3 Roma tomatoes or small vine-ripened
    tomatoes, chopped
1/2 cup dried cranberries

1/4 cup pine nuts, toasted
1 1/2 to 2 ounces goat cheese, crumbled
1 head butter, red leaf or green leaf lettuce,
    torn and chilled
Freshly ground pepper to taste

VINAIGRETTE
Combine the olive oil, vinegar, mustard, garlic, salt and pepper in a jar with a tight-fitting lid and seal tightly. Shake to mix.

SALAD
Toss the avocado, tomatoes, cranberries, pine nuts and goat cheese with 1/4 cup of the vinaigrette in a salad bowl. Let stand for 10 minutes. Add the lettuce to the avocado mixture and toss to coat. Divide the salad evenly among 4 serving plates and sprinkle with pepper. Serve immediately.

California Sol Food
Junior League of San Diego, Inc., San Diego, California

Belgian Endive Salad with Smoked Bacon

Serves 6 to 8

6 heads Belgian endive
12 slices smoked bacon, crisp-cooked and crumbled
3/4 cup chopped tomato, drained
1/3 cup crumbled feta cheese

1/4 cup walnut pieces
2 tablespoons finely chopped fresh basil
Balsamic Vinaigrette (below)

Slice the root bottom off the endive. Separate into spears and tear into bite-size pieces. Combine the endive, bacon, tomato, cheese, walnuts and basil in a bowl. Add the Balsamic Vinaigrette and toss until coated.

Balsamic Vinaigrette

Makes 3/4 cup

3 tablespoons balsamic vinegar
1 teaspoon Dijon mustard
1/2 cup olive oil

1 garlic clove, minced
1/4 teaspoon thyme
Salt and freshly ground pepper to taste

Whisk the vinegar and Dijon mustard in a bowl until combined. Add the olive oil gradually, whisking constantly until the olive oil is incorporated. Whisk in the garlic, thyme, salt and pepper.

The Cook's Canvas 2
Cameron Art Museum, Wilmington, North Carolina

Make-Ahead Romaine Salad

Serves 4 to 6

Juice of 2 lemons
2 large Haas avocados, chopped
6 green onions, sliced
2 heaping teaspoons Beau Monde seasoning
1/2 to 3/4 cup freshly grated or shredded
   Parmesan cheese

2 heads romaine
3/4 cup corn oil
Salt to taste

Place the lemon juice, avocados, green onions, Beau Monde seasoning and one-half of the Parmesan cheese in a large deep salad bowl. Do not mix. Tear the romaine into bite-size pieces and place on top. Sprinkle with the remaining Parmesan cheese. Chill, covered, for 6 to 8 hours. To serve, drizzle with the corn oil and sprinkle with the salt. Toss the salad to mix.

Now Serving
Junior League of Wichita Falls, Wichita Falls, Texas

Café Salad

1 head green leaf lettuce or red leaf lettuce
1 head Boston lettuce or butter lettuce
1 red bell pepper, cut into thin strips
1 (16-ounce) package sliced fresh mushrooms

1 (4- to 6-ounce) package crumbled blue cheese
1 heaping cup toasted walnuts
Cherry tomatoes, halved
Dressing (below)

Combine the leaf lettuce, Boston lettuce, bell pepper, mushrooms, cheese, walnuts and cherry tomatoes in a large salad bowl. Toss to mix. Add the Dressing and toss to coat.

DRESSING
3/4 cup olive oil
1/4 cup balsamic vinegar
2 to 3 garlic cloves, minced

1 shallot, chopped
1 tablespoon spicy Dijon mustard
Salt and freshly ground black pepper to taste
Seasoned pepper to taste

Whisk the olive oil, vinegar, garlic, shallot and mustard in a bowl. Season with salt, black pepper and seasoned pepper to taste. Cover and chill for at least 24 hours.

A League of Our Own: From Blue Jeans to Ball Gowns
Rockwall Women's League, Rockwall, Texas

Crunchy Romaine Toss

1 (3-ounce) package ramen noodles
1 cup walnuts, chopped
1/4 cup (1/2 stick) unsalted butter
1 bunch broccoli, coarsely chopped

1 head romaine, rinsed and torn into pieces
4 green onions, chopped
1 cup Sweet-and-Sour Dressing (below)

Crumble the ramen noodles; discard the seasoning packet. Brown the ramen noodles and walnuts in the butter in a skillet. Remove to paper towels to drain. Combine the ramen noodles, walnuts, broccoli, romaine and green onions in a salad bowl and toss to mix. Pour the Sweet-and-Sour Dressing over the salad and toss to coat.

Sweet-and-Sour Dressing

1 cup vegetable oil
1 cup sugar
1/2 cup wine vinegar

1 tablespoon soy sauce
Salt and pepper to taste

Process the oil, sugar, vinegar, soy sauce, salt and pepper in a blender until blended.

Down Home: Treasured Recipes from our House to Yours
West Point Junior Auxiliary, West Point, Mississippi

Broccoli Slaw

Serves 8 to 10

1 package broccoli slaw
3 ribs celery, chopped
4 or 5 green onions, chopped
1/2 cup sunflower oil
2 teaspoons soy sauce

1/4 cup white vinegar
1/2 cup sugar
3/4 cup sliced almonds
1/2 cup sunflower seeds
1 can rice noodles

Mix the broccoli, celery and green onions in a large bowl. For the dressing, combine the sunflower oil, soy sauce, vinegar and sugar in a covered jar and shake to mix well. Add to the salad and toss lightly. Chill until serving time. Add the almonds, sunflower seeds and rice noodles just before serving; toss gently.

Downtown Savannah Style
Junior League of Savannah, Savannah, Georgia

Coleslaw

Serves 12

3 pounds cabbage, trimmed
2 green bell peppers, seeded
3 onions, cut into wedges
1 (4-ounce) jar chopped pimentos, drained
2 cups water

2 cups sugar
2 cups vinegar
1 tablespoon salt
1 tablespoon mustard seeds
1 tablespoon prepared horseradish

Pulse the cabbage, bell peppers and onions separately in a food processor until ground. Spoon the vegetables into a bowl and stir in the pimentos. Combine the water, sugar, vinegar, salt, mustard seeds and horseradish in a saucepan and mix well. Cook until heated through, stirring frequently. Let stand until cool. Pour the vinegar dressing over the cabbage mixture and toss until coated.

Note: Store indefinitely in the refrigerator.

The Cook's Canvas 2
Cameron Art Museum, Wilmington, North Carolina

Mardi Gras Slaw

1 teaspoon salt
1/2 medium head green cabbage, chopped
1/2 medium head purple cabbage, chopped
3 ribs celery, chopped
1/2 yellow bell pepper, chopped

1 cup white vinegar
2 cups sugar
1 teaspoon celery seeds
1 teaspoon mustard

Sprinkle the salt over the chopped green and purple cabbage in a bowl. Let stand for 1 hour. Squeeze out all liquid. Mix the cabbage, celery and bell pepper in a bowl. Combine the vinegar, sugar, celery seeds and mustard in a saucepan. Bring to a boil and boil for 1 minute. Let cool. Pour over cabbage mixture and mix well. Place in an airtight container and place in the freezer for 30 to 45 minutes. Remove from the freezer and let stand at room temperature to thaw. The slaw will be crisp when thawed.

Crescent City Collection
The Junior League of New Orleans, New Orleans, Louisiana

Fruited Winter Slaw

1 1/3 cups vegetable or peanut oil
1/2 cup cider vinegar
1/2 cup lemon juice
1/4 cup honey
1/2 teaspoon ground ginger
1 garlic clove, peeled and halved
2 teaspoons salt
1/2 teaspoon ground pepper

1 small head red cabbage, shredded (1 1/2 pounds)
1 small head green cabbage, shredded (1 1/2 pounds)
1 small onion, shredded
Salt and pepper to taste
Sliced dried apricots to taste
Sliced dried bananas to taste
Cashews to taste

Combine the oil, vinegar, lemon juice, honey, ginger, garlic, remaining salt and pepper in a jar with a tight-fitting lid and shake well. Chill for 2 to 12 hours. Remove and let stand at room temperature for 15 minutes. Remove the garlic and shake well. Layer the red and green cabbage in a large salad bowl. Add the onion, salt and pepper to taste. Arrange the apricots, bananas and cashews in the center. Pour the honey mixture over the vegetables and toss well.

Between the Lakes
The Junior League of Saginaw Valley, Saginaw, Michigan

Cold Asparagus with Pecans

Serves 6 to 8

1 1/2 pounds fresh asparagus, as young and
tender as possible, or 2 (10-ounce) packages
frozen asparagus
3/4 cup finely chopped pecans
2 tablespoons vegetable oil

1/4 cup cider vinegar
1/4 cup soy sauce
1/4 cup sugar
Pepper to taste

Cook asparagus in boiling water 6 to 7 minutes, or until tender and still bright green. Drain and rinse under cold water. Drain again. Arrange in 1 or 2 layers in oblong serving dish. Mix remaining ingredients and pour over asparagus, lifting asparagus so mixture penetrates to bottom. Sprinkle with pepper. Serve chilled. May be marinated up to 36 hours ahead.

Magic
Junior League of Birmingham, Inc., Birmingham, Alabama

Sweet Basil and Tomato Corn Salad

Serves 6 to 8

6 ears corn, shucked
1/2 cup chopped orange bell pepper
1/2 cup chopped shallots
1/2 cup chopped cherry tomatoes
3 tablespoons apple cider vinegar

3 tablespoons olive oil
1/2 teaspoon kosher salt
1/2 teaspoon freshly ground pepper
1 1/2 cup thinly sliced fresh basil leaves

Bring enough water to cover the corn to a boil in a large saucepan. Add the corn and cook for 3 minutes. Drain and rinse with cold water. Cut the kernels off the cob when the corn is cool enough to handle. Combine the bell pepper, corn, shallots, tomatoes, vinegar, olive oil, salt and pepper in a large bowl and mix well. Stir in the basil just before serving.

Life is Delicious
Hinsdale Junior Woman's Club, Hinsdale, Illinois

Fresh Corn and Tomato Salad

Serves 10

12 large ears of white corn
7 tablespoons olive oil
2 tablespoons finely chopped garlic
1 cup packed julienned fresh basil

10 Roma tomatoes, chopped
3 tablespoons balsamic vinegar
Salt and pepper to taste

Cut the tops of the corn kernels off the cob with a sharp knife and put into a bowl. Heat 2 tablespoons of the olive oil in each of 2 large skillets. Add ½ of the garlic and ½ of the corn to each of the skillets. Sauté for 5 minutes or until the corn is tender. Remove from the heat. Add ½ of the basil to each skillet and mix well. Spoon the corn mixture into 2 large bowls. Cool slightly, stirring occasionally. Add ½ of the remaining olive oil, ½ of the tomatoes, ½ of the vinegar and ½ of the remaining basil to each bowl and mix gently. Season with salt and pepper. Chill, covered, for 3 to 8 hours.

California Sol Food
Junior League of San Diego, Inc., San Diego, California

Corn Bread Salad

Serves 8 to 10

RANCH DRESSING
1 cup mayonnaise

1 cup sour cream
1 envelope ranch salad dressing mix

SALAD
1 recipe corn bread, cooled and crumbled
1 (14-ounce) can black beans, drained
1 (14-ounce) can Shoe Peg corn, drained
1 medium red onion, chopped

3 large tomatoes, chopped
8 ounces (2 cups) shredded Cheddar cheese
1 (2-ounce) jar real bacon bits
1 small bunch green onions, chopped

To prepare the dressing, combine the mayonnaise, sour cream and salad dressing mix in a small bowl and mix well.

To prepare the salad, layer the corn bread, beans, corn, onion and tomatoes ½ at a time in a large glass salad bowl. Spread the dressing over the layers. Sprinkle with the cheese, bacon and green onions.

Notably Nashville
Junior League of Nashville, Nashville, Tennessee

Summer Pepper Salad

Serves 8 to 10

1/2 red onion, finely chopped
1 medium cucumber, peeled and
   cut into 1-inch pieces
1 tomato, cut into 1-inch pieces
1 red bell pepper, cut into 1-inch pieces
1 orange bell pepper, cut into 1-inch pieces

1 yellow bell pepper, cut into 1-inch pieces
1 green bell pepper, cut into 1-inch pieces
1 cup (4 ounces) crumbled feta cheese
1/3 cup balsamic vinegar
1/4 cup extra-virgin olive oil

Toss the onion, cucumber, tomato and bell peppers in a salad bowl. Sprinkle with the cheese. Whisk the vinegar and olive oil in a small bowl. Add the oil mixture to the bell pepper mixture and toss to coat.

An Occasion to Gather
Junior League of Milwaukee, Milwaukee, Wisconsin

Mediterranean Potato Salad

Serves 6

OLIVE OIL VINAIGRETTE
1/4 cup olive oil

1/4 cup red wine vinegar
Kosher salt and pepper to taste

POTATO SALAD
1 pound unpeeled small white creamer potatoes
1 pound unpeeled small red creamer potatoes
3/4 cup chopped tomato

1/2 cup chopped fresh parsley
1/2 green bell pepper, chopped
1 shallot, finely chopped
3/4 teaspoon salt

For the vinaigrette, combine the olive oil, vinegar, salt and pepper in a jar with a tight-fitting lid and seal tightly. Shake to blend.

For the salad, combine the potatoes with enough water to cover in a saucepan and bring to a boil. Boil for 10 minutes or until tender and drain. Mix the potatoes, tomato, parsley, bell pepper, shallot and salt in a bowl. Add the vinaigrette to the potato mixture and toss to coat. Serve at room temperature. For a variation, cut the potatoes into bite-size pieces.

Tables of Content
Junior League of Birmingham, Inc., Birmingham, Alabama

New Potatoes with Dill

5 cups new potatoes, cooked in their jackets until just tender, quartered
3/4 cup sour cream
1/4 cup mayonnaise
2 tablespoons vinegar
1/2 teaspoon prepared mustard
1 1/2 tablespoons minced onion

1/2 cup peeled and diced cucumber
3/4 teaspoon salt
1/4 teaspoon pepper
1/4 teaspoon celery seeds (maybe a little more)
1/2 teaspoon chopped dill weed
2 hard-boiled eggs, chopped
1/8 cup minced fresh parsley

Place quartered potatoes in a bowl. Whisk together the sour cream, mayonnaise, vinegar, and mustard in a bowl, adding the onion, cucumber and spices. Pour over potatoes and mix lightly. Gently fold in eggs. Refrigerate. Garnish with parsley.

A Southern Collection Then and Now
Junior League of Columbus, Columbus, Georgia

Seurat Salad

1 (14-ounce) can artichoke hearts, drained, sliced
1 (14-ounce) can hearts of palm drained, sliced
1/4 cup chopped green onions
2 tablespoons finely chopped fresh parsley
6 tablespoons salad oil
2 tablespoons fresh lemon juice

Juice of 2 garlic cloves
4 ounces bleu cheese, crumbled
Salt and pepper to taste
Romaine leaves
2 large tomatoes, cut into 12 slices
1/4 cup crumbled crisp-cooked bacon

Combine the artichokes, hearts of palm, green onions and parsley in a bowl and mix gently. Add a mixture of the salad oil, lemon juice, garlic juice and bleu cheese and toss to mix. Season with salt and pepper. Chill, covered, in the refrigerator until serving time. The salad may be prepared to this point 1 day in advance. Line 6 chilled salad plates with romaine. Arrange 2 tomato slices on each salad plate. Top with the artichoke mixture. Sprinkle with the bacon just before serving.

Art Fare
Toledo Museum of Art Aides, Toledo, Ohio

Tomato Salad with Basil Oil Dressing

BASIL OIL DRESSING
3 cups loosely packed fresh basil leaves (3 ounces)
3/4 cup extra-virgin olive oil

1 tablespoon fresh lemon juice
1 teaspoon kosher salt
1 garlic clove

TOMATO SALAD
3 pounds fresh heirloom tomatoes of various
    assortments and sizes

3 ounces goat cheese
Salt and freshly ground pepper to taste
6 sprigs of basil for garnish

For the dressing, combine the basil, olive oil, lemon juice, salt and garlic in a blender or food processor and process until smooth.

For the salad, core each tomato and cut into halves. Cut each half into quarters. Arrange the tomatoes evenly on 6 salad plates. Crumble 1/2 ounce of the goat cheese over each serving and season to taste with salt and pepper. Drizzle about 2 tablespoons of the dressing over each salad and garnish with a sprig of basil. Serve immediately.

Note: The Basil Oil Dressing is a snap to make and will keep in the refrigerator for up to one week. The oil will solidify in the refrigerator. Bring to room temperature before serving.

Tables of Content
Junior League of Birmingham, Inc., Birmingham, Alabama

Marinated Winter Salad

Serves 8

1 (16-ounce) jar whole baby carrots, drained
2 cups sliced zucchini (about 1 medium)
1 (14-ounce) can hearts of palm, drained and sliced
1 (7-ounce) jar pickled baby corn, drained
    (optional)
2/3 cup vegetable oil

1/4 cup vinegar
1 clove garlic, minced
1 teaspoon sugar
3/4 teaspoon salt
3/4 teaspoon dry mustard
2 ounces crumbled blue cheese

Combine carrots, zucchini, and hearts of palm. Add picked baby corn, if desired. Combine oil and next 5 ingredients in a jar. Pour over vegetables. Marinate in refrigerator several hours or overnight. To serve, drain vegetables. Serve on Boston or Bibb lettuce leaves. Sprinkle with blue cheese.

Food for Thought
The Junior League of Birmingham, Inc., Birmingham, Alabama

Fruit and Cheese Tortellini

Serves 8

1 (7-ounce) package frozen cheese tortellini
1 cup halved grapes
1 cup blueberries

1 cup strawberries, sliced
Poppy seed salad dressing to taste

Cook the tortellini according to the package directions; drain and cool. Combine the tortellini, grapes, blueberries, strawberries and salad dressing in a bowl. Serve immediately.

Note: An easy take-along for a summertime potluck. Try using green grapes for some red, white and blue Fourth of July fun!

Once Upon A Time
Junior League of Evansville, Evansville, Indiana

Lemony Orzo Salad

Serves 6

1 cup orzo
1/3 cup chopped zucchini
1/3 cup chopped red onion
1/3 cup minced fresh parsley
3 tablespoons fresh lemon juice
1 tablespoon minced fresh basil, or
   1 teaspoon dried basil

1 tablespoon olive oil
2 teaspoons minced fresh mint
1/2 teaspoon salt
1/4 teaspoon pepper
1 cup chopped tomato
1/3 cup crumbled feta cheese
2 tablespoons chopped kalamata olives

Cook the pasta using the package directions, omitting the salt and butter; drain. Combine the pasta, zucchini and onion in a bowl and toss to mix. Whisk the parsley, lemon juice, basil, olive oil, mint, salt and pepper in a bowl until mixed. Add the pasta mixture to the olive oil mixture and toss to coat. Stir in the tomato, cheese and olives. Serve at room temperature or chilled.

California Sol Food
Junior League of San Diego, Inc., San Diego, California

Chicken and Wild Rice Salad

Serves 4 to 6

DIJON VINAIGRETTE
3/4 cup rice wine vinegar
3 tablespoons Dijon mustard
1 teaspoon granulated sugar

2 garlic cloves, minced
1 1/2 cups canola oil
Salt and black pepper to taste

To prepare the vinaigrette, mix the vinegar, Dijon mustard, sugar and garlic in a medium bowl. Add the canola oil gradually, whisking constantly until incorporated. Season with salt and pepper.

WILD RICE SALAD
3 cups cooked wild rice, chilled
2 cups chopped grilled chicken breasts
1/2 cup chopped red bell pepper

1/2 cup chopped red onion
1/2 cup golden raisins
2 tablespoons minced green onions
1 cup cashews

To prepare the salad, combine the rice, chicken, bell pepper, red onion, raisins, green onions and cashews in a bowl and mix well. Add the vinaigrette and toss until coated.

Starfish Café: Changing Lives One Recipe at a Time ...
Union Mission/Starfish Café, Savannah, Georgia

Cilantro Chicken Salad

Serves 8

4 cups chicken broth
6 skinless chicken breasts
1/2 cup lime juice
2 tablespoons red wine vinegar
2 tablespoons vegetable oil
2 teaspoons salt
1 tablespoon sugar
2 tablespoons minced garlic

1/2 cup chopped cilantro
1/2 cup chopped red onion
3 small tomatoes, peeled, seeded, chopped
2 to 3 small Anaheim chiles, chopped
1 cup cooked black beans
2 small avocados, cut into bite-size pieces
Leaf lettuce

Bring the broth to a simmer; add the chicken. Simmer, covered, until the chicken is tender. Cool in the broth. Remove the chicken and cut into bite-size pieces. Chill the broth, covered. Skim the fat. Reserve 1/2 cup broth. Combine the next 10 ingredients and reserved broth in a large bowl, tossing gently. Add the chicken and black beans; toss to combine. Marinate, covered, in the refrigerator for 4 to 12 hours. Add the avocados just before serving; toss lightly to combine. Serve on leaf lettuce.

A Thyme to Remember
The Dallas County Medical Society Alliance, Dallas, Texas

Citrus Chicken and Feta Cheese Caesar Salad

Serves 6

4 boneless, skinless chicken breast halves
6 cups torn romaine lettuce
6 ounces feta cheese, crumbled
1/2 cup thinly sliced red onion
1/2 orange bell pepper, cut into rings

1/4 cup olive oil
3 tablespoons orange juice concentrate
1 tablespoon white wine vinegar
2 teaspoons finely chopped green onions

Place the chicken on a grill rack. Grill over hot coals until cooked through. Cut into 1/4-inch strips. Combine the lettuce, chicken, cheese, onion and pepper rings in a large salad bowl and toss to mix well. Mix the olive oil, orange juice concentrate, vinegar and green onions in a bowl. Pour over the chicken mixture and toss lightly. Serve immediately.

A Sunsational Encore
Junior League of Greater Orlando, Orlando, Florida

Cran-Raspberry Chicken Salad

Serves 10

4 cups chopped cooked chicken
1/2 cup mayonnaise
12 ounces raspberry yogurt
1/2 cup pecans, chopped
1 (6-ounce) package sweetened dried cranberries
3 to 4 ribs celery, finely chopped

1/4 cup minced green onions
1 1/2 teaspoons lemon juice, or to taste
1 1/2 teaspoons salt, or to taste
1 1/2 teaspoons curry powder, or to taste
Cayenne pepper to taste
10 croissants or lettuce leaves

Combine the chicken, mayonnaise, yogurt, pecans, cranberries, celery, green onions, lemon juice, salt and curry powder in a bowl. Season with cayenne pepper and mix well. Spread between split croissants for sandwiches or serve over lettuce leaves.

Marshes to Mansions
Junior League of Lake Charles, LA, Lake Charles, Louisiana

Grilled Chicken and Peach Salad

PEACH SALAD DRESSING
1 peach, peeled and chopped
1 cup white wine vinegar
2 tablespoons sugar

1 tablespoon Dijon mustard
1 teaspoon salt
1 cup olive oil

SALAD
4 boneless skinless chicken breasts
4 peaches, peeled and cut into halves
2 tablespoons olive oil
1 teaspoon salt
1/2 teaspoon pepper

2 cups mixed salad greens
1/2 cup chopped celery
1/2 cup chopped pecans or slivered
  almonds, toasted
1/4 cup sliced green onions

To prepare the dressing, process the peach, vinegar, sugar, Dijon mustard and salt in a blender. Add the olive oil gradually, processing constantly at low speed until incorporated.

To prepare the salad, brush the chicken and peaches with the olive oil. Season the chicken with the salt and pepper. Place the chicken on a grill rack and grill until cooked through. Place the peaches cut side down on a grill rack and grill for 3 minutes or until lightly charred. Let the chicken and peaches stand until cool. Slice one peach and set aside. Chop the chicken and remaining three peaches and place in a large salad bowl. Add the salad greens, celery, pecans and green onions. Add the dressing and toss until well coated. Divide among four salad plates. Garnish with reserved peach slices.

Shall We Gather
Trinity Episcopal Church, Wetumpka, Alabama

Since the 1961 publication of *The Gasparilla Cookbook*, The Junior League of Tampa has sold more than 400,000 cookbooks. The profits from cookbook sales directly fund our community projects, which focus on education, literacy, basic needs, and foster care.

For each of Tampa's Culinary Collection titles sold, three books will go home with a kindergarten student who has few, if any, other books at home. One child exclaimed when he received his books from a volunteer, "This is better than Christmas!" The teacher explained later that the books he was taking home were more presents than he had received at Christmas.

Crab and Orzo Salad

1 (6-ounce) jar quartered marinated artichoke
   hearts, drained
1 pound jumbo lump crab meat
1 pound orzo
1/2 cup white wine vinegar
1 shallot, chopped
2 garlic cloves

2 basil leaves
1 teaspoon Dijon mustard
1 teaspoon dried oregano
3/4 cup olive oil
10 drained oil-pack sun-dried tomatoes, sliced
1 bunch green onions, sliced
2 tablespoons chopped parsley

Reserve four of the artichoke hearts. Chop the remaining artichoke hearts; set aside. Drain the crab meat and flake; set aside. Cook the orzo in boiling salted water until al dente. Drain the orzo and rinse under cold water. Spoon into a serving bowl and set aside. Combine the reserved artichoke hearts, vinegar, shallot, garlic, basil, mustard and oregano in a blender and process until smooth. Add the oil in a fine stream, processing constantly at high speed until incorporated. Stir 1 cup of the vinaigrette into the orzo. Add the chopped artichokes, sun-dried tomatoes, green onions, crab meat and parsley and toss gently to combine. Season with salt and pepper to taste. Serve with the remaining vinaigrette on the side.

A Thyme to Entertain
Junior League of Annapolis, Inc., Annapolis, Maryland

Sensation Salad Dressing

1/2 pound finely ground Romano cheese
1 pint salad oil

Juice of 2 lemons
Juice of 3 cloves of garlic

Shake all ingredients in a quart jar. Dressing will keep indefinitely in refrigerator. Especially good tossed with lettuce, water cress, and parsley leaves. Salt and pepper greens as desired before adding dressing.

River Road Recipes: The Textbook of Louisiana Cuisine
Junior League of Baton Rouge, Baton Rouge, Louisiana

Beer and Nut Greek Burgers

Serves 8

2 pounds extra-lean ground beef
1/3 cup beer
1 envelope onion soup mix
1 to 2 tablespoons pine nuts, chopped

1/3 teaspoon Greek seasoning
1/4 teaspoon garlic salt
1/4 teaspoon pepper
Hamburger buns, lightly toasted

Preheat the grill to 350 to 400 degrees or to medium-high. Combine the ground beef, beer, soup mix, pine nuts, Greek seasoning, garlic salt and pepper in a bowl and mix well. Shape the ground beef mixture into 8 patties. Arrange the patties on the grill rack and grill for 15 minutes, turning once. Serve on toasted buns with feta cheese, roasted red peppers and spinach, if desired.

Tables of Content
Junior League of Birmingham, Inc., Birmingham, Alabama

Cuban Wraps

Makes 4 wraps

10 cloves roasted garlic
1/3 cup mayonnaise
1/3 cup mustard
4 (6- to 7-inch) flour tortillas or wraps
4 large romaine lettuce leaves

4 ounces deli ham, thinly sliced
4 ounces roasted pork, thinly sliced
4 ounces (1 cup) shredded Swiss cheese
Sandwich-style sliced sour pickles

Mash the garlic in a small bowl. Add the mayonnaise and mustard and mix well. Spread the mixture on the tortillas, leaving a 1/2-inch border. Place a lettuce leaf on the lower 1/3 of each tortilla. Top each with 1 ounce ham, 1 ounce pork, 2 tablespoons cheese and a pickle slice. Fold in the sides of the tortilla and roll tightly to enclose the filling. May be prepared several hours in advance and chilled, wrapped in parchment paper or plastic wrap, until ready to serve.

Every Day Feasts
The Junior League of Tampa, Tampa, Florida

Ham-Wiches

Serves 6

⅓ cup butter, melted
2 tablespoons prepared mustard
1 small chopped onion
1 tablespoon poppy seeds

6 hamburger buns
6 slices ham
6 slices Swiss or American cheese

Combine butter, mustard, onion, and poppy seeds. Spread on inside of hamburger buns. Place 1 slice ham and 1 slice cheese on each bun. Spread sauce on top of buns. Heat in oven on cookie sheet 15 minutes at 350 degrees.

The Gasparilla Cookbook
The Junior League of Tampa, Tampa, Florida

Hot Ham Sandwiches

Serves 16

½ cup (1 stick) butter, softened
⅓ cup mayonnaise
4½ teaspoons Dijon mustard
½ teaspoon Worcestershire sauce
1 tablespoon poppy seeds

16 large or 32 small croissants
2 to 3 pounds very thinly sliced Black Forest ham
1 to 2 pounds thinly sliced Monterey Jack cheese
 with peppers

Combine the butter, mayonnaise, Dijon mustard, Worcestershire sauce and poppy seeds in a bowl. Stir to mix well. Cut the croissants into halves. Spread the butter mixture on both halves of each croissant. Layer half the croissants with the ham and cheese. Top each with half a croissant. Wrap the sandwiches in foil and place on a baking sheet. Bake at 325 degrees for 30 minutes or until the cheese melts.

For Such A Time As This: A Cookbook
Park Cities Baptist Church, Dallas, Texas

Pork Tenderloin Sandwiches with Herb Mayonnaise

Serves 10 to 12

1 (1½-pound) pork tenderloin
3 tablespoons jerk seasoning
¼ cup olive oil
½ cup water
1 cup mayonnaise
2 tablespoons chopped basil

2 tablespoons chopped chives
2 tablespoons chopped rosemary
2 tablespoons chopped thyme
Salt and pepper to taste
10 to 12 Hawaiian bread rolls

Rub the pork with the jerk seasoning. Brown the pork on all sides in the hot olive oil in a Dutch oven. Add the water. Bake at 350 degrees for 30 minutes. Remove from the oven and let stand until cool. Chill, covered, until ready to serve. Combine the mayonnaise, basil, chives, rosemary and thyme in a bowl and mix well. Season with salt and pepper. Slice the pork. Slice the rolls horizontally and arrange the pork on the bottom halves. Spread some of the herb mayonnaise on the top halves and place mayonnaise side down on top of the pork.

Shall We Gather

Trinity Episcopal Church, Wetumpka, Alabama

Toasted Brie Chicken Tea Sandwiches

Makes 12 to 24 sandwiches

2 pounds boneless skinless chicken breasts, cubed
2 cups chicken broth
1 cup mayonnaise
1 cup red grapes, sliced
3 ribs celery, finely chopped
2 teaspoons Italian herbs

2 teaspoons pepper
1 teaspoon onion powder
6 to 12 croissants
2 (8-ounce) wheels Brie cheese, rind removed and cheese sliced

Preheat the oven to 375 degrees. Combine the chicken and broth in a roasting pan. Roast for 12 to 18 minutes or until cooked through. Do not allow the chicken to brown. Drain and discard the broth. Place the chicken in a large bowl and let stand until cool. Mix the mayonnaise, grapes, celery, Italian herbs, pepper and onion powder in a bowl. Stir in the chicken. Cut each croissant into haves crosswise and cut each half into halves horizontally. Toast the croissants. Place a slice of Brie on half of the croissant pieces. Top with the chicken mixture and the remaining croissant pieces.

Savor the Seasons

The Junior League of Tampa, Tampa, Florida

MJC Executive Croissant Sandwiches

Serves 6

2 Bartlett pears
1 teaspoon lemon juice
1/4 cup water
6 (2 1/2-ounce) butter croissants
Curry Sauce with Capers

18 ounces smoked turkey, thinly sliced
6 ounces mixed spring greens
1 large red onion, thinly sliced
6 (1-ounce) slices Provolone cheese

Slice the pears thinly. Combine the lemon juice and water in a large bowl. Add the pears and toss to coat; drain. Cut the croissants into halves. Spread the curry sauce evenly over each half. Layer the turkey, mixed spring greens, onion and cheese evenly over the 6 bottom halves of the croissants. Arrange the pear slices in a fan shape over the layers. Top with the 6 top halves of the croissants.

CURRY SAUCE WITH CAPERS
1/2 cup mayonnaise
1/4 cup sour cream
1/2 teaspoon chopped dried herbs
1/8 teaspoon salt
3/8 teaspoon curry powder

1 tablespoon minced dried onion
1/2 tablespoon chopped fresh parsley
1 teaspoon lemon juice
1 tablespoon capers, drained
1/4 teaspoon Worcestershire sauce

Combine the mayonnaise, sour cream, herbs, salt, curry powder, onion, parsley, lemon juice, capers and Worcestershire sauce in a bowl and mix well. Chill, covered, for 8 to 12 hours.

If You Can't Stand the Heat, Get Out of the Kitchen
Junior Service League of Independence, Independence, Missouri

Chicken and Almond Sandwich Spread

1 cup chopped chicken
1 cup chopped almonds
8 tablespoons cream
Salt and pepper to taste

Mix chopped chicken with finely chopped almonds and cream. Season to taste and make into sandwiches.

Charleston Receipts
Junior League of Charleston, Charleston, South Carolina

Thai Turkey Roll-Ups

Serves 4

PEANUT MAYONNAISE
1 tablespoon peanut butter
2 tablespoons lime juice
2 tablespoons mayonnaise

1 garlic clove, crushed
1/2 teaspoon ground ginger
1/8 teaspoon (or more) ground or flaked red pepper

ROLL-UPS
4 (10-inch) flour tortillas
1/2 cup chopped fresh basil

4 large green cabbage leaves
8 thin slices cooked turkey, about 8 to 10 ounces
1 cup red bell pepper slices

To prepare the mayonnaise, combine the peanut butter, lime juice, mayonnaise, garlic, ginger and red pepper in a bowl and mix well.

To prepare the roll-ups, spread the mayonnaise on the tortillas. Top each with 2 tablespoons basil, 1 cabbage leaf, 2 slices turkey and 1/4 cup red bell pepper. Roll the tortillas to enclose the filling. Wrap each tortilla in plastic wrap and chill until serving time.

Lone Star to Five Star
The Junior League of Plano, Plano, Texas

Tortilla Roll-Ups

Serves 4

1 (2-ounce) tub herb-seasoned cheese spread
Mayonnaise
4 (12-inch) sun-dried tomato, spinach, wheat or
  flour tortillas

1 pound roasted turkey breast, sliced
2 bunches green onions, chopped
10 ounces baby spinach leaves, stemmed
8 ounces bacon, crisp-cooked and crumbled

Combine the herbed cheese spread with enough mayonnaise in a bowl until a spreading consistency. Spread the cheese mixture over 1 side of each tortilla. Layer the tortillas evenly with the turkey, green onions, spinach and bacon. Roll tightly and wrap each roll individually in plastic wrap. Chill for several hours. Cut each roll diagonally into halves and stand on ends on serving plates, or cut each roll into 1/2-inch slices and secure with wooden picks. Substitute ham or roast beef for the turkey and fresh basil for the spinach if desired.

Compliments of
The Woman's Exchange of Memphis, Memphis, Tennessee

Gourmet Pimento Cheese

Makes 3 cups

1 1/2 cups (6 ounces) grated Parmesan cheese
1 cup (4 ounces) shredded Cheddar cheese
1 cup (4 ounces) shredded smoked Gouda cheese
1 (7-ounce) jar diced pimentos, drained
1 cup mayonnaise

1 jalapeño, seeded and minced
1 tablespoon vinegar
1 teaspoon salt
1 teaspoon black pepper
Cayenne pepper to taste

Combine the Parmesan cheese, Cheddar cheese, Gouda cheese and pimentos in a bowl and mix well. Mix the mayonnaise, jalapeño, vinegar, salt, black pepper and cayenne pepper in a bowl and stir into the cheese mixture. Chill, covered, in the refrigerator. Use as a sandwich filling or a spread for crackers or as a dip. Substitute Colby cheese or Monterey Jack cheese for 1 of the cheeses listed above if desired.

Compliments of
The Woman's Exchange of Memphis, Memphis, Tennessee

Pimiento Cheese Spread

Makes 4 cups

1 pound mild Cheddar cheese, grated
1 (4-ounce) jar diced pimientos, drained
Seasoned salt to taste

Cayenne pepper to taste
1/2 cup mayonnaise or to taste

Combine all above ingredients. Add ingredients from variations below if desired. Refrigerate and chill thoroughly until ready to serve.

Variations: Choose one of the following:

Add 1 chopped, roasted and peeled red pepper.

Add 1/3 cup finely chopped walnuts.

Add 1 small clove minced garlic.

Add finely chopped jalapeños to taste.

Add 1/4 cup chopped black olives and 1/4 cup dried green chives.

Add 2 hard-cooked, finely chopped eggs, 1/2 cup thinly sliced celery and 3 tablespoons sweet pickle relish.

Necessities and Temptations
The Junior League of Austin, Austin, Texas

Miniature Tomato Sandwiches

Makes 16 sandwiches

1/4 cup mayonnaise
3 ounces cream cheese, softened
2 teaspoons chopped fresh basil
1/4 teaspoon salt

1/4 teaspoon pepper
1 baguette
4 plum tomatoes, sliced and drained

Combine the mayonnaise, cream cheese, basil, 1/8 teaspoon salt and 1/8 teaspoon pepper in a bowl and mix well. Chill, covered, for 8 hours. Cut the baguette into sixteen slices. Spread the cream cheese mixture on one side of each slice and top each with one or two tomato slices. Sprinkle with the remaining 1/8 teaspoon salt and 1/8 teaspoon pepper and serve immediately.

Note: When adding tomatoes to your sandwiches, first salt them on both sides. Drain them on a rack or in a colander for 15 minutes and pat dry with paper towels. This will prevent soggy sandwiches.

Mardi Gras to Mistletoe
Junior League of Shreveport-Bossier, Shreveport, Louisiana

Entrées

"'What's for dinner?' Someone asked this question daily at our house growing up. For us, mealtime was the time my family turned off the television, came together to share a meal, and talked about their day. As a parent, I discovered that not everyone sat down to home-cooked meals, but I desperately wanted to carry on this important tradition for my family. The only hitch? I couldn't cook.

I called my mom, and she gave me some solid advice. 'Use a Junior League cookbook—you'll find great recipes.' She went on to reveal that all her best recipes came from Junior League books, and in following her advice, I became a seasoned cook and discovered a true passion.

Years later, I joined the Junior League and became involved in the development of our latest cookbook, *Tables of Content*. My love of cooking coupled with an organization committed to improving our community inspired me to also work on publishing a quarterly cooking magazine benefiting the Junior League's community projects.

What a transition—from somebody lost in the kitchen to a cookbook committee member—all because of Junior League cookbooks! What I love most is how the Junior League works to better lives, including both the quality of my own family and the quality of others' lives all across the community and country."

Christine Velezis
Junior League of Birmingham, Alabama

Grandmother's Texas Barbecued Brisket

Serves 8

2 teaspoons celery salt
1 teaspoon garlic powder
1 teaspoon onion salt
1 (3- to 4-pound) beef brisket

1/2 cup barbecue sauce
2 tablespoons ketchup
2 tablespoons Worcestershire sauce
1/2 teaspoon liquid smoke

Mix the celery salt, garlic powder and onion salt in a bowl and rub evenly over the brisket. Combine the barbecue sauce, ketchup, Worcestershire sauce and liquid smoke in a bowl and mix well. Brush the barbecue sauce mixture over the brisket and wrap in heavy-duty foil. Chill for 8 hours or longer. Preheat the oven to 300 degrees. Arrange the foil-wrapped brisket in a heavy roasting pan and bake for 5 hours or until the brisket is tender. Slice or shred as desired.

Barbecue Sauce

Makes 2 cups

1 1/2 cups ketchup
1/4 cup vinegar
3 tablespoons brown sugar
2 tablespoons Worcestershire sauce
1 small onion, finely chopped
1 tablespoon minced garlic

1 tablespoon molasses
1 teaspoon prepared mustard
1 teaspoon fresh lemon juice
1/4 teaspoon salt
1/4 teaspoon Tabasco sauce
1/8 teaspoon ground red pepper

Combine the ketchup, vinegar, brown sugar, Worcestershire sauce, onion, garlic, molasses, prepared mustard and lemon juice in a large saucepan and mix well. Stir in the salt, Tabasco sauce and red pepper. Bring to a boil and reduce the heat to low. Simmer for 40 to 50 minutes or to the desired consistency, stirring occasionally. Let stand until cool. Store in an airtight container in the refrigerator.

Tables of Content
Junior League of Birmingham, Inc., Birmingham, Alabama

Sunday Favorite Brisket

Serves 8 to 10

1 (6- to 8-pound) beef brisket
1/2 to 3/4 cup ketchup
1/4 cup low-sodium soy sauce

6 garlic cloves, minced
1 large onion, thinly sliced
1 bay leaf

Trim off and discard any excess fat from the brisket. Place fat side up in a shallow roasting pan. Combine the ketchup, soy sauce and garlic in a bowl. Using your hands, coat the brisket thoroughly on both sides with the ketchup mixture. Arrange the onion slices under and over the brisket. Add the bay leaf. Cover with foil. Roast at 350 degrees for 2 to 2 1/2 hours or until cooked through. Let stand for 15 minutes. Reduce the oven temperature to 300 degrees. Remove the brisket from the pan, reserving the juices in the pan. Slice into long thin pieces. Return the slices to the pan. Bake for 20 to 30 minutes. (Or, chill in the pan until serving time and reheat at 300 degrees until heated through.) Remove and discard the bay leaf. Serve with a robust red wine.

Once Upon A Time
Junior League of Evansville, Evansville, Indiana

Slow-Cooker Pot Roast

Serves 6

1 (3-pound) boneless beef chuck roast
2 large garlic cloves, sliced
1/4 cup all-purpose flour
1/2 teaspoon salt
1/2 teaspoon pepper
1/3 cup olive oil
1 1/2 cups red wine
1 onion, sliced
1 (8-ounce) can tomato sauce

1 tablespoon brown sugar
1 teaspoon oregano
1 teaspoon prepared horseradish
1 teaspoon prepared mustard
1 bay leaf
8 small red potatoes, peeled (about 1 1/2 pounds)
8 carrots, peeled and quartered
3 ribs celery, chopped

Cut the roast into halves and make small slits in the top of each half. Insert a garlic slice into each slit. Coat the roast with a mixture of the flour, salt and pepper. Heat the olive oil in a large skillet and brown the roast on all sides in the hot oil. Place the roast in a 6-quart slow cooker and add the wine and onion. Mix the tomato sauce, brown sugar, oregano, prepared horseradish, prepared mustard and bay leaf in a bowl and pour over the roast. Add the potatoes, carrots and celery and cook, covered, on Low for 8 hours. Discard the bay leaf before serving.

Tables of Content
Junior League of Birmingham, Inc., Birmingham, Alabama

Beef Tenderloin with Mango Salsa

MANGO SALSA
2 1/2 cups chopped mangoes or peaches
1 cup chopped red bell pepper
1/2 cup chopped red onion
1/3 cup chopped fresh cilantro

1/2 cup jalapeño jelly
1/4 cup lime juice
2 teaspoons grated lime zest
1 jalapeño chile, seeded (optional) and chopped

SPICE RUB
1/4 cup olive oil
1 1/2 tablespoons cinnamon
1 tablespoon coriander

1 tablespoon sugar
1 tablespoon paprika
1 teaspoon salt
1/2 teaspoon cayenne pepper

BEEF TENDERLOIN
1 1/2 to 2 pounds beef tenderloin, or
   6 (6-ounce) beef fillet steaks
Olive oil

For the salsa, combine the mangoes, bell pepper, onion and cilantro in a bowl and mix well. Stir in the jalapeño jelly, lime juice, lime zest and jalapeño chile. Chill, covered, in the refrigerator. The salsa may be prepared several hours in advance of serving.

For the rub, combine the olive oil, cinnamon, coriander, sugar, paprika, salt and cayenne pepper in a bowl and mix well.

For the tenderloin, brush the tenderloin with olive oil and pat the rub over the surface, pressing lightly. Grill the tenderloin over medium-high heat to the desired degree of doneness, turning occasionally. Slice as desired and serve with the salsa. A red wine, such as merlot or Spanish tempranillo, would be a nice accompaniment.

An Occasion to Gather
Junior League of Milwaukee, Milwaukee, Wisconsin

Beef Tenderloin

1 beef tenderloin, room temperature
Salt and pepper
Butter or margarine

Trim tenderloin of excess fat and place on a rack in pan. Season with salt and pepper. Bake tenderloin uncovered in a preheated 450-degree oven for 20 minutes. Reduce heat to 350 degrees and bake an additional 15 minutes. Remove tenderloin from oven and spread butter over top and cover with foil. Allow to stand 10 to 15 minutes before slicing.

A Southern Collection Then and Now
Junior League of Columbus, Columbus, Georgia

Lobster-Stuffed Beef Tenderloin　　Serves 8

1 (3- to 4-pound) beef tenderloin
2 (8-ounce) frozen lobster tails
Salt to taste
2 tablespoons butter, melted
1 tablespoon lemon juice
6 slices bacon, partially cooked

1/2 cup sliced green onions
1/2 cup (1 stick) butter
1/2 to 3/4 cup dry white wine
3 garlic cloves, minced
Mushrooms
Sprigs of fresh parsley

Cut the beef lengthwise to but not through the bottom to butterfly. Cook the frozen lobster tails in boiling salted water to cover in a large saucepan. Return to a boil and reduce the heat. Simmer for 5 to 6 minutes or until the lobster meat is opaque. Remove the lobster from the shells and cut into halves lengthwise. Place the lobster end to end inside the beef. Mix 2 tablespoons melted butter and the lemon juice together and drizzle over the lobster. Wrap the beef around the lobster to enclose and tie together with string at 1-inch intervals. Place on a rack in a shallow roasting pan. Roast at 425 degrees for 45 to 50 minutes for rare. Lay the bacon slices on top of the beef and roast for 5 minutes. Sauté the green onions in 1/2 cup butter in a saucepan until tender. Add the wine and garlic and sauté until heated through. To serve, cut the roast into slices and place on a serving platter. Spoon the sauce over the roast and garnish with mushrooms and parsley.

Now Serving
Junior League of Wichita Falls, Wichita Falls, Texas

Spicy Enchiladas

1 (2- to 3-pound) chuck roast
1 (16-ounce) can chopped tomatoes
1/4 cup hot salsa
1/4 cup water
5 garlic cloves, minced
2 1/2 tablespoons chili powder
2 tablespoons oregano
1 1/2 teaspoons cumin
Salt and pepper to taste

12 flour tortillas
1 small onion, chopped
Chopped jalapeño chiles (optional)
Chopped green chiles
1 (10-ounce) can enchilada sauce
1 (8-ounce) can tomato sauce
Shredded Cheddar and Monterey Jack cheese
    to taste
Chopped fresh cilantro (optional)

Place the roast in a baking pan. Combine the undrained tomatoes, salsa, water, garlic, chili powder, oregano, cumin, salt and pepper in a bowl and mix well. Pour the tomato mixture over the roast. Bake, tightly covered, at 300 degrees for 3 hours. Remove the roast from the oven and shred. May be prepared 1 day in advance and stored, covered, in the refrigerator.

Dip the tortillas in hot water for 1 second and pat dry with paper towels. Spoon some of the beef, onion, jalapeño chiles and green chiles onto the center of each tortilla. Roll to enclose the filling. Arrange seam side down in a greased 10×15-inch baking dish.

Mix the enchilada sauce and tomato sauce in a bowl. Pour over the top of the enchiladas. Sprinkle with cheese. Bake, covered tightly, at 350 degrees for 25 minutes. Remove cover and sprinkle with more cheese. Bake for 10 minutes longer. Sprinkle with cilantro.

Cooking by the Bootstraps
Junior Welfare League of Enid, Enid, Oklahoma

Asian-Grilled Flank Steak

1/2 cup soy sauce
2 tablespoons brown sugar
2 tablespoons lemon juice
2 tablespoons vegetable oil
2 tablespoons minced onion

1 large garlic clove, minced
1 teaspoon ground ginger
1/4 teaspoon pepper
1 1/2 pounds flank steak

Combine the soy sauce, brown sugar, lemon juice, oil, onion, garlic, ginger and pepper in a bowl and mix well. Pour the soy sauce mixture over the steak in a dish just large enough to hold the steak, turning to coat. Marinate, covered, in the refrigerator for 6 to 10 hours, turning occasionally. Drain, reserving the marinade. Arrange the steak on a rack in a broiler pan. Broil 3 inches from the heat source for 5 minutes per side for rare or to the desired degree of doneness. Bring the reserved marinade to a boil in a saucepan and boil for 2 minutes. Cut the steak across the grain into thin slices and serve with the reserved marinade. You may grill over hot coals if desired.

Worth Tasting
Junior League of the Palm Beaches, West Palm Beach, Florida

Marinated Flank Steak

Serves 4 to 6

1 flank steak
1/2 cup olive oil
1 large garlic clove, crushed
2 tablespoons crumbled Roquefort cheese
2 tablespoons dry vermouth

2 teaspoons instant coffee granules
1 teaspoon kosher salt
1/2 teaspoon freshly ground pepper
1/2 teaspoon Dijon mustard

Score the flank steak. Combine the olive oil, garlic, cheese, vermouth, coffee granules, salt, pepper and Dijon mustard in a bowl and mix well. Pour the olive oil mixture over the steak in a shallow dish, turning and rubbing to coat. Marinate at room temperature for 1 hour. Preheat the broiler or grill. Drain the steak, reserving the marinade. Broil or grill the steak for 5 minutes per side or to the desired degree of doneness. Bring the reserved marinade to a boil in a saucepan and boil for 5 minutes. Add the steak to the hot marinade and turn to coat. Cut the steak diagonally into slices and serve with the remaining warm marinade.

Compliments of
The Woman's Exchange of Memphis, Memphis, Tennessee

Savory Steak Sauté

Serves 4 to 6

1 1/2 pounds sirloin steak, trimmed
2 small garlic cloves, minced
2 tablespoons Dijon mustard
1 tablespoon olive oil
Juice of 1/2 lemon
1 teaspoon salt
1/4 teaspoon pepper

1 tablespoon brandy
2 tablespoons butter
2 tablespoons olive oil
1/2 cup chopped onion
1/2 pound mushrooms, sliced
1/2 cup dry red wine
1 tablespoon Worcestershire sauce

Cut the steak across the grain into very thin bite-size pieces. Combine the garlic, Dijon mustard, olive oil, lemon juice, salt, pepper and brandy in a bowl and mix to a paste consistency. Add the steak and toss to coat. Let stand for 30 minutes. Heat 1 tablespoon of the butter and 1 tablespoon of the olive oil in a large skillet over medium-high heat. Sear a few pieces of the steak at a time for 1 minute on each side, adding the remaining butter and olive oil to the skillet as needed. Remove the steak to a dish. Reduce the heat to low. Add the onion and sauté until tender. Add the mushrooms and cook until tender. Stir in the wine. Cook for 1 or 2 minutes, scraping up all the browned bits on the bottom of the skillet. Stir in the Worcestershire sauce. Return the steak to the skillet. Reduce the heat and simmer, covered, for 5 minutes or until heated through. Adjust the seasonings. Garnish each serving with chopped fresh parsley.

Tastes, Tales and Traditions
Palo Alto Auxiliary for Children, Palo Alto, California

French Market Meat Loaf

Serves 8

2 tablespoons olive oil
8 ounces andouille sausage, finely chopped
1 cup chopped onion
1 red bell pepper, finely chopped
1 cayenne or other hot red pepper, seeded, minced
2 garlic cloves, minced
$\frac{1}{2}$ teaspoon dried thyme

$\frac{1}{2}$ teaspoon dried oregano
$\frac{1}{2}$ cup tomato sauce
$\frac{1}{2}$ cup beef broth
$\frac{1}{4}$ cup fresh bread crumbs
2 pounds ground beef
1 teaspoon salt
Pepper to taste

Heat the olive oil in a large skillet over low heat. Add the sausage, onion, bell pepper, hot pepper, garlic, thyme and oregano and mix well. Cover and cook for 15 minutes. Remove to a bowl and let cool to room temperature. Add the tomato sauce, broth and bread crumbs to the sausage mixture. Crumble the ground beef into the bowl. Add the salt and season with pepper. Mix gently until combined. Pack into a 5×9-inch loaf pan. Bake at 350 degrees for 45 minutes or until cooked through. Pour off the drippings from the pan. Cover the pan loosely with foil and let stand for 10 minutes. Slice and serve.

Crescent City Collection
The Junior League of New Orleans, New Orleans, Louisiana

Taglarina (Ti-ger-ree-ny)

Serves 12

1 large onion, chopped
1 bell pepper, chopped
3 cloves of garlic, chopped
Small amount of oil
2 pounds lean ground beef
2 teaspoons chili powder
Dash Worcestershire sauce
Salt and pepper

1 (16-ounce) can of tomatoes
1 (16-ounce) can cream-style corn
1 (8-ounce) can tomato sauce
1 ($3\frac{1}{2}$-ounce) can ripe olives and juice
6 to 8 ounces shell macaroni, cooked
$\frac{1}{4}$ teaspoon oregano
Cheddar cheese

Sauté chopped onion, bell pepper, and garlic in small amount of oil until clear. Remove from pan, sauté ground beef and add chili powder, Worcestershire sauce, salt, and pepper. Add sautéed seasonings, tomatoes, corn, and tomato sauce. Add olives cut from seeds and olive juice. Taste to adjust salt. Add macaroni which has been cooked in salt water as directed on package. Add oregano. Place in 9×13-inch casserole. Refrigerate 6 to 8 hours to allow flavors to blend. One hour before serving, slice cheese on top. Bake at 350 degrees for 1 hour. If glass baking dish is used, remove from refrigerator sooner and bake at 325 degrees.

A Taste of Georgia
Newnan Junior Service League, Newnan, Georgia

Two-Potato and Apricot Stew in a Pumpkin Shell

Serves 6

2 pounds lean beef stew meat,
    cut into 1 1/2-inch cubes
1 large onion, chopped
2 cloves of garlic, minced
3 tablespoons vegetable oil
2 large tomatoes, chopped
1 large green bell pepper, chopped
1 tablespoon salt
1/2 teaspoon pepper
1 teaspoon sugar

1 cup dried apricots
3 white potatoes, peeled, diced
3 sweet potatoes, peeled, diced
2 cups beef broth
1 medium pumpkin
Melted butter
Salt and pepper to taste
1/4 cup dry sherry
1 (16-ounce) can whole kernel corn, drained

Cook the beef, onion and garlic in the oil in a stockpot until the beef is browned. Add the tomatoes, green pepper, 1 tablespoon salt, 1/2 teaspoon pepper, sugar, apricots, potatoes, sweet potatoes and broth and mix well. Simmer, covered, for 1 hour.

Cut off and discard the pumpkin top. Scoop out the seeds and stringy membrane. Brush the inside of the pumpkin with butter. Sprinkle lightly with salt and pepper to taste.

Stir the sherry and corn into the stew. Spoon into the pumpkin shell. Place the pumpkin shell in a shallow baking pan. Bake at 325 degrees for 1 hour or until the pumpkin pulp is tender.

Place the pumpkin in a large bowl to stabilize it on the table. Ladle the stew into individual bowls, scooping out some of the pumpkin with each serving of stew.

Beyond Burlap
Junior League of Boise, Boise, Idaho

Grillades

2 1/2 to 3 pounds veal rounds, sliced or slivered
   (sirloin tip or round steak may be used)
5 tablespoons bacon drippings
3 tablespoons flour
3 medium onions, chopped
6 green onions, chopped
2 medium bell peppers, chopped
2 cloves garlic, chopped
1/3 bunch celery with leaves, chopped

1/3 bunch parsley, chopped
2 cups canned tomatoes
2 cups beef or veal stock (broth)
1 tablespoon or more Worcestershire sauce
2 teaspoons Kitchen Bouquet (optional)
1 small bay leaf
1/2 teaspoon thyme, crushed
Salt and pepper to taste
Burgundy (optional)

Brown meat in bacon drippings. Remove to a platter. Add flour to drippings and stir until a rich brown. Add vegetables (except tomatoes) and sauté until transparent. Add meat and all remaining ingredients. Cover and simmer for 3 hours, adding water as necessary. (You may add burgundy instead of water.) Remove bay leaf before serving. Serve over hot grits, garlic grits, rice, or potatoes.

River Road Recipes III: A Healthy Collection
Junior League of Baton Rouge, Baton Rouge, Louisiana

Tuscan Veal Piccata

1/2 cup all-purpose flour
1 pound veal cutlets, pounded to 1/4 inch thick
2 tablespoons olive oil, more if needed
5 tablespoons unsalted butter, divided,
   more if needed
2 ounces prosciutto, julienned

1 tablespoon minced shallot
3/4 cup chicken broth
1/4 cup dry white wine
1/4 cup freshly squeezed lemon juice
2 tablespoons capers, drained and rinsed
3 tablespoons minced fresh parsley

Put the flour in a shallow dish, dredge the veal in the four, and pat to remove the excess. Heat a large skillet over medium-high heat, add 1 tablespoon of the olive oil and 1 tablespoon of the butter, and swirl to coat the pan. When sizzling, add the veal to the pan in a single layer (do this in batches) and sauté until lightly browned, about 1 minute per side. Transfer the veal to a platter or individual plates and keep warm in a low oven. Repeat with the remaining veal cutlets, adding more butter and oil to the skillet with each batch.

Add the prosciutto and shallot to the skillet and sauté until tender and aromatic, scraping up remaining browned bits from the pan, about 30 seconds. Add the broth and wine and bring to a boil, then simmer to reduce the liquid to about 1/3 cup, about 3 minutes. Add the lemon juice and capers and reduce again to about 1/3 cup, about 3 minutes. Swirl in the remaining 3 tablespoons butter and parsley and stir until evenly blended and the sauce thickens slightly. Spoon the sauce over the veal and serve right away.

Celebrate the Rain
The Junior League of Seattle, Seattle, Washington

Veal Royale

Serves 6 to 8

2 pounds veal, sliced thin
1 cup flour
1/2 teaspoon paprika
1/2 teaspoon salt
1/2 teaspoon sage
1/3 cup oil
1/3 cup butter
1/2 cup currant jelly

4 tablespoons catsup
1 (10-ounce) can consommé
1/3 cup dry sherry
Pinch of cayenne pepper
Pinch of garlic salt
Pinch of pepper
1 to 2 cups sliced mushrooms,
   enough to cover veal

Dry veal on paper towel. Dredge slices in mixture of flour, paprika, salt, and sage. Heat butter and oil together in a frying pan until very hot. Water should bead when sprinkled in pan. Brown veal slices very quickly and remove them to a 9×13-inch casserole dish. In same frying pan, combine currant jelly, catsup, consommé, sherry, cayenne, garlic salt, and pepper. Stir and bring to a boil. Pour this mixture over veal. Add mushrooms to casserole. Cover with foil and bake at 325 degrees for 60 minutes or at 400 degrees for 30 minutes, or refrigerate, and bake later.

Applehood & Motherpie
Junior League of Rochester, Inc., Rochester, New York

Braised Lamb Shanks

Serves 8

8 lamb shanks
All-purpose flour
1/4 cup vegetable oil
1 onion, sliced
4 garlic cloves, minced
1 cup ketchup

1 cup water
2 tablespoons Worcestershire sauce
1/2 cup cider vinegar
1/4 cup packed brown sugar
2 teaspoon dry mustard
1 cup raisins

Coat the lamb with flour. Heat the oil in a large Dutch oven on the stovetop. Add the lamb and brown on all sides. Drain off any excess oil. Place the onion over the lamb shanks. Combine the garlic, ketchup, water, Worcestershire sauce, vinegar, brown sugar, dry mustard and raisins in a saucepan and mix well. Cook until heated through, stirring frequently.

Pour over the lamb and onion. Bake, covered, at 350 degrees for 2 hours or until the lamb is tender. Baste the lamb with the sauce. Bake, uncovered, for 15 minutes longer.

Note: This recipe can be made 1 day ahead. Chill, covered, in the refrigerator. This also freezes well.

Popovers to Panache
The Village Club, Bloomfield Hills, Michigan

Grilled Tenderloin with Blueberry Barbecue Sauce

Serves 12 to 15

TENDERLOINS
3 venison, beef or pork tenderloins
1 cup vegetable oil
3/4 cup soy sauce
1/2 cup red wine vinegar
1/3 cup fresh lemon juice

1/4 cup Worcestershire sauce
2 tablespoons dry mustard
2 tablespoons chopped fresh parsley
1 tablespoon freshly ground pepper
2 teaspoons salt
2 garlic cloves, crushed

BLUEBERRY BARBECUE SAUCE
1 tablespoon olive oil
1/4 cup minced onion
1 tablespoon chopped fresh jalapeño chile
1 pint fresh blueberries
3 tablespoons brown sugar

1/4 cup rice vinegar
1/4 cup ketchup
3 tablespoons Dijon mustard
1 teaspoon Tabasco sauce
1/4 cup (1/2 stick) unsalted butter
Salt and pepper to taste

TENDERLOINS
Arrange the tenderloins in a shallow dish. Whisk the oil, soy sauce, vinegar, lemon juice, Worcestershire sauce, dry mustard, parsley, pepper, salt and garlic in a bowl and pour over the tenderloins, turning to coat. Marinate, covered, in the refrigerator for 4 to 5 hours, turning occasionally; drain.

Grill the venison tenderloins over medium-hot coals for 14 to 15 minutes, turning once. If using beef tenderloins, grill for at least 30 minutes. Remove the tenderloins to a serving platter and slice as desired.

SAUCE
Heat the olive oil in a large skillet and add the onion and jalapeño chile. Sauté until the onion is tender and stir in the blueberries, brown sugar, vinegar, ketchup, Dijon mustard and Tabasco sauce. Bring to a low boil and cook for 15 minutes, stirring constantly.

Pour the blueberry mixture into a blender and process until puréed. Strain the purée into a small saucepan, discarding the solids. Cook until heated through, stirring frequently. Stir in the butter and cook until blended. Season with salt and pepper and serve immediately with the tenderloins. You may prepare the sauce in advance, adding the butter just before serving.

Mardi Gras to Mistletoe
Junior League of Shreveport-Bossier, Shreveport, Louisiana

Bacon-Wrapped Pork Tenderloin

Serves 4

2 pork tenderloins, cut into halves
8 slices bacon
1 (8-ounce) bottle Russian salad dressing

Wrap 2 bacon slices around each tenderloin half and secure with wooden picks. Place in a baking dish. Pour the salad dressing over the top. Marinate, covered, in refrigerator for 24 hours. Bake, uncovered, at 350 degrees for 1 hour or until the pork is cooked through.

Down Home: Treasured Recipes from Our House to Yours
West Point Junior Auxiliary, West Point, Mississippi

Maple- and Pecan-Glazed Pork Tenderloin

Serves 6

1/2 cup chopped pecans
1/2 cup real maple syrup
2 tablespoons stone-ground mustard
2 tablespoons bourbon

2 (1-pound) pork tenderloins
1/2 teaspoon salt
1 tablespoon butter or margarine
1 tablespoon vegetable oil

Bring the pecans, maple syrup and stone-ground mustard to a boil in a saucepan, stirring frequently. Reduce the heat and simmer for 3 minutes or until thickened. Stir in the bourbon and remove from the heat.

Sprinkle the pork tenderloins with the salt. Heat the butter and oil in a large ovenproof skillet over medium-high heat. Add the tenderloins and cook for 3 minutes per side or until brown. Spread the maple sauce over the tenderloins and place the skillet in a preheated 450-degree oven. Bake for 12 to 15 minutes or to 160 degrees on a meat thermometer. Remove the tenderloins to a serving platter and cover loosely with foil. Let stand for 10 minutes. Slice the pork and serve with the sauce remaining in the skillet.

Marshes to Mansions
Junior League of Lake Charles, LA, Lake Charles, Louisiana

Rosemary Ginger Pork Tenderloin

Makes 8 (3-ounce) servings

2 (1-pound) pork tenderloins, trimmed
1 (12-ounce) jar apricot preserves
1 (5-ounce) bottle light teriyaki sauce

3 tablespoons chopped fresh rosemary
2 tablespoons chopped fresh ginger

Place the tenderloins in a large heavy-duty sealable plastic bag or in a shallow dish. Mix the preserves, teriyaki sauce, rosemary and ginger in a bowl and pour over the tenderloins. Seal tightly and turn to coat. Marinate in the refrigerator for 30 minutes or for up to 8 hours, turning occasionally. Drain the tenderloins, reserving the marinade. Preheat the oven to 425 degrees. Bring the reserved marinade to a boil in a small saucepan and set aside. Arrange the tenderloins in a baking pan and bake for 25 minutes or until a meat thermometer inserted in the thickest portion registers 155 degrees, basting frequently with the reserved marinade. Remove from the oven and let stand, covered, for 10 minutes or until a meat thermometer registers 160 degrees.

Tables of Content
Junior League of Birmingham, Inc., Birmingham, Alabama

Pork Tenderloin Waldorf

Serves 4 to 6

2 pork tenderloins (1 1/2 pounds)
3/4 cup apple jelly
1/4 cup lemon juice concentrate
1/4 cup soy sauce
1/4 cup oil
1 tablespoon ginger root, grated

1 cup apple, chopped
1 cup fresh bread crumbs
1/4 cup celery, chopped
1/4 cup pecans, chopped
Apple wedges
Parsley sprigs

Partially slit tenderloins lengthwise, being careful not to cut all the way through. Place tenderloins in zippered plastic bag; set aside. In a small saucepan, combine jelly, lemon juice, soy sauce, oil, and ginger root. Cook and stir until jelly melts; reserve 3 tablespoons. Carefully pour jelly mixture over tenderloins and seal bag. Refrigerate 4 hours or overnight. When ready to cook, combine the apple, bread crumbs, celery, pecans, and reserved jelly mixture in a small bowl. Place tenderloins in baking dish; spoon apple mixture into the slits of tenderloins. Bake at 350 degrees for 30 minutes. Loosely cover and bake 10 minutes longer or until meat thermometer reaches 160 degrees. Garnish with apple wedges and parsley.

The Bess Collection
Junior Service League of Independence, Independence, Missouri

Mapled Pork Chops

Serves 6

6 pork chops
1 tablespoon dried minced onion
1 tablespoon vinegar
1 tablespoon Worcestershire sauce
1 teaspoon salt

½ teaspoon chili powder
⅛ teaspoon pepper
¼ cup maple syrup
¼ cup water

Place the pork chops in a single layer in a 9×13-inch baking dish. Combine the onion, vinegar, Worcestershire sauce, salt, chili powder, pepper, syrup and water in a bowl and mix well. Pour over the pork chops. Bake the pork chops, covered, at 400 degrees for 45 minutes, basting occasionally with the syrup mixture. Bake, uncovered, for 15 minutes longer or until cooked through.

If You Can't Stand the Heat, Get Out of the Kitchen
Junior Service League of Independence, Independence, Missouri

The Best Barbecued Ribs

Serves 4

½ cup (1 stick) butter
¾ cup ketchup
½ cup packed brown sugar
3 tablespoons lemon juice
1 tablespoon Dijon mustard

2 teaspoons steak sauce
2 teaspoons hot pepper sauce
2 teaspoons Worcestershire sauce
4 pounds baby back ribs, lightly salted

Melt the butter in a saucepan. Stir in the ketchup, brown sugar, lemon juice, Dijon mustard, steak sauce, hot pepper sauce and Worcestershire sauce. Cook until the sugar is melted, stirring frequently. Keep warm. Place the ribs on a rack in a roasting pan. Spread with some of the sauce. Bake at 325 degrees for 30 minutes. Baste with the sauce. Bake for 2 hours longer or until cooked through and tender, brushing with the remaining sauce every 15 minutes.

For Such A Time As This: A Cookbook
Park Cities Baptist Church, Dallas, Texas

Chinese Ribs

2 racks of baby back ribs
Peanut oil
Chinese five-spice powder to taste
1 cup soy sauce
1 cup fresh or canned grapefruit juice
1/4 cup ketchup

1/4 cup oyster sauce
1/4 cup packed light brown sugar
3 tablespoons rice wine vinegar
2 green onions, chopped
2 slices green chile

Preheat the oven to 300 degrees. Brush the surface of the ribs with peanut oil and sprinkle with five-spice powder. Arrange the ribs on a baking sheet and bake for 2 hours. Combine the soy sauce, grapefruit juice, ketchup, oyster sauce, brown sugar, vinegar, green onions and green chile slices in a saucepan and simmer for 20 to 30 minutes, stirring occasionally. Strain the sauce into a bowl, discarding the solids. Remove the ribs from the oven and brush liberally with the sauce. Bake for 15 to 20 minutes longer and serve.

Compliments of
The Woman's Exchange of Memphis, Memphis, Tennessee

Daddy's Best Texas Pork Ribs

Serves 6

18 pork ribs, fat trimmed
Garlic powder to taste
Seasoned salt to taste

Pepper to taste
1 1/2 cups honey
1/2 cup soy sauce

Season both sides of the ribs with the garlic powder, seasoned salt and pepper. Fill the charcoal pan of an upright smoker with charcoal briquettes. Soak 4 or 5 chunks of hickory in water for a few minutes and place around the edge of the charcoal pan. Pour odorless starter fluid on the top of 4 or 5 briquettes. Light. Immediately place a pan of water in its position above the charcoal. Arrange the ribs in the rib racks. Cover with dome lid. Cook for 4 to 5 hours.

Mix honey and soy sauce in a bowl until smooth. Apply the honey sauce to both sides of the ribs with a basting brush. Cook for 20 minutes longer. Do not cook longer then 30 minutes after applying the sauce or the ribs may taste bitter.

A Thyme to Remember
The Dallas County Medical Society Alliance, Dallas, Texas

Real Cajun Red Beans and Rice

Serves 6 to 8

1 pound dried red beans
2 quarts water
8 ounces salt pork
Salt to taste
3 cups chopped onions
1 bunch green onions, chopped
1 cup fresh parsley, chopped
1 cup chopped bell pepper
1 (4-ounce) can tomato sauce
2 large garlic cloves, crushed

1 tablespoon salt
1 tablespoon Worcestershire sauce
1 teaspoon black pepper
1 teaspoon red pepper
1/4 teaspoon oregano
1/4 teaspoon thyme
3 dashes of Tabasco sauce
1 pound link sausage, sliced
Hot cooked rice

Sort and rinse the beans. Combine the beans with a generous amount of water in a bowl and soak for 8 to 10 hours; drain. Combine the beans, 2 quarts water, the salt pork and salt to taste in a large stockpot and bring to a boil. Reduce the heat and simmer for 45 minutes. Stir in the onions, green onions, parsley, bell pepper, tomato sauce and garlic. Add 1 tablespoon salt, the Worcestershire sauce, black pepper, red pepper, oregano, thyme and Tabasco sauce and mix well.

Simmer for 1 hour, stirring occasionally. Add the sausage and cook for 45 minutes. Remove from the heat and let stand until cool; do not chill. Return the bean mixture to the heat and bring to a boil. Reduce the heat to low and simmer for 30 to 40 minutes or to the desired consistency, stirring occasionally. Serve over hot cooked rice.

Mardi Gras to Mistletoe
Junior League of Shreveport-Bossier, Shreveport, Louisiana

"Googling recipes pays off in convenience, but cooks miss the flavor packed in the pages of cookbooks from church groups, parent-teacher associations, women's groups and other nonprofit organizations."

Sandra Kallio
Wisconsin State Journal

Roasted Chicken

1 (5- to 6-pound) chicken
1 lemon, cut into halves
4 garlic cloves
1/4 cup (1/2 stick) unsalted butter (optional)
Olive oil
Kosher salt and freshly ground pepper to taste
1 tablespoon all-purpose flour
1 cup (or more) chicken stock, water, fruit juice or wine

Preheat the oven to 500 degrees. Remove the wing tips from the chicken. Stuff the cavity with the lemon, garlic and butter. Drizzle with olive oil and season inside and out with kosher salt and pepper. Place breast side up in an 8×12-inch roasting pan. Place legs first in the oven and roast for 10 minutes. Move the chicken slightly in the pan to prevent sticking. Roast for 40 to 50 minutes or until the juices run clear. Remove to a platter, tilting the chicken over the roasting pan to allow all the cooking juices to drain into the pan.

Pour the cooking juices into a gravy separator, leaving any browned bits in the pan. Allow the juices to separate and spoon 1 tablespoon of the drippings from the top into the roasting pan. Place on the stovetop and stir the flour into the drippings. Cook over medium heat until slightly brown, stirring constantly.

Pour the juice from the bottom of the gravy separator into a 2-cup measure, taking care not to get any of the grease. Add enough stock to measure 1 1/2 cups. Add to the roasting pan and cook for 4 minutes or until thickened, stirring constantly. Serve with the chicken.

The Bells Are Ringing: A Call to Table
Mission San Juan Capistrano Women's Guild, San Juan Capistrano, California

"Community cookbooks are a voyeur's treat, a window into the everyday life and foods of a group of churchgoers, a clutch of quilters, or a league of ladies inclined toward service."

John T. Edge, A Gracious Plenty

Chicken Jambalaya

1 (4- to 5-pound) hen, cut up
1 teaspoon black pepper
1/2 cup vegetable oil
3 medium onions, chopped
1 teaspoon garlic powder
8 cups water
2 teaspoons salt
1 teaspoon black pepper
1 teaspoon Tabasco sauce, or 1 tablespoon Cajun Chef
1 teaspoon garlic powder
1/2 teaspoon MSG (optional)
1/4 teaspoon red pepper
4 cups long grain rice

Sprinkle the hen with 1 teaspoon black pepper. Heat the oil in a 5-quart cast-iron Dutch oven over high heat. Brown the hen on all sides in the hot oil. Reduce the heat to medium when the oil clears. Continue to brown until the bottom of the Dutch oven has a layer of browned bits. Stir in the onions and 1 teaspoon garlic powder.

Cook over low heat until the onions are tender, stirring constantly. Stir in the water. Bring to a boil over high heat. Remove from heat. Let stand for 5 to 10 minutes to allow the oil to rise.

Skim off as much oil as possible. Stir in the salt, 1 teaspoon black pepper, Tabasco sauce, 1 teaspoon garlic powder, MSG and red pepper. Bring to a boil over high heat. Stir in the rice; reduce the heat to low.

Cook, covered, for 10 minutes and stir. Cool, covered, for 20 minutes longer. Serve with a green salad, Cajun white beans and crusty French bread. Substitute 3 pounds cubed boneless pork and 1 pound sliced tube sausage for the hen for Pork and Sausage Jambalaya.

Serving Louisiana
LSU Foundation, Baton Rouge, Louisiana

Baked Chicken Supreme

Serves 8

4 chicken breasts, split and boned
1/2 cup flour
1 teaspoon salt
1/4 teaspoon pepper
1 stick butter, divided

1/4 cup minced green onions
1/4 cup chicken broth
3/4 cup dry white wine
1/2 pound fresh mushrooms, sliced
2 cups seedless grapes

Preheat oven to 350 degrees. Coat chicken breast with flour seasoned with salt and pepper; brown in 5 tablespoons butter and remove. Arrange breasts close together in shallow pan. Add onions to pan drippings; cook until tender. Stir in chicken broth and wine; bring to boil and pour over chicken. Cover and bake for 1 hour or more until chicken is tender. Cook mushrooms in remaining 3 tablespoons of butter. Add to chicken along with grapes. Cover and continue to bake for 10 minutes or until grapes are just heated.

Magic
Junior League of Birmingham, Inc., Birmingham, Alabama

Chicken Diablo

Serves 4

4 chicken breasts
1/4 cup butter
1/2 cup honey

1/4 cup Dijon mustard
1 teaspoon curry powder
1 teaspoon salt

Preheat the oven to 350 degrees. Rinse the chicken and pat dry. Arrange in a shallow baking pan. Melt the butter in a small saucepan. Stir in the honey, mustard, curry powder and salt. Pour over the chicken, turning to coat evenly. Bake, covered, for 45 minutes. Bake, uncovered, for 15 minutes longer or until the chicken is tender and brown, basting frequently with the pan juices.

Apron Strings
Junior League of Little Rock, Little Rock, Arkansas

Cranberry- and Apple-Stuffed Chicken Breasts with Raspberry Balsamic Drizzle

Serves 6

CHICKEN
6 (4-ounce) boneless skin-on chicken breasts
1 1/2 cups olive oil
3/4 cup white wine
Juice of 2 lemons

1 tablespoon chopped garlic
1/2 cup chopped onion
1 tablespoon kosher salt
1 1/2 teaspoons freshly ground black pepper
1/3 cup flat-leaf parsley

STUFFING
1/2 cup chopped onion
1/2 cup chopped celery
3/4 cup peeled chopped Granny Smith apple
3/4 cup (1 1/2 sticks) melted butter
1 1/2 teaspoons rubbed sage

3/4 cup dried cranberries
1/2 teaspoon kosher salt
1/4 teaspoon freshly ground black pepper
2 1/4 cups chicken stock
1 (14-ounce) package herb stuffing mix

RASPBERRY BALSAMIC DRIZZLE
1 cup balsamic vinegar

1/2 cup seedless raspberry preserves
Sage for garnish

For the chicken, arrange the chicken in a single layer in a shallow dish. Combine the olive oil, wine, lemon juice, garlic, onion, salt, pepper and parsley in a bowl and mix well. Pour over the chicken. Chill, covered, for 12 hours or longer.

For the stuffing, sauté the onion, celery and apple in the butter in a saucepan until tender. Stir in the sage, cranberries, salt, pepper and stock. Bring to a boil. Add the stuffing mix and mix well. Drain the chicken, discarding the marinade. Stuff each chicken breast generously between the skin and the meat with the stuffing. Arrange the stuffed chicken in a baking dish. Spoon any remaining stuffing around the chicken. Bake at 375 degrees for 1 hour, covering for the last 15 minutes if necessary. Arrange on a platter.

For the drizzle, pour the vinegar in a small saucepan. Cook over low heat for 8 to 10 minutes or until the vinegar is thick and syrupy and reduced to 2 tablespoons; do not boil. Stir in the preserves. Drizzle over the chicken. Garnish with sage.

Life is Delicious
Hinsdale Junior Woman's Club, Hinsdale, Illinois

Oven-Fried Chicken

6 whole chicken breasts, split, skinned
3 ¹/₂ cups ice water
1 cup plain nonfat yogurt
1 cup Italian-seasoned bread crumbs
1 cup flour
1 tablespoon Old Bay seasoning
¹/₄ teaspoon garlic powder

¹/₂ teaspoon Creole seasoning or
    Cajun seasoning
¹/₂ teaspoon thyme
¹/₂ teaspoon basil
¹/₂ teaspoon oregano
¹/₈ teaspoon freshly ground black pepper
Cayenne to taste

Spray a baking sheet 3 times with nonstick cooking spray. Rinse the chicken. Place the chicken in the ice water in a bowl. Spoon the yogurt into a medium bowl. Combine the bread crumbs, flour, Old Bay seasoning, garlic powder, Creole seasoning, thyme, basil, oregano, black pepper and cayenne in a sealable plastic bag, shaking to mix. Remove 2 pieces of the chicken from the water; coat with the yogurt. Place the chicken in the plastic bag, shaking to coat. Arrange on the prepared baking sheet. Repeat the process with the remaining chicken. Spray the chicken lightly with nonstick cooking spray. Place the baking sheet on the bottom oven rack. Bake at 400 degrees for 1 hour, turning every 20 minutes to assure even browning.

A Taste of the Good Life: From the Heart of Tennessee
Saint Thomas Hospital, Nashville, Tennessee

Lowcountry Cinnamon Chicken

¹/₂ cup raisins
2 medium apples, peeled, cored, and chopped fine
¹/₂ cup sliced almonds
1 can water chestnuts, chopped fine
¹/₂ to 3/4 cup brown sugar

1 stick melted butter
1 teaspoon cinnamon, or more to taste
2 teaspoons curry powder, or more to taste
8 chicken breasts, skinned and boned

Preheat oven to 350 degrees. Mix all ingredients, except chicken in small mixing bowl. Place a full tablespoon of apple mixture on each chicken breast. Bring up corners and secure with toothpick. Turn over and place in medium-sized baking dish. Place remaining apple mixture on top of each breast. Cover tightly with foil and bake at 350 degrees for 35 to 40 minutes, basting at least twice with juices.

Charleston Receipts Repeats
Junior League of Charleston, Charleston, South Carolina

Siesta Grilled Chicken

Serves 4

4 (5-ounce) boneless skinless chicken breasts
1/2 cup chopped fresh cilantro
1/4 cup olive oil
Juice of 2 limes

2 tablespoons chopped bottled jalapeño chiles
2 garlic cloves, minced
1 teaspoon salt
1 teaspoon black pepper

Arrange the chicken in a shallow dish. Mix the cilantro, olive oil, lime juice, jalapeño chiles and garlic in a bowl and pour over the chicken, turning to coat. Sprinkle with the salt and pepper. Marinate, covered, in the refrigerator for 8 to 10 hours, turning occasionally. Preheat the grill, arrange the chicken on the grill rack. Grill for 20 minutes or until cooked through, turning halfway through the grilling process.

Simply Sarasota
Junior League of Sarasota, Sarasota, Florida

Southwestern Grilled Chicken

Serves 4

1/8 cup apple cider vinegar
1/8 cup olive oil
1 tablespoon Dijon mustard
1/4 teaspoon onion salt
1/2 teaspoon coarsely ground pepper
1/2 teaspoon dried dillweed

1/2 teaspoon dried basil
4 skinless boneless chicken breasts
1 ripe avocado, sliced
1 cup grated Monterey Jack cheese
Salsa
Lime slices

For marinade, combine first 7 ingredients, and mix well. Place chicken in heavy-duty zip-top plastic bag. Pour marinade over chicken. Squeeze out air and seal bag. Refrigerate at least 30 minutes. Remove chicken from bag, discarding marinade. Grill chicken over medium coals until done, turning once. Arrange chicken on a baking sheet. Top each breast with slice of avocado and grated Monterey Jack cheese. Broil until cheese is melted. Top with salsa. Garnish each serving with lime slice. Serve with refried beans, brown rice, and a salad.

Food For Thought
The Junior League of Birmingham, Inc., Birmingham, Alabama

Chicken Asiago with Hickory Smoked Bacon

Serves 6 to 8

4 slices hickory smoked bacon, chopped
1 onion, chopped
4 cloves garlic, minced
4 boneless, skinless chicken breasts, cut into bite-sized pieces
1/4 to 1/2 teaspoon cayenne pepper
Kosher salt and freshly ground black pepper to taste

Olive oil
1/3 cup white wine
1/2 cup cream
3/4 cup grated Asiago cheese
2 ounces cream cheese, cut into cubes
8 ounces penne pasta, cooked and drained

Sauté the bacon with the onion in a large skillet over medium-high heat until the onion is limp; add garlic and continue to cook until bacon is crisp; drain and remove to a bowl. Season the chicken with the cayenne pepper, salt and black pepper. Sauté in a small amount of olive oil in the skillet until cooked through. Add the wine, cream, Asiago cheese and cream cheese. Simmer until the cheeses are melted, stirring gently. Stir in the bacon mixture. Fold in the pasta. Spoon into a serving dish.

Be Present At Our Table
Germantown United Methodist Women, Germantown, Tennessee

Southwest Chicken Bake

Serves 4

1 (2 1/2-pound) chicken, poached
2 (4-ounce) cans green chiles
2 cups sour cream
1 medium onion, chopped
16 ounces Cheddar cheese, shredded
16 ounces Monterey Jack cheese, shredded

1 teaspoon garlic powder
Salt and pepper to taste
4 small cans enchilada sauce
1 (2-ounce) package small corn tortillas
1/2 cup vegetable oil, heated or melted butter

Chop the chicken, discarding the skin and bones. Combine the chicken, chiles, sour cream, onion, half the Cheddar cheese, half the Monterey Jack cheese, garlic powder, salt and pepper in a bowl and mix well. Grease a 9×13-inch baking dish. Spread the bottom with just enough of the enchilada sauce to cover. Dip the tortillas in the oil and then in the enchilada sauce. Spoon some of the chicken mixture in the center of each tortilla. Roll to enclose the filling. Arrange the tortillas seam side down in the prepared dish, allowing the tortillas to touch. Sprinkle with the remaining Cheddar cheese and Monterey Jack cheese. Bake at 350 degrees for 45 minutes.

Made in the Shade
Junior League of Greater Fort Lauderdale, Fort Lauderdale, Florida

Coconut Chicken with African Spices and Couscous

Serves 5 to 6

CHICKEN
1 tablespoon olive oil
5 boneless skinless chicken breasts, chopped
1 yellow onion, finely chopped
2 red bell peppers, finely chopped
1 carrot, finely chopped
1 teaspoon curry powder
1 teaspoon brown sugar
1/2 teaspoon ground ginger

1 cup canned diced tomatoes
1 cup coconut milk
1 cup chicken broth
2 garlic cloves, minced
1 tablespoon grated lemon zest
2 whole cloves
1 golden potato, peeled and chopped
1 sweet potato, peeled and chopped

COUSCOUS AND ASSEMBLY
2/3 cup olive oil
2 cups couscous
1/2 cup golden raisins

1/2 cup chick-peas
1/4 cup pine nuts, toasted
3 cups chicken broth
Salt and pepper to taste

To prepare the chicken, heat the olive oil in a large stockpot over medium heat. Add the chicken, onion, bell peppers, carrot, curry powder, brown sugar and ginger to the hot oil and sauté for 5 to 7 minutes, until the vegetables are tender. Stir in the tomatoes, coconut milk, broth, garlic, lemon zest and cloves. Bring to a boil and reduce the heat. Stir in the potatoes and simmer for 30 minutes or until the potatoes are tender and the chicken is cooked through, stirring occasionally. Discard the cloves.

To prepare the couscous, combine olive oil, couscous, raisins, chick-peas and pine nuts in a heatproof bowl and mix well. Bring the broth to a boil in a saucepan and pour over the couscous mixture, mixing well. Let stand, covered with plastic wrap, for about 15 minutes. Season with salt and pepper and fluff with a fork. Ladle the coconut chicken over the couscous on a serving platter. Serve immediately.

Starfish Café: Changing Lives One Recipe at a Time...
Union Mission/Starfish Café, Savannah, Georgia

Elegant Party Casserole

2 to 4 tablespoons butter	2/3 cup flour
3 pounds fresh mushrooms, thickly sliced	1 tablespoon salt
8 whole chicken breasts, cooked, coarsely chopped	1 1/2 teaspoons pepper
2 pounds deveined peeled cooked shrimp	6 cups milk
3 (14-ounce) cans artichoke hearts, drained,	1 cup sherry or white wine
cut into quarters	2 tablespoons Worcestershire sauce
3/4 cup (1 1/2 sticks) butter	1/2 cup freshly grated Parmesan cheese

Heat 2 to 4 tablespoons butter in a skillet. Sauté the mushrooms in the butter until tender. Layer equal amounts of the chicken, shrimp, mushrooms and artichokes in 2 greased 9×13-inch baking dishes. Preheat the oven to 375 degrees. Heat 3/4 cup butter in a saucepan over low heat until melted. Add the flour, salt and pepper and stir until blended. Cook over low heat until bubbly and smooth, stirring constantly. Remove from heat. Add the milk gradually, stirring constantly. Bring to a boil, stirring constantly. Boil for 1 minute, stirring constantly. Stir in the sherry and Worcestershire sauce. Pour over the prepared layers. Sprinkle with the cheese. Bake for 45 minutes.

Art Fare
Toledo Museum of Art Aides, Toledo, Ohio

Slow-Roasted N' Awlins Turkey

1 (14- to 18-pound) turkey	2 tablespoons black pepper
1/4 cup poultry seasoning	1/2 cup (1 stick) margarine, softened
2 tablespoons salt	

Remove the giblets and rinse the turkey inside and out. Pat dry inside and out with paper towels. Mix the poultry seasoning, salt and pepper in a small bowl. Rub the mixture on the inside and outside of the turkey. Rub the margarine on the inside, outside and under the skin. Coat all surfaces of the turkey with the seasonings and margarine. Place the turkey in a high-sided baking pan large enough to hold it. Wrap foil around the wing tips and ends of the drumsticks. Roast, uncovered, at 500 degrees for 20 minutes or just until the turkey turns a honey brown color. Reduce the temperature to 200 degrees and roast for 40 to 50 minutes per pound or until cooked through. Place on a platter and cover loosely with foil. Let stand for 15 to 20 minutes before carving.

Crescent City Collection
The Junior League of New Orleans, New Orleans, Louisiana

Turkey Lasagna with Goat Cheese and Basil

1 tablespoon olive oil
1 tablespoon butter
1 cup chopped onion
1 garlic clove, chopped
1/4 teaspoon freshly grated nutmeg
1 1/2 pounds ground turkey
1 (28-ounce) can crushed tomatoes in tomato purée
1 (6-ounce) can tomato paste
1/4 cup chopped fresh flat-leaf parsley
1/2 cup chopped fresh basil leaves

2 teaspoons kosher salt
1 teaspoon freshly ground black pepper
8 ounces lasagna noodles
15 ounces ricotta cheese
4 ounces goat cheese, crumbled
1 1/4 cups grated Parmesan cheese
1 egg, lightly beaten
1 pound fresh mozzarella cheese, thinly sliced
Fresh basil for garnish

Heat the olive oil and butter in a large skillet over medium heat. Add the onion. Cook for 3 to 4 minutes or until tender. Add the garlic and nutmeg and cook for 1 minute. Add the turkey. Cook over medium-low heat for 8 to 10 minutes or until brown and crumbly, stirring frequently. Stir in the tomatoes, tomato paste, 2 tablespoons of the parsley, basil, 1 1/2 teaspoons of the salt and 1/2 teaspoon of the pepper. Bring to a simmer. Cook for 15 to 20 minutes or until thickened.

Place the noodles in a bowl and cover with very hot water. Let stand for 20 minutes; drain.

Combine the ricotta cheese, goat cheese, 1 cup of the Parmesan cheese, egg, remaining 2 tablespoons parsley, remaining 1/2 teaspoon salt, and remaining 1/2 teaspoon pepper in a bowl and mix well.

Spread 1/3 of the sauce evenly over the bottom of a 9×12-inch baking dish. Layer the pasta, mozzarella cheese, ricotta mixture and remaining sauce one-half at a time over the sauce. Sprinkle with the remaining 1/4 cup Parmesan cheese. Bake at 400 degrees for 30 minutes or until hot and bubbly. Garnish with fresh basil.

Life is Delicious
Hinsdale Junior Woman's Club, Hinsdale, Illinois

Life is Delicious honors the many women who have served Hinsdale Junior Woman's Club throughout its nearly sixty-year history. Since its inception, HJWC has sponsored both small and large-scale events, all with one goal in mind: to raise funds to help support children and families. In addition to raising large financial contributions, our members have donated their time through hands-on service projects to make life better for others. They have pulled weeds, planted flowers, cooked meals, held clothing drives, and helped the community in countless other ways. In the process, they have enjoyed some laughs and created friendships that have lasted a lifetime. HJWC has proven through over half a century of commitment to service that women coming together for a higher cause can truly make a difference in the world. *Life is Delicious* celebrates these relationships and helps fund the many projects of HJWC.

Megan McCleary
Hinsdale Junior Woman's Club
Hinsdale, Illinois

Wild Turkey with Ginger Barbecue Sauce

Serves 4 to 6

1 pound wild white turkey meat,
 cut into 1/4-inch slices
1 tablespoon canola oil
1 green bell pepper, chopped
1 yellow onion, chopped
2 teaspoons minced garlic
1 teaspoon coriander
1 teaspoon red pepper
1/4 teaspoon allspice

1/2 cup ketchup
Juice of 1 large lemon
2 tablespoons honey
2 tablespoons Worcestershire sauce
1 tablespoon finely minced fresh gingerroot
Salt to taste
White wine (optional)
Hot cooked rice

Sauté the turkey in the canola oil in a large heavy skillet over medium-low heat for 15 to 20 minutes per side. Push the turkey to the edge of the skillet. Add the bell pepper, onion, garlic, coriander, red pepper and allspice to the skillet. Cook over low heat for 15 minutes, stirring frequently. Stir the turkey into the bell pepper mixture and add the ketchup, lemon juice, honey, Worcestershire sauce, gingerroot and salt. Simmer, covered, for 20 to 30 minutes, stirring occasionally. Add wine if desired to increase the sauce quantity and mix well. Simmer just until heated through, stirring frequently. Spoon over hot cooked rice on a serving platter.

MariThyme Treasures
Texas Maritime Museum, Houston, Texas

Grilled Cornish Game Hens

Serves 8

4 Cornish game hens
Kosher salt to taste
Freshly ground pepper to taste
3/4 cup stone-ground mustard

6 tablespoons Dijon mustard
6 tablespoons soy sauce
2 tablespoons Pickapeppa Sauce

Split the game hens into halves and remove the backbones. Press lightly to flatten and sprinkle with salt and pepper. Combine the stone-ground mustard, Dijon mustard, soy sauce and Pickapeppa Sauce in a bowl and mix well. Brush each side of the game hens with some of the mustard mixture and arrange in a shallow baking dish. Marinate, covered, in the refrigerator for 2 hours or longer. Remove the game hens from the refrigerator 30 minutes before baking. Preheat the oven to 375 degrees and bake for 30 minutes or until the juices run clear, turning once. Preheat the grill and arrange the game hens bone side down on the grill rack. Grill for 5 to 10 minutes and turn. Grill about 10 minutes longer or until the skin is crisp. Serve with a spinach salad, corn and crusty French bread.

Compliments of
The Woman's Exchange of Memphis, Memphis, Tennessee

Deadly Duck

3 or 4 whole duck breasts
1/2 cup Worcestershire sauce
1/2 cup zesty Italian salad dressing
1 tablespoon soy sauce

1 tablespoon frozen lemon juice concentrate, or
2 tablespoons fresh lemon juice
8 to 10 slices bacon, cut into halves

Debone the duck breasts and reserve the bones for preparing homemade stock. Cut the duck into 1- to 1 1/2-inch-thick strips. Combine the Worcestershire sauce, salad dressing, soy sauce and lemon juice concentrate in a bowl and mix well. Add the duck and turn to coat. Marinate, covered, in the refrigerator for 8 to 10 hours; drain.

Preheat the grill. Roll the duck strips into pinwheels and wrap each with bacon; secure with wooden picks. Grill over hot coals for 3 to 5 minutes per side.

Compliments of
The Woman's Exchange of Memphis, Memphis, Tennessee

Black Bean Pasta

Serves 6

1 large onion, sliced
1 small red bell pepper, cut into strips
1 yellow bell pepper, cut into strips
8 ounces fresh mushrooms, sliced
2 tablespoons olive oil
1 (15-ounce) can black beans, drained, rinsed
1 (16-ounce) can whole tomatoes, chopped
1 (15 1/2-ounce) can kidney beans

1 1/2 ounces capers, drained
1/4 cup sliced black olives
1/4 teaspoon rosemary
1/4 teaspoon basil
1/4 teaspoon pepper
12 ounces angel hair pasta, cooked, drained
Fat-free Parmesan cheese
Fresh basil leaves

Sauté the onion, red pepper, yellow pepper and mushrooms in the olive oil in a skillet over medium-high heat until tender. Stir in the black beans, undrained tomatoes, undrained kidney beans, capers, black olives, rosemary, basil and pepper. Bring to a boil; reduce heat. Simmer for 30 minutes, stirring occasionally. Spoon over the angel hair pasta on a serving platter. Garnish with freshly grated fat-free Parmesan cheese and basil leaves.

A Taste of the Good Life: From the Heart of Tennessee
Saint Thomas Hospital, Nashville, Tennessee

Spinach, Penne and Asparagus Toss

Serves 12

GREEN ONION VINAIGRETTE
3/4 cup sliced green onions
1/2 cup olive oil

6 tablespoons white wine vinegar
2 tablespoons soy sauce

PASTA
1 1/2 pounds fresh asparagus spears
24 ounces penne or rigatoni
Salt to taste

1 tablespoon olive oil
6 ounces baby spinach, trimmed
1 cup salted roasted cashews, coarsely chopped
Pepper to taste

For the vinaigrette, process the green onions, olive oil, vinegar and soy sauce in a blender for 2 minutes or until smooth.

For the pasta, snap off the woody ends of the asparagus spears. Cut the spears into 1-inch pieces. Place the asparagus in a microwave-safe dish and add a small amount of water. Microwave, loosely covered, for 10 minutes; drain. Let stand until cool.

Cook the pasta in boiling salted water in a large saucepan using package directions; drain. Toss the hot pasta with the olive oil in a bowl until coated. Let stand until cool. Drizzle the vinaigrette over the pasta. Add the asparagus, spinach and cashews and toss to mix. Season with salt and pepper.

MariThyme Treasures
Texas Maritime Museum, Houston, Texas

Fresh Tomatoes on Fettuccine

Serves 4 to 6

4 ripe tomatoes, diced
3 to 4 tablespoons chopped fresh basil
3 to 4 tablespoons chopped fresh parsley
4 tablespoons capers (with juice)
2 cloves garlic, minced

4 tablespoons extra-virgin olive oil
Salt and pepper
3/4 pound fettuccine
1/4 cup freshly grated Parmesan cheese

Toss tomatoes with next 5 ingredients. Add salt and pepper to taste. Cover and leave at room temperature until ready to serve. Cook pasta according to package directions; drain. Serve tomato mixture on fettuccine. Sprinkle with fresh Parmesan.

Food for Thought
Junior League of Birmingham, Inc., Birmingham, Alabama

Orecchiette with Lentil Gravy

Serves 2 to 3

½ onion, chopped
1 garlic clove, minced
1 tablespoon olive oil
1 (15-ounce) can tomato sauce
½ cup chopped fresh tomato
¼ cup lentils, drained and rinsed

¼ teaspoon oregano
¼ teaspoon basil
¼ teaspoon thyme
¼ teaspoon salt
⅛ teaspoon Tabasco sauce
Hot cooked orecchiette

Sauté the onion and garlic in the olive oil in a large skillet until the onion is tender. Stir in the tomato sauce, tomato, lentils, oregano, basil, thyme, salt and Tabasco sauce. Simmer, covered, for 45 to 60 minutes or to the desired consistency, stirring occasionally. Spoon the lentil sauce over hot cooked pasta on a serving platter.

Compliments of
The Woman's Exchange of Memphis, Memphis, Tennessee

Julie's Vegetable Lasagna

Serves 8 to 12

1 (16-ounce) package of large lasagna noodles
2 thawed packages chopped spinach
2 cups grated Parmesan or Romano cheese
2⅔ cups ricotta cheese
1 teaspoon salt
1 teaspoon pepper
½ teaspoon ground nutmeg

2 cloves minced garlic
1 large chopped onion
3 tablespoons olive or salad oil
1 (30-ounce) can tomato sauce
¼ cup dry red wine
½ teaspoon basil
½ teaspoon oregano

Cook noodles according to package directions, drain and rinse twice in cold water, set aside. Squeeze excess moisture from spinach. In bowl, mix spinach and 1½ cups Romano/Parmesan cheeses. Add ricotta cheese, salt, ½ teaspoon pepper and nutmeg; mix well. Spread mixture along each noodle and roll in jelly roll. Stand rolled and filled noodles up on end, making sure they are not packed in, in 9×13-inch buttered baking dish. Sauté garlic and onion in oil on medium heat. Add tomato sauce, wine, basil, oregano and remaining ½ teaspoon pepper. Simmer, uncovered, for 10 minutes, spoon sauce on top of each noodle and pour remaining sauce on top. Bake, uncovered, at 350 degrees for 10 minutes. After cooking, sprinkle leftover grated cheese on top.

Of Tide & Thyme
Junior League of Annapolis, Inc., Annapolis, Maryland

Penne Rigate with Mushroom Sauce

1 tablespoon butter
1/2 cup finely chopped onion
1/4 cup finely chopped celery
1/4 cup finely chopped carrots
1 1/2 teaspoons tomato paste
1 cup dry red wine
1 (10-ounce) can beef consommé
1/8 teaspoon each thyme and pepper

1 tablespoon butter
8 ounces fresh mushrooms, sliced
1 tablespoon water
1 teaspoon cornstarch
1/8 teaspoon salt
8 ounces penne rigate, cooked and drained
Sprigs of flat-leaf parsley

Heat 1 tablespoon butter in a medium skillet over medium-high heat and add the onion, celery and carrots. Sauté for 5 minutes and stir in the tomato paste. Cook for 2 minutes, stirring constantly. Mix in the wine and cook for 10 minutes or until most of the liquid evaporates, stirring frequently. Stir in the consommé, thyme and pepper.

Bring to a boil and cook for 3 minutes or until the mixture is reduced to 1 cup, stirring frequently. Strain through a sieve into a heatproof bowl, discarding the solids. Cover to keep warm.

Heat 1 tablespoon butter in a saucepan over medium-high heat. Add the mushrooms to the hot butter and sauté for 5 minutes. Stir in the consommé mixture and bring to a boil. Reduce the heat to low and simmer for 5 minutes. Mix together the water and cornstarch in a small bowl and add to the sauce. Add salt and bring to a boil. Boil for 1 minute, stirring constantly. Toss the mushroom sauce with the pasta in a pasta bowl and garnish with sprigs of parsley. Serve with warm baguettes and red wine.

Compliments of
The Woman's Exchange of Memphis, Memphis, Tennessee

Zucchini Pasta Bake

8 ounces penne
Salt to taste
1/2 cup crushed saltine crackers
1/4 cup (1 ounce) grated Parmesan cheese
1/2 onion, chopped
1 tablespoon olive oil
2 cups chopped zucchini
1 tomato, chopped
2 garlic cloves, minced
1/2 teaspoon dried oregano
1/2 teaspoon dried basil
1 pinch celery seeds
Pepper to taste
1 cup (4 ounces) shredded mozzarella cheese

Cook the pasta in boiling salted water in a saucepan for 10 to 12 minutes or until al dente; drain. Process the crackers and Parmesan cheese in a blender or food processor until combined. Sauté the onion in the hot olive oil in a large skillet over medium heat until tender. Add the zucchini, tomato, garlic, oregano, basil and celery seeds. Season with salt and pepper. Sauté until the zucchini is tender. Remove from the heat and fold in the pasta and mozzarella cheese. Spoon into a lightly greased baking dish. Sprinkle evenly with the cracker mixture. Bake at 350 degrees for 25 minutes or until the top is light brown. Let stand for 5 minutes.

Shall We Gather
Trinity Episcopal Church, Wetumpka, Alabama

Vegetable Tian

6 potatoes, sliced (about 2 1/2 pounds)
Salt to taste
4 leeks (white and green portions), sliced
1 tablespoon olive oil
Freshly ground pepper to taste
1 tablespoon olive oil
1 pound fresh mushrooms, sliced
3 garlic cloves, minced
1/4 cup minced fresh parsley
1 tablespoon olive oil

3 red and/or yellow bell peppers, cut into strips
1/4 cup minced fresh basil
6 zucchini, sliced
1 tablespoon olive oil
1/2 cup milk or half-and-half (optional)
2 eggs, beaten (optional)
1 cup (4 ounces) freshly grated Parmesan cheese
   (optional)
Fresh herbs or fresh tomato sauce

Preheat the oven to 350 degrees. Parboil the potatoes in salted water in a saucepan for 7 to 8 minutes; drain. Layer the potatoes in a lightly oiled 3-quart baking dish. Sauté the leeks in 1 tablespoon olive oil in a skillet until tender. Season to taste with salt and pepper and spoon over the potato layer, reserving the pan drippings.

Heat 1 tablespoon olive oil with the reserved pan drippings and add the mushrooms and garlic. Sauté until the mushrooms are tender and season to taste with salt and pepper. Stir in the parsley and spoon the mushroom mixture over the prepared layers, reserving the pan drippings.

Heat 1 tablespoon olive oil with the reserved pan drippings and add the bell peppers. Sauté for 2 to 3 minutes and spoon the bell peppers over the prepared layers. Sprinkle with the basil and top with the zucchini, overlapping the slices. Drizzle with 1 tablespoon olive oil and sprinkle with salt and pepper.

Whisk the milk and eggs in a bowl until blended and pour over the prepared layers. Sprinkle with the cheese and bake on the center oven rack until the potatoes are tender and the mixture is set, if using the egg mixture. Cool on a wire rack for 10 minutes. Serve garnished with fresh herbs or fresh tomato sauce.

Compliments of
The Woman's Exchange of Memphis, Memphis, Tennessee

Fish and Seafood

"Since opening the café, our real-life culinary lab for those at-risk for homelessness in the Savannah area, I have enjoyed getting to know the students in each class. They are really the ones who make it fun for me. They start out insecure, struggling to look me in the eye or shake my hand. During their time at the café, I watch a change take place as they become confident chefs who assertively hold my stare and firmly shake my hand.

When we decided to publish a cookbook, we thought it would be interesting to find some of our graduates and see how their lives had changed as a result of their experience. I was completely taken aback by how their lives have continued to change. They were each prouder, more confident, and had stabilized their lives further. Yet, I was humbled by how modest they were as they told me of the changes in their lives for the better. It was great testimony to the effectiveness of the program. The cookbook became a celebration of the very tangible ways that good cooking can make someone's life much, much better than they ever dreamed possible."

Micheal Elliott
President and CEO
Union Mission, Inc.
Starfish Café, Savannah, Georgia

Baked Catfish Parmesan

Serves 6

6 skinned catfish filets
1 cup dry bread crumbs (plain, whole wheat
   or Italian)
3/4 cup grated Parmesan cheese
1/4 cup chopped parsley
1 teaspoon paprika
1/2 teaspoon oregano

1/4 teaspoon basil
2 teaspoons salt
1/2 teaspoon pepper
1/3 cup butter or margarine, melted
Lemon wedges
Parsley

Clean, wash and pat fish dry. Combine bread crumbs, Parmesan cheese, parsley, paprika, oregano, basil, salt and pepper. Dip catfish in melted butter and roll in crumb mixture. Arrange fish in a well greased 9×13-inch baking dish. Bake at 375 degrees for about 30 minutes or until fish flakes easily when tested with a fork. Garnish with lemon wedges and parsley.

Traditions: A Taste of the Good Life
Junior League of Little Rock, Little Rock, Arkansas

Oven-Fried Catfish

Serves 4

Nonstick cooking spray
1/4 cup cornmeal
1 teaspoon dried thyme
1 teaspoon dried basil
1/2 teaspoon garlic powder

1/2 teaspoon lemon pepper
3 teaspoons blackening seasoning
4 (4-ounce) catfish fillets
1/2 teaspoon paprika

Preheat oven to 400 degrees. Spray nonstick cooking spray over baking sheet 3 times to coat. Place cornmeal, thyme, and basil on a large plate or in a plastic bag and mix well. Sprinkle garlic powder, lemon pepper, and blackening seasoning evenly on to each of the 4 fillets. Coat fillets thoroughly with the cornmeal mixture and transfer to baking sheet. Dust each fillet with paprika. Coat fish lightly with cooking spray. Bake on bottom rack of oven for 20 minutes. Reduce heat to 350 degrees and bake 5 minutes more, until crust is golden and fish flakes easily.

A Taste of the Good Life: From the Heart of Tennessee
Saint Thomas Hospital, Nashville, Tennessee

Catfish with Shrimp Sauce

CATFISH
4 catfish fillets
Juice of 2 lemons

All-purpose flour
Olive oil or butter

SHRIMP SAUCE
Juice of 1/2 lemon
8 ounces shrimp, peeled and deveined
2 tablespoons olive oil or butter
8 mushrooms, thinly sliced

2 whole scallions, finely chopped
1 tablespoon all-purpose flour
1 teaspoon chicken broth concentrate
1 cup hot water
1/2 cup white wine

For the catfish, arrange the fillets in a shallow dish and drizzle with the lemon juice, turning to coat. Marinate, covered, in the refrigerator for 2 hours. Coat the fillets with flour and sauté in olive oil in a skillet until the fillets flake easily. Cover to keep warm.

For the sauce, drizzle the lemon juice over the shrimp in a shallow dish. Marinate, covered, in the refrigerator for 30 minutes. Drain, reserving the liquid. Sauté the shrimp in the olive oil in a skillet until pink. Remove the shrimp to a bowl using a slotted spoon, reserving the pan drippings. Cool and cut the shrimp lengthwise into halves. Add the reserved liquid, mushrooms and scallions to the reserved pan drippings and sauté until the scallions are tender. Sprinkle the flour over the mushroom mixture and cook over medium heat for 5 minutes, stirring constantly. Mix the broth concentrate and hot water in a bowl and add to the mushroom mixture along with the wine. Increase the heat and cook until the mixture is reduced by 1/2, stirring constantly. Stir in the shrimp and drizzle over the catfish.

Compliments of
The Woman's Exchange of Memphis, Memphis, Tennessee

"Community cookbooks have a voice that is authentic to the community. Not just one voice; they have many voices coming to the table together. In every culture, the meal table is where the values, beliefs, and traditions are passed on."

Ellen Rolfes

Lemony Stuffed Flounder

Serves 4

1/3 cup chopped celery
2 tablespoons chopped onion
1/3 cup butter
1 cup herb-seasoned stuffing mix
1 tablespoon chopped fresh parsley
1 tablespoon lemon juice
1 teaspoon grated lemon zest

1/4 teaspoon salt
1/4 teaspoon pepper
4 medium fresh flounder fillets or thawed frozen
   flounder fillets
1/3 cup butter
1/2 teaspoon dillweed

Sauté the celery and onion in 1/3 cup butter in a saucepan over medium heat. Add the stuffing mix, parsley, lemon juice, lemon zest, salt and pepper and mix well. Cut the flounder fillets into halves and arrange 4 of the halves in an ungreased 9×9-inch baking dish. Spread the stuffing mixture over the fillet halves and top with the remaining halves. Melt 1/3 cup butter in small saucepan and stir in the dillweed. Pour over the fish. Bake at 350 degrees on the center oven rack for 20 to 30 minutes or until the fish flakes easily.

Oh My Stars!
Junior League of Roanoke Valley, Roanoke, Virginia

Grouper Piccata

Serves 2

2 (8-ounce) grouper fillets
Flour
4 tablespoons olive oil
1/2 cup white wine
Juice of 1 lemon

1/2 cup (1 stick) butter, sliced
2 tablespoons capers
2 teaspoons minced garlic
2 teaspoons minced shallot
Salt and pepper to taste

Coat the grouper lightly with flour. Heat the olive oil in a sauté pan and add the fish. Sauté for 3 to 5 minutes on each side or until cooked through. Remove to a platter. Add the wine to the sauté pan , stirring to deglaze. Cook until reduced by 1/2. Stir in the lemon juice and cook until reduced by 1/4. Add the butter, capers, garlic and shallot and mix well. Simmer for 2 minutes. Season with salt and pepper. Serve with the fish.

From Grouper to Grits
The Junior League of Clearwater-Dunedin, Clearwater, Florida

Grilled Halibut with Pineapple Mango Salsa

Serves 6

TROPICAL SALSA
1 cup chunks fresh pineapple
3/4 cup chunks fresh mango
2/3 cup chunks fresh papaya
1/2 cup chunks seeded tomato
1/3 cup chunks seeded cucumber

1/3 cup chunks red onion
3 tablespoons minced fresh cilantro
2 tablespoons minced fresh mint
2 tablespoons minced seeded jalapeño chile
2 tablespoons fresh lime juice
Salt to taste

HALIBUT
6 (6-ounce) halibut fillets,
    or any firm white fish

Olive oil
Salt and pepper to taste

For the salsa, combine the pineapple, mango, papaya, tomato, cucumber, onion, cilantro, mint, jalapeño chile and lime juice in a bowl and mix well. Season with salt. Chill, covered, for 1 to 4 hours, stirring occasionally.

For the halibut, preheat the grill to medium-high. Brush the fillets with olive oil and sprinkle with salt and pepper. Grill over hot coals for about 5 minutes per side or just until the fillets are opaque in the center. Arrange 1 fillet on each of 6 dinner plates and top each with some of the salsa. Serve immediately. To prevent the fillets from sticking to the grill rack, place the fillets in a grill basket coated with nonstick cooking spray before placing on the grill rack.

California Sol Food
Junior League of San Diego, Inc., San Diego, California

Zesty Orange Roughy Almandine

Serves 4

1 tablespoon plus 1 teaspoon sliced almonds
2 tablespoons margarine
2 tablespoons minced fresh parsley
1 tablespoon grated lemon rind

3 tablespoons lemon juice
1/4 teaspoon salt
4 (6-ounce) orange roughy filets

Brown almonds in a small nonstick skillet over low heat until lightly toasted, and set aside. Melt margarine in a skillet over low heat. Add parsley, lemon juice, rind and salt, stirring well. Remove from heat and set aside. Cover broiler pan with aluminum foil. Place in oven 6 inches from the heating element; preheat pan for 3 minutes. Arrange filets in preheated pan, and baste evenly with margarine mixture. Broil 6 inches from heat for 8 minutes or until fish flakes when fork tested. Sprinkle almonds over fish before serving.

Of Tide & Thyme
Junior League of Annapolis, Inc., Annapolis, Maryland

Rockfish Tacos

Serves 4

1 to 1 1/2 pounds rockfish fillets
Salt and pepper to taste
Chesapeake Bay seasoning to taste
1 1/2 tablespoons olive oil
1/2 cup diced tomato
1/2 cup green salsa
2 tablespoons chopped fresh cilantro
1 tablespoon fresh lime juice

8 corn or flour tortillas
1 cup chopped romaine
1 cup chopped red cabbage
1/2 cup thinly sliced red onion
1/2 cup (2 ounces) shredded Monterey Jack cheese
1 avocado, sliced
Cilantro leaves
1 lime, cut into wedges

Season the rockfish with salt, pepper and Chesapeake Bay seasoning. Place in a 9×13-inch baking dish and drizzle with the olive oil. Bake at 325 degrees for 30 minutes or until the fish begins to flake. Flake the fish apart with a fork and place in a bowl. Add the tomato, salsa, 2 tablespoons cilantro and the lime juice and toss until coated. Layer the tortillas between dampened nonrecycled paper towels. Microwave on High for 1 minute. Spoon the fish mixture onto each tortilla. Top with the romaine, cabbage, onion and cheese. Garnish with the avocado and a few cilantro leaves. Serve the lime wedges on the side. (Note: For a variation, use 12 ounces peeled cooked large shrimp instead of the rockfish.)

A Thyme to Entertain
Junior League of Annapolis, Inc., Annapolis, Maryland

Mahogany Glazed Salmon

Serves 4

1/2 cup plain yogurt
2 tablespoons soy sauce
1 tablespoon olive oil
1 tablespoon minced fresh ginger

1 tablespoon lemon juice
Pinch of pepper
4 (6-ounce) salmon fillets
1 1/2 teaspoons chopped fresh chives

Combine the yogurt, soy sauce, olive oil, ginger, lemon juice and pepper in a shallow dish and mix well. Lay the salmon on top and turn to coat. Let stand, covered, for 20 to 30 minutes. Remove the salmon to a rack on a broiler pan. Broil 3 inches from the heat source for 4 to 5 minutes or until the fish flakes easily. Remove to warm serving plates and sprinkle with the chives. You may grill the salmon instead of broiling and may also use a whole salmon fillet instead of 4 salmon fillets.

Recipes of Note
Greensboro Symphony Guild, Greensboro, North Carolina

Pistachio-Crusted Salmon with Wilted Greens

Serves 6

2 1/2 pounds salmon, cut into 6 fillets
3/4 cup pistachios
1 1/2 cups mayonnaise
1 1/2 teaspoons horseradish
1 1/2 teaspoons ground pepper

1 1/2 teaspoons lemon juice
1/4 teaspoon salt
2 pounds baby bok choy, sliced, or 1 1/2 pounds baby
    spinach leaves
Olive oil

Place the salmon skin side down on a baking sheet. Pulse the pistachios in a food processor with a sharp blade until coarsely ground. Do not overprocess. Combine the pistachios, mayonnaise, horseradish, pepper, lemon juice and salt in a bowl and mix well. Spread on top of the salmon. Bake at 425 degrees for 20 minutes. Remove the salmon from the baking sheet with a spatula, letting the skin stick to the baking sheet. (For easier cleanup, place baking sheet immediately in hot water to loosen the skin.) Sauté the bok choy or baby spinach in batches in hot olive oil in a skillet until each batch is wilted before adding the next. Divide among six dinner plates, topping each with a salmon fillet.

The Cook's Canvas 2
Cameron Art Museum, Wilmington, North Carolina

Pasta with Salmon, Spinach and Tomatoes

Serves 6

16 ounces bow tie pasta
1/2 cup chicken broth
1 pound salmon, cooked, bones removed and
    salmon broken into chunks
8 ounces cream cheese, cut into cubes
1 (10-ounce) package frozen chopped spinach,
    thawed and drained

1 teaspoon minced garlic
1 teaspoon salt
1 teaspoon pepper
1 tablespoon lemon juice
15 cherry tomatoes, cut into halves
1/2 cup (2 ounces) grated Parmesan cheese

Cook the pasta using the package directions; drain. Heat one-half of the broth and the salmon in a large skillet. Add the cream cheese and cook until the cream cheese melts, stirring frequently. Add the remaining broth, the spinach, garlic, salt, pepper and lemon juice. Cook for 3 to 5 minutes or until combined. Add the cherry tomatoes and cook for 2 minutes or until softened. Add the hot cooked pasta and toss to coat. Spoon into a serving bowl and sprinkle with the Parmesan cheese. You may use cream cheese with 1/3 less fat.

Great Women, Great Food
Junior League of Kankakee County, Kankakee, Illinois

Sole with Lemon Cream

2 tablespoons unsalted butter
2 pounds sole fillets, cut to make 4 pieces
1/2 teaspoon salt
1/4 teaspoon freshly ground pepper
1/4 cup all-purpose flour

3/4 cup cream or heavy cream
Grated zest of 1 lemon
1/4 teaspoon salt
1 tablespoon lemon juice
2 tablespoons chopped fresh parsley

Melt the butter in a skillet over medium heat. Sprinkle the sole fillet with 1/2 teaspoon salt and the pepper. Dredge the fillets in the flour and shake to remove any excess. Sauté the fillets in the butter for 2 minutes per side or until the fish flakes easily; do not overcook. Remove to a serving dish and keep warm. Add the cream and lemon zest to the skillet. Simmer for 2 minutes or until the cream begins to thicken, stirring constantly. Stir in 1/4 teaspoon salt, the lemon juice and parsley. Spoon over the fillets.

The Bells are Ringing: A Call to Table
Mission San Juan Capistrano Women's Guild, San Juan Capistrano, California

Grilled Marinated Swordfish

1 cup vegetable oil
1 lemon, juice only
4 cloves garlic, minced
2 tablespoons dried basil
1 tablespoon dried oregano

1 teaspoon celery salt
1/2 teaspoon ground black pepper
6 (1-inch-thick) swordfish steaks
1/2 cup butter, melted
Fresh parsley for garnish

Combine oil, the juice of one lemon, garlic, basil, oregano, celery salt and pepper. Mix well. Brush both sides of the steaks generously with the mixture. Place the steaks in a shallow dish and pour remaining marinade over steaks. Refrigerate for 2 hours, turning steaks every half hour. Grill about 6 inches from the coals for 5 minutes. Turn and baste with marinade. Grill 6 to 7 more minutes. Serve brushed with melted butter and topped with fresh parsley.

Of Tide & Thyme
Junior League of Annapolis, Inc., Annapolis, Maryland

Lemon Soy Swordfish

Serves 8

8 small swordfish steaks, or 4 large swordfish steaks,
   cut into halves
1/3 cup soy sauce
1/4 cup lemon juice

1 teaspoon grated lemon zest
1 garlic clove, crushed
2 teaspoons Dijon mustard
1/2 cup vegetable oil

GARNISH
Lemon wedges
Parsley sprigs

Pierce the fish with a fork and place in a shallow 9×13-inch dish. Combine the soy sauce, lemon juice, lemon zest, garlic, Dijon mustard and oil in a small bowl and mix well. Pour over the fish. Marinate in the refrigerator for 1 to 3 hours, turning occasionally and piercing again with a fork. Drain the fish and place in a preheated broiler pan. Broil for 5 to 6 minutes on each side or until the fish flakes easily. Garnish with lemon wedges and parsley.

Note: To grill the fish, reserve the marinade. Grill over medium coals for 5 to 6 minutes on each side, brushing occasionally with the reserved marinade.

Savor the Moment
Junior League of Boca Raton, Boca Raton, Florida

Sunk Boat Trout

Serves 6

1/3 cup grated Parmesan cheese
1/3 cup all-purpose flour
1/4 teaspoon salt
1/2 teaspoon pepper
1 1/2 teaspoons paprika

1/4 cup skim milk
1 egg white, beaten
Six 6-ounce trout or catfish fillets
3 tablespoons sliced almonds

Combine cheese, flour, salt, pepper, and paprika. Set aside. Combine milk and beaten egg. Dip fillets in egg-milk mixture and dredge in flour mixture. Arrange in a 9×13-inch baking dish. Spray each fillet with vegetable oil cooking spray and sprinkle with almonds. Bake, covered, at 350 degrees for 35 to 40 minutes.

River Road Recipes III: A Healthy Collection
Junior League of Baton Rouge, Baton Rouge, Louisiana

Tuna with Mango Relish

Serves 4

MANGO RELISH
2 very ripe mangoes
1 ripe avocado

1/2 cup chopped fresh cilantro
1/4 cup chopped red onion or green onions

TUNA
1/4 cup soy sauce
1/4 cup teriyaki sauce

2 teaspoons chopped fresh gingerroot
2 teaspoons chopped garlic
4 medium tuna steaks

For the relish, cut the mangoes and avocado into 1/4-inch chunks. Combine the mangoes, avocado, cilantro and onion in a bowl and mix well.

For the tuna, mix the soy sauce, teriyaki sauce, gingerroot and garlic in a shallow pan. Add the tuna and turn several times to coat. Marinate, covered, in the refrigerator for 1 hour. Remove the tuna and discard the marinade. Place the tuna on a grill rack or in a pan on top of the stove and cook for 2 to 3 minutes per side. Serve the tuna topped with the relish.

Toast of the Coast
Junior League of Jacksonville, Jacksonville, Florida

Lime-Marinated Fish with Black Bean Sauce

Serves 6

3 tablespoons butter, melted
Juice of 2 limes
2 tablespoons Creole seasoning
Fresh fish (enough for 6 servings)
1 (16-ounce) can black beans, drained
Salt

2 tablespoons sour cream
1 medium ripe tomato, chopped
1/2 cup hot salsa

GARNISHES: sour cream, 4 chopped green onions

Combine the butter, lime juice and Creole seasoning. Marinate fish in butter mixture. Process black beans 5 seconds, just until chopped. Add salt to taste. Stir in 2 tablespoons sour cream. Combine tomato and salsa. Set aside. Broil fish until white and flaky. To serve, layer black bean sauce, broiled fish, and salsa mixture on a plate. Garnish with sour cream and chopped green onions, if desired.

Food For Thought
Junior League of Birmingham, Inc., Birmingham, Alabama

Parmesan Baked Fish Fillets

Serves 4

4 sole, tilapia or orange roughy fillets
Juice of 1 large lemon
Salt and pepper to taste
1 cup mayonnaise

5 tablespoons grated Parmesan cheese
3 tablespoons chopped fresh parsley
1 tablespoon chopped fresh chives
2 egg whites, stiffly beaten

Place the fish in a baking dish and sprinkle with the lemon juice. Cover and chill for 30 minutes. Season lightly with salt and pepper. Mix the mayonnaise, cheese, parsley and chives in a bowl. Fold in the egg whites. Spread over the fish. Cover the dish with foil but do not let it touch the topping. Broil for 10 minutes. Remove the foil and broil until golden brown and the fish flakes easily.

A League of Our Own: From Blue Jeans to Ball Gowns
Rockwall Women's League, Rockwall, Texas

Pierside Maryland Steamed Blue Crabs

Makes 3 dozen

1 cup beer or water
1 cup vinegar
3 dozen Maryland blue crabs

1 cup Chesapeake-style seafood seasoning
Cider vinegar, melted butter and crab seasoning
  for serving

Plunge crabs into hot water for one minute. In a large crab pot with a rack, place the liquid in the bottom of the pan, just level with the bottom of the rack. If more liquid is needed, add more until the level is reached. Layer 6 crabs and 6 tablespoons of crab seasoning. Repeat until all of the crabs are in the pot. Bring to a boil, uncovered. Reduce heat and simmer for 20 minutes, covered. Serve hot onto a table covered with a layer of newspaper. Eat the crab pieces plain or dip them in vinegar or melted butter. Extra crab seasoning may be sprinkled on the crabs if desired.

Of Tide & Thyme
The Junior League of Annapolis, Inc., Annapolis, Maryland

Crab Cakes with Tequila Sauce

CREOLE CRAB CAKES

3 tablespoons olive oil
1/3 cup chopped onion
1/4 cup chopped green bell pepper
1/4 teaspoon white pepper
Black pepper to taste
1/4 cup chopped green onions
1 tablespoon minced garlic
1 tablespoon plus 1 teaspoon of your favorite
    Creole seasoning

2 eggs
2 teaspoons Creole mustard
1/2 cup Italian-style bread crumbs
6 tablespoons coarsely grated
    Parmesan cheese
8 ounces jumbo lump crab meat
5 tablespoons olive oil

TEQUILA SAUCE

1/4 cup tequila
1 tablespoon fresh lime juice
1 1/2 tablespoons minced onion
1/2 teaspoon minced garlic

1 1/2 tablespoons chopped fresh cilantro
1/4 teaspoon salt
Pepper to taste
2 tablespoons heavy cream
1/4 cup (1/2 stick) unsalted butter

For the crab cakes, heat 3 tablespoons olive oil in a large skillet over high heat. Add the onion, bell pepper, white pepper and black pepper and sauté for 1 minute. Remove the mixture to a bowl and let cool. Whisk the eggs into the vegetable mixture. Stir in the Creole mustard, bread crumbs and cheese. Fold in the crab meat gently. Shape into patties and place on a baking sheet. Chill, covered, until ready to cook. Heat 5 tablespoons olive oil in a large skillet over high heat. Add the crab cakes and cook until golden brown on both sides.

For the sauce, combine the tequila, lime juice, onion, garlic, cilantro, salt and pepper in a skillet. Bring to a boil, stirring occasionally. Stir in the cream and simmer for a few minutes. Whisk in the butter and remove from the heat. Spoon the sauce onto serving plates and top with the crab cakes. The sauce may be made without the butter the day before serving. Chill, covered, until almost ready to serve. Bring to a simmer over low heat and whisk in the butter.

Marshes to Mansions
Junior League of Lake Charles, LA, Lake Charles, Louisiana

Gulf Coast Crab Cakes

Makes 6 crab cakes

1/4 cup chopped onion
2 tablespoons butter
1 pound lump crab meat, shells removed and flaked
1/3 cup bread crumbs
1 egg, beaten

1/4 teaspoon hot pepper sauce
Salt and pepper to taste
Vegetable oil
2 tablespoons butter, melted
Lemon wedges

Sauté the onion in 2 tablespoons butter in a skillet over medium heat until tender. Combine the sautéed onion, crab meat and bread crumbs in a bowl and mix gently. Add the egg, hot pepper sauce, salt and pepper and mix gently.

Shape the crab meat mixture into six 3-inch cakes. Arrange the crab cakes in a single layer on a baking sheet lined with waxed paper. Chill, covered with plastic wrap, for 1 hour.

Place the oven rack 6 inches from the heat source. Preheat a broiler pan and brush lightly with oil. Arrange the crab cakes in a single layer in the prepared pan and brush the tops with 2 tablespoons melted butter. Broil for 4 minutes or until golden brown; turn. Broil for 4 minutes longer or until golden brown. Serve immediately with lemon wedges.

MariThyme Treasures
Texas Maritime Museum, Houston, Texas

Bank's Channel Crab Casserole

Serves 6

2 cups seasoned croutons
1 cup chopped celery
1/2 cup chopped onion
1 cup mayonnaise
Juice of 1 lemon
Dash of hot red pepper sauce

Salt and freshly ground pepper to taste
1 pound fresh crab meat, cleaned
1/2 cup freshly grated Parmesan cheese
1/2 cup (1 stick) butter, softened
1/2 cup fine bread crumbs

Combine the croutons, celery, onion, mayonnaise, lemon juice, hot sauce, salt and pepper in a bowl and mix well. Fold in the crab meat and spoon into a 2-quart baking dish. Mix the cheese, butter and bread crumbs in a bowl until crumbly. Sprinkle the crumb mixture over the crab meat mixture. Bake at 350 degrees for 50 to 60 minutes or until brown and bubbly.

The Cook's Canvas 2
Cameron Art Museum, Wilmington, North Carolina

Crabmeat Mornay

1 stick butter
1 small bunch green onions, chopped
½ cup finely chopped parsley
2 tablespoons flour
1 pint breakfast cream

½ pound grated Swiss cheese
1 tablespoon sherry wine
Red pepper to taste
Salt to taste
1 pound white crabmeat

Melt butter in heavy pot and sauté onions and parsley. Blend in flour, cream, and cheese, until cheese is melted. Add other ingredients and gently fold in crab meat. This may be served in a chafing dish with Melba toast or in patty shells.

River Roads Recipes: The Textbook of Louisiana Cuisine
Junior League of Baton Rouge, Baton Rouge, Louisiana

Classic Crawfish Monica
Serves 6

2 cups (1 pint) half-and-half
1 cup (½ pint) heavy cream
6 green onions, chopped
½ cup (1 stick) butter
1 pound crawfish tails with fat

2 garlic cloves, minced (optional)
Thyme, salt, black pepper, cayenne pepper and
   Creole seasoning to taste (optional)
1 pound fresh fettuccini, cooked and drained
3/4 cup (3 ounces) freshly grated Parmesan cheese

Combine the half-and-half and heavy cream in a saucepan. Cook for 10 minutes or until slightly reduced. Sauté the green onions in the butter in a skillet. Add the crawfish, garlic, thyme, salt, black pepper, cayenne pepper and Creole seasoning to taste. Stir in the cream mixture. Cook until creamy and reduced slightly, stirring frequently. Pour over the hot fettuccini in a large serving bowl. Add the cheese and toss to mix well.

Roux To Do
Junior League of Greater Covington, Covington, Louisiana

Crawfish Pies

Serves 18

1 1/2 cups chopped onions
1 1/2 cups chopped celery
6 garlic cloves, minced
1/2 cup (1 stick) butter
1 (10-ounce) can cream of mushroom soup
1 (12-ounce) can evaporated milk
2 tablespoons cold water

2 teaspoons cornstarch
1/2 cup chopped green onions
1 bunch parsley, trimmed and chopped or minced
3 pounds Louisiana crawfish tails
8 ounces Parmesan cheese, grated
Salt and pepper to taste
6 refrigerator pie pastries

Sauté the onions, celery and garlic in the butter in a large saucepan until the vegetables are tender. Stir in the soup and evaporated milk. Mix the cold water and cornstarch in a small bowl and stir into the soup mixture. Add the green onions, parsley and crawfish and mix well. Cook over medium heat for 15 minutes, stirring occasionally. Stir in the cheese, salt and pepper.

Line three 9-inch pie plates with 3 of the pastries. Spoon the crawfish mixture evenly into the 3 pastry-lined pie plates. Top with the remaining pastries, fluting the edges and cutting vents. Bake at 350 degrees for 30 minutes or until light brown. Let stand for 15 minutes before serving. You may prepare and bake in advance and freeze for future use. Reheat at 325 degrees for 25 minutes or until heated through.

River Road Recipes IV: Warm Welcomes
Junior League of Baton Rouge, Baton Rouge, Louisiana

Broiled Curried Sea Scallops

Serves 5 to 6

2 pounds sea scallops
1/4 cup maple syrup
1/4 cup mustard

1 teaspoon lemon juice
2 teaspoons curry powder

Place the scallops on a broiler pan lined with foil. Combine the maple syrup, mustard, lemon juice and curry powder in a bowl and mix well. Brush the tops of the scallops with half the curry mixture. Broil the scallops at the lowest level of the broiler for 10 minutes. Remove the scallops from the oven. Turn over the scallops and brush with the remaining curry mixture. Broil for 10 minutes longer.

Between the Lakes
The Junior League of Saginaw Valley, Saginaw, Michigan

Low Country Shrimp Boil

Serves 12 to 14

6 pounds raw shrimp (headed), in shells
5 pounds smoked sausage links or sweet
  Italian sausage
1 pound butter, (reserve 3/4 pound for serving
  with corn)

1/2 cup salt
Tabasco sauce
16 ears of corn, broken in half

SAUCE:
3 cups catsup
1 teaspoon horseradish, or to taste

Dash lemon, to taste
Dash Worcestershire sauce, if desired

Wash and rinse shrimp. Cut sausage in 2- to 3-inch lengths. Fill one 8- to 10-quart pot (or two smaller ones) half full of water. Add 1/2 cup butter and salt to water and bring to boil. Add Tabasco to taste. Put corn in water and boil 5 minutes. Add sausage to water and boil 2 to 3 minutes. Add shrimp to water and boil 3 minutes or until shells begin to separate from shrimp. Drain and serve from one large bowl, serving butter with corn and sauce with shrimp.

This is great cooked outdoors if you have a gas burner. In the low country, this is often served poured in a heap on newspapers spread on tables—no plates . . . no forks.

Savannah Style
Junior League of Savannah, Savannah, Georgia

Hampton Plantation Shrimp Pilau

Serves 6

4 slices bacon
1 cup rice (raw)
3 tablespoons butter
1/2 cup celery (cut small)
2 tablespoons chopped bell pepper

2 cups shrimp (cleaned)
1 teaspoon Worcestershire
1 tablespoon flour
Salt and pepper to taste

Fry bacon until crisp. Save to use later. Add bacon grease to water in which you cook rice. In another pot, melt butter, add celery and bell pepper. Cook a few minutes; add shrimp which have been sprinkled with Worcestershire sauce and dredged with four. Stir and simmer until flour is cooked. Season with salt and pepper. Now add cooked rice and mix until rice is "all buttery" and "shrimpy." You may want to add more butter. Into this stir the crisp bacon, crumbled. Serve hot.

Charleston Receipts
Junior League of Charleston, Charleston, South Carolina

Shrimp Cakes

1/4 cup (1/2 stick) butter
1/2 cup chopped onion
1/2 cup chopped celery
1 pound shrimp, cooked, peeled and chopped
1/3 cup fine dry bread crumbs
1/2 cup mayonnaise
2 tablespoons minced fresh parsley

1/2 teaspoon Old Bay Seasoning
1/2 teaspoon Worcestershire sauce
Tabasco sauce to taste
Salt and freshly ground pepper to taste
1/3 cup fine dry bread crumbs
2 tablespoons butter
Lemon wedges

Melt 1/4 cup butter in a skillet and add the onion and celery. Sauté until tender and spoon into a bowl. Stir the shrimp and 1/3 cup bread crumbs into the onion mixture. Mix the mayonnaise, parsley, Old Bay seasoning, Worcestershire sauce, Tabasco sauce, salt and pepper in a bowl and stir into the shrimp mixture.

Shape the shrimp mixture into 8 cakes and arrange in a single layer on a baking sheet lined with waxed paper. Chill, covered with plastic wrap, for 1 to 4 hours.

Coat the cakes with 1/3 cup bread crumbs. Melt 2 tablespoons butter in a heavy skillet over medium heat and add the cakes. Cook for 2 to 3 minutes per side or until golden brown. Serve the cakes warm with lemon wedges or Lemon Butter Sauce.

Lemon Butter Sauce

Sauté 2 minced garlic cloves in 1/2 cup butter in a small saucepan for 1 minute. Whisk in 1 1/2 tablespoons cornstarch until combined. Stir in 1/2 cup dry white wine and bring to a boil. Cook for 1 minute or until thickened, stirring constantly. Remove from the heat and stir in 1 tablespoon fresh lemon juice, 3 chopped green onions, 1/2 teaspoon salt and 1/4 teaspoon ground red pepper. Serve with Shrimp Cakes. Omit the cornstarch for a simple butter sauce that pairs well with most any fish.

Tables of Content
Junior League of Birmingham, Inc., Birmingham, Alabama

Mayport Shrimp and Grits

GRITS
1 1/2 cups chicken stock
1/2 cup milk
1/2 cup stone-ground or quick-cooking grits
1 tablespoon butter

1 to 1 1/2 cups (4 to 6 ounces) shredded extra-sharp
    Vermont white Cheddar cheese or
    Monterey Jack cheese
1 to 2 teaspoons cayenne pepper
Salt and black pepper to taste

SHRIMP
6 to 8 slices bacon, chopped
3 garlic cloves, chopped
1 sweet onion, chopped
5 jalapeño chiles, seeded and finely chopped
1/2 cup dry white wine
3 tomatoes, chopped

1 teaspoon paprika
1 to 2 tablespoons Old Bay seasoning
Salt and pepper to taste
1 pound large shrimp, peeled
1/4 cup finely chopped parsley
1/4 cup sliced scallions

For the grits, bring the chicken stock and milk to a boil in a large saucepan. Whisk in the grits. Reduce the heat and simmer for 20 to 30 minutes or until the mixture is thick, stirring frequently. Stir in the butter, cheese, cayenne pepper, salt and black pepper.

For the shrimp, cook the bacon in a large skillet until crisp. Add the garlic, onion and jalapeño chiles. Sauté over medium heat until the onion is golden brown. Add the wine, stirring to loosen any browned bits from the bottom of the skillet. Cook over medium-high heat for 3 to 5 minutes. Reduce the heat to medium-low. Stir in the tomatoes, paprika, Old Bay seasoning, salt and pepper. Add the shrimp. Cook for 5 minutes or until the shrimp turn pink. Remove from the heat. Stir in the parsley and scallions; drain well. Serve over the grits.

Toast of the Coast
Junior League of Jacksonville, Jacksonville, Florida

The Junior League of Jacksonville is committed to promoting voluntarism, developing the potential of women, and improving the community. The proceeds from the sale of *Toast of the Coast* make it possible for their volunteers to make an impact with projects such as foster care, literacy, and Done-In-A-Day workdays.

Sautéed Shrimp and Peppers over Cheese Grits

Serves 6 to 8

½ cup chopped Canadian bacon
1 cup red bell pepper strips
1 cup green bell pepper strips
1 (10-ounce) can diced tomatoes with
    green chiles, drained
1½ pounds shrimp, peeled and deveined

½ cup chopped green onions
1⅔ cups milk
1 (16-ounce) can chicken broth
1 cup quick-cooking golden grits
1 cup (4 ounces) shredded sharp Cheddar cheese

Brown the bacon in a skillet. Stir in the bell peppers and cook for 10 minutes, stirring frequently. Add the tomatoes and mix well. Cook for 5 minutes, stirring occasionally. Stir in the shrimp and cook for 3 minutes longer or until the shrimp turn pink, stirring occasionally. Mix in the green onions. Remove from the heat and cover to keep warm. Bring the milk and broth to a boil in a saucepan and stir in the grits. Return the grits mixture to a boil; reduce the heat. Cook for 5 minutes, stirring occasionally. Add the cheese to the grits and stir until melted. Spoon the shrimp mixture over the grits on a serving platter.

River Road Recipes IV: Warm Welcomes
Junior League of Baton Rouge, Baton Rouge, Louisiana

Shrimp and Wild Rice Casserole

Serves 6 to 8

1½ pounds mushrooms, sliced
1 small bell pepper, chopped
¼ cup chopped onion
¼ cup (½ stick) butter, melted
2 pounds shrimp, peeled and deveined
3 cups cooked wild rice
2 (10-ounce) cans cream of mushroom soup

½ cup half-and-half
1 garlic clove, minced
1 tablespoon Worcestershire sauce
¼ teaspoon thyme
Salt and pepper to taste
1 cup (4 ounces) shredded Monterey Jack cheese

Sauté the mushrooms, bell pepper and onion in the butter in a skillet until the vegetables are tender. Add the shrimp and sauté until the shrimp turn pink. Remove from the heat and stir in the wild rice, soup, half-and-half, garlic, Worcestershire sauce and thyme. Season with salt and pepper. Spoon into a greased baking dish. Sprinkle with the cheese. Bake at 350 degrees for 30 to 45 minutes.

Shall We Gather
Trinity Episcopal Church, Wetumpka, Alabama

Fais Do-Do Drunken Shrimp

¼ cup olive oil
¼ cup minced onion
5 garlic cloves, minced
2 pounds shrimp, peeled and deveined with
    tails left on

¼ cup tequila
¼ cup lime juice
Salt to taste
Creole seasoning to taste
2 tablespoons chopped cilantro

Heat the olive oil in a large skillet. Add the onion and garlic. Cook over medium heat for 3 minutes or until tender. Add the shrimp and tequila. Simmer for 3 to 5 minutes or until the shrimp turn pink. Spoon into a nonreactive bowl. Add the lime juice and toss to coat. Season with salt, Creole seasoning and cilantro. Chill, covered, in the refrigerator.

Roux To Do
Junior League of Greater Covington, Covington, Louisiana

Tequila Lime Shrimp

¼ cup fresh lime juice
¼ cup tequila
½ cup olive oil
2 cloves of garlic, chopped
2 shallots, chopped

1 teaspoon cumin
1 teaspoon salt
½ teaspoon pepper
2 ½ pounds large shrimp, peeled, deveined

Whisk the lime juice, tequila and olive oil in a bowl. Stir in the garlic, shallots, cumin, salt and pepper. Pour over the shrimp in a bowl. Marinate, covered, in the refrigerator for 1 to 4 hours. Drain the shrimp, discarding the marinade. Place the shrimp in a baking dish. Bake at 400 degrees for 20 minutes or until the shrimp turn pink.

Note: For kabobs, soak bamboo skewers in water for 1 hour. Thread the shrimp onto the soaked skewers. Place on a grill rack. Grill until the shrimp turn pink.

A Sunsational Encore
Junior League of Greater Orlando, Orlando, Florida

Tradd Street Shrimp

Serves 6 to 8

2 to 3 pounds shrimp, cooked and peeled
1 box wild and white rice mix, cooked
1 cup Cheddar cheese, grated
1 cup Swiss cheese, grated
1 can cream of mushroom soup
1 cup onion, chopped

1 cup green pepper, chopped
1 cup celery, chopped
6 tablespoons butter
4 lemons, thinly sliced
Salt to taste
Black pepper, freshly ground, to taste

Mix together first five ingredients. Set aside. Sauté onions, pepper and celery in butter until soft. Add to shrimp mixture. Place in a long flat 3-quart casserole dish. Season to taste with salt and pepper. Cover the top completely with lemon slices. Sprinkle with more pepper. Cover with foil. Bake until thoroughly heated (about 20 minutes.)

Note: 3 to 4 cups cooked chicken can be substituted or a mixture of both.

Charleston Receipts Repeats
Junior League of Charleston, Charleston, South Carolina

Shrimp with Feta Cheese over Angel Hair Pasta

Serves 4

1 pound medium shrimp, peeled and deveined
1/4 cup fresh lemon juice
1/4 cup olive oil
3/4 cup finely chopped green onions
1 tablespoon minced garlic
5 plum tomatoes, peeled and chopped
   (about 2 cups)
1/4 cup clam juice

3 tablespoons butter
1 teaspoon basil
1/2 teaspoon oregano
1/4 teaspoon kosher salt
1/4 cup white wine
3/4 cup crumbled feta cheese
12 ounces angel hair pasta

Toss the shrimp and lemon juice in a bowl. Heat the olive oil in a skillet over medium-high heat and add the green onions and garlic. Sauté until the green onions are tender. Stir in 1 1/2 cups of the tomatoes and bring to a boil. Reduce the heat to medium-low and simmer, covered, for 20 minutes, stirring occasionally. Stir in the clam juice and simmer for 5 minutes longer.

Preheat the oven to 350 degrees. Melt the butter in a skillet over medium heat. Add the shrimp and sauté for 5 minutes or until the shrimp turn pink. Pour the tomato mixture into a shallow 2-quart baking dish. Place the remaining tomatoes in the center of the tomato mixture and surround with the shrimp. Sprinkle the basil, oregano and salt over the shrimp and drizzle with the wine. Sprinkle with the feta cheese and bake for 15 minutes or until heated through. Cook the pasta using the package directions and drain. Spoon the shrimp mixture over the hot pasta on a serving platter and serve immediately.

Tables of Content
Junior League of Birmingham, Inc., Birmingham, Alabama

Roasted Red Pepper and Pesto Shrimp over Pasta

Serves 4 to 6

12 to 16 ounces angel hair pasta
1 (12-ounce) jar roasted red peppers, drained
8 ounces cream cheese, softened
1/2 cup chicken broth

1/2 teaspoon salt
1/4 teaspoon red pepper
1/4 cup prepared fresh pesto
2 pounds deveined peeled cooked fresh shrimp

Cook the pasta using the package directions. Drain and cover to keep warm. Combine the roasted peppers, cream cheese and broth in a blender and process until smooth. Spoon the roasted pepper mixture into a large skillet and cook over medium to medium-high heat until heated through. Stir in the salt and red pepper and bring to a boil. Cook for 4 minutes, stirring frequently. Remove from the heat and stir in the pesto. Stir in the shrimp and simmer for 4 minutes or until heated through. Serve immediately over the hot cooked pasta.

Tables of Content
Junior League of Birmingham, Inc., Birmingham, Alabama

Seafood Gumbo 2

Serves 8 to 10

1/2 cup salad oil
1/2 cup flour
1 large onion, chopped
2 to 3 garlic cloves, minced
One 1-pound can tomatoes, undrained
1 1/2 pounds frozen okra or equivalent fresh
Oil for frying okra
2 quarts hot water
3 1/2 tablespoons salt
3/4 teaspoon red pepper

1 large bay leaf
1/4 teaspoon thyme
8 to 10 allspice berries
Few grains chili pepper
2 pounds headless raw shrimp, peeled
1 pound claw crab meat, picked
1 pint oysters
1/2 cup chopped green onions
1/2 cup chopped parsley

Make a very dark roux in a large heavy pot. Add onion and garlic. Cook slowly until onion is transparent. Add tomatoes and cook on low heat until oil rises to the top (about 30 minutes), stirring frequently. In separate skillet, fry okra in oil on moderately high heat, stirring constantly until okra is no longer stringy. Add the okra to the other mixture, stir and simmer about 10 minutes. Add water, salt and pepper. Simmer partially covered for 45 minutes. Add other seasonings and simmer an additional 20 minutes, then add shrimp—simmer 15 minutes; then add crab meat, simmering 15 minutes more. Add the oysters the last 5 minutes of cooking. Taste carefully for seasoning, adding more if necessary. Remove from fire and stir in green onions and parsley. Serve over rice. Variations may be made by adding different seafoods, sausages or poultry.

River Road Recipes II: Second Helping
Junior League of Baton Rouge, Baton Rouge, Louisiana

Seafood Stew

1/4 cup olive oil
2 tablespoons unsalted butter
1 yellow onion, finely chopped
2 ribs celery, finely chopped
2 leek bulbs, thinly sliced
2 carrots, finely chopped
5 garlic cloves, minced
1/2 cup dry white wine
1 quart (4 cups) vegetable broth
2 cups tomato juice

4 plum tomatoes, finely chopped
1 teaspoon saffron
Grated zest and juice of 2 lemons
1 pound mussels, scrubbed
1 pound littleneck clams, scrubbed
1 pound halibut, cut into large pieces
8 ounces scallops
8 large shrimp, peeled and deveined
Salt and pepper to taste
1/4 cup chopped Italian parsley

Heat the olive oil and butter in a large stockpot over medium heat. Add the onion, celery, leeks and carrots to the butter mixture and cook for 7 minutes, stirring frequently. Stir in the garlic and cook for 1 minute. Stir in the wine, broth, tomato juice and tomatoes.

Bring to a simmer and then stir in the saffron, lemon zest and lemon juice. Simmer for 20 minutes, stirring occasionally. Add the mussels and clams and bring to a boil. Reduce the heat to low and add the halibut, scallops and shrimp. Simmer for 4 minutes and season with salt and pepper. Ladle the stew into bowls and sprinkle with the parsley. Serve immediately with crusty bread.

Starfish Café: Changing Lives One Recipe at a Time …
Union Mission/Starfish Café, Savannah, Georgia

Simply Sarasota: Creatively Casual Cuisine created a revolution in our fund-raising, pushing the Junior League of Sarasota's income to its highest level in our fifty-year history during the first year of cookbook sales. The proceeds are going towards our signature project, improving the lives of children in our community. Not only has this beautiful, already well-loved cookbook brought great attention to the League's involvement in the community, it has also brought attention to the people and projects in our community that need it most.

Seafood Lasagna

6 lasagna noodles
1 cup chopped onion
1 cup sliced mushrooms
1/4 cup (1/2 stick) butter or margarine
8 ounces cream cheese, cubed and softened
1 1/2 cups cottage cheese
1/2 cup (2 ounces) grated Parmesan cheese
1 egg, beaten
1 tablespoon parsley flakes
2 teaspoons basil
Salt and pepper to taste
1 (10-ounce) can cream of mushroom soup
1/3 cup dry white wine
1 pound deveined peeled boiled shrimp
1 pound lump crab meat, drained and shells removed
1 cup (4 ounces) shredded mozzarella cheese

Cook the noodles using the package directions; drain. Sauté the onion and mushrooms in the butter in a large skillet until tender. Remove from the heat. Add the cream cheese and mix well. Stir in the cottage cheese, Parmesan cheese, egg, parsley flakes, basil, salt and pepper. Combine the soup and wine in a bowl and mix well. Fold the shrimp and crab meat into the soup mixture. Layer the noodles, cream cheese mixture and shrimp mixture 1/2 at a time in a greased 9×13-inch baking dish and sprinkle with the mozzarella cheese. Bake at 350 degrees for 45 minutes.

River Road Recipes IV: Warm Welcomes
Junior League of Baton Rouge, Baton Rouge, Louisiana

"Though the majority of American women may no longer slaughter pigs, preserve peaches, or make their own tortillas, the effort of cooking continues to largely be women's work, a major force in the rhythm of our lives, keeping us alive, and bringing us together around the table with those we like, those we love, and those we need."

Laura Schenone
A Thousand Years Over a Hot Stove

Vegetables and Sides

Nashville—a city rich in history, music, and Southern charm. It's the heart of Tennessee and home of the meat and three (that's Southern shorthand for a meat and three vegetables, for those of you not fortunate enough to have lived in the land of country ham and red-eye gravy).

While living a heart-healthy lifestyle is something most of us aspire to, it's not always what we practice when it comes to eating. Flavorful cooking may even seem incompatible with foods that are good for the heart.

Not so. That's why we decided to compile our cookbooks. For years we've been showing cardiac rehabilitation patients there are a lot of good eats that are good for you, too. People who want to eat a heart-healthy diet can still enjoy many traditional Southern favorites with just a few changes here and there.

All of the recipes in our cookbooks have been carefully analyzed to make sure they fall within the guidelines of heart-healthy food. Best of all, the recipes have been taste-tested by people who love Southern home cooking.

All proceeds from the sale of our books are used to further Saint Thomas Heart Hospital Institute cardiac research and education so that more people can benefit from the joys of living a heart-healthy lifestyle without sacrificing the flavors of the South.

Connie Rafalowski

Kitty Fawaz
Saint Thomas Hospital
Nashville, Tennessee

Marinated Asparagus with Cherry Tomatoes

Serves 6 to 8

2 pounds asparagus, steamed
15 cherry tomatoes, cut into halves
1/2 garlic clove, minced
1 cup olive oil
1/2 cup balsamic vinegar
1/4 cup sugar

2 teaspoons orange juice
1/8 teaspoon salt
1/8 teaspoon pepper
6 green onions, chopped
1 green bell pepper, chopped
1/4 cup chopped pimento

Place the asparagus and tomatoes in a large sealable plastic bag. Combine the garlic, olive oil, balsamic vinegar, sugar, orange juice, salt and pepper in a bowl and whisk until blended. Pour over the asparagus and tomatoes. Add the green onions, bell pepper and pimento. Chill in the refrigerator for 8 to 10 hours.

Savor the Seasons
The Junior League of Tampa, Tampa, Florida

Asparagus Casserole

Serves 4

1 can asparagus
1 1/2 cups heavy cream sauce
Worcestershire to taste

Salt and pepper to taste
1 cup grated sharp cheese
1/2 cup split blanched almonds

Cut asparagus in thirds. Flavor cream sauce with Worcestershire sauce, salt and pepper. Put all ingredients together in layers in a casserole dish and bake for 40 minutes at 325 degrees.

Charleston Receipts
Junior League of Charleston, Charleston, South Carolina

Asparagus Tart

1 (9-inch) refrigerator pie pastry
1 pound asparagus spears
2 thick slices hickory-smoked bacon
1 tablespoon butter
1/4 cup chopped sweet onion
1/4 cup chopped red bell pepper
4 ounces cream cheese, softened

1/2 cup mayonnaise
1/2 cup half-and-half
2 tablespoons all-purpose flour
2 eggs
2 cups (8 ounces) shredded Swiss cheese
1 cup (4 ounces) grated Parmesan cheese

Preheat the oven to 350 degrees. Fit the pie pastry into a lightly greased tart pan and bake for 5 to 7 minutes. Let stand until cool. Maintain the oven temperature.

Snap off the thick woody ends of the asparagus spears and discard. Cut the spears into 3-inch pieces. Bring 1 inch of water to a boil in a saucepan and place the asparagus in a steamer basket over the boiling water. Steam, covered, for 4 to 6 minutes or until tender-crisp and drain.

Cook the bacon in a skillet over medium-high heat until crisp. Remove the bacon to a paper towel to drain, reserving the pan drippings. Cool the bacon and crumble. Melt the butter with the reserved pan drippings and add the onion and bell pepper. Sauté until tender.

Combine the cream cheese, mayonnaise, half-and-half, flour and eggs in a mixing bowl and beat until blended. Stir in the bacon, onion mixture and Swiss cheese. Arrange the asparagus in the baked shell and pour the cream cheese mixture over the top. Sprinkle with the Parmesan cheese and bake for 30 to 35 minutes or until a knife inserted near the center comes out clean.

Tables of Content
Junior League of Birmingham, Inc., Birmingham, Alabama

In 1950, after trying various fund-raisers, the Junior League of Charleston decided to create a cookbook as a fund-raiser. This effort proved more than successful, resulting in the renowned *Charleston Receipts*. It quickly won national acclaim and today holds the title of oldest Junior League cookbook still in print, with more than 792,000 copies sold.

Black Bean Tart

POTATO CRUST
2 cups frozen shredded hash brown
   potatoes, thawed

3 tablespoons butter, melted
¹/₂ teaspoon each salt and pepper

BEAN FILLING
1 tablespoon vegetable oil
1 red bell pepper, finely chopped (about 1 cup)
¹/₂ cup finely chopped purple onion
1 (15-ounce) can black beans, drained and rinsed
1 (15-ounce) can whole kernel corn, drained

2 jalapeño chiles, seeded and finely chopped
¹/₂ teaspoon ground cumin
¹/₂ teaspoon chili powder
1 ¹/₂ cups (6 ounces) shredded Monterey Jack cheese
1 teaspoon chopped fresh cilantro

CREAMY LIME TOPPING
1 cup sour cream
2 teaspoons fresh lime juice

¹/₄ teaspoon each salt and pepper
Chopped fresh cilantro for garnish

For the crust, preheat the oven to 350 degrees. Press the potatoes between paper towels to remove any excess moisture. Mix the potatoes, butter, salt and pepper in a bowl. Pat the potato mixture over the bottom and up the side of a greased 9-inch pie plate and bake for 20 to 25 minutes or until light brown. Maintain the oven temperature.

For the filling, heat the oil in a skillet and add the bell pepper and onion. Sauté until tender and remove from the heat. Stir in the beans, corn, jalapeño chiles, cumin and chili powder. Fold in the cheese and cilantro. Spoon the bean mixture into the potato crust and bake for 20 minutes. Cool in the pan on a wire rack for 10 minutes.

For the topping, mix the sour cream, lime juice, salt and pepper in a bowl. Top the tart with the topping and garnish with the cilantro.

Tables of Content
Junior League of Birmingham, Inc., Birmingham, Alabama

Boston Baked Beans

3 cups dried small white beans
12 ounces salt pork
1 large onion, peeled
6 tablespoons molasses

$^1\!/_2$ teaspoon salt
$^1\!/_2$ teaspoon prepared mustard
$^1\!/_2$ teaspoon pepper
Boiling water

Sort and rinse the beans. Place in a large saucepan and add enough water to cover. Soak for 8 to 12 hours. Drain the beans; return to the saucepan and cover with fresh water. Cook over medium heat until a thick layer appears on the surface of the water. Remove from the heat; drain.

Score the rind on the salt pork at $^1\!/_2$-inch intervals. Place the salt pork and onion in the bottom of a bean pot. Spoon the beans over the pork. Top with the molasses, salt, prepared mustard and pepper. Pour enough boiling water over the beans to cover.

Bake, covered, at 250 degrees for 4 hours, adding more boiling water to cover the beans every hour if necessary. Uncover the beans; move the salt pork to the top. Bake, uncovered, for 1 hour longer or until the salt pork is crisp. Do not add any water during the final baking time.

Boston Uncommon
The Junior League of Boston, Boston, Massachusetts

Balsamic Green Beans

1 $^1\!/_2$ pounds green beans, trimmed and cut into
   1 $^1\!/_2$-inch pieces
$^1\!/_2$ cup olive oil
3 tablespoons balsamic vinegar
$^1\!/_2$ teaspoon Dijon mustard

1 garlic clove, minced (optional)
1 small onion, finely chopped
Pepper to taste
$^1\!/_2$ cup (2 ounces) shredded Parmesan cheese

Steam the green beans in a steamer until tender-crisp. Plunge immediately into ice water in a bowl to stop the cooking process; drain and pat dry. Place the green beans in a serving bowl. Whisk the olive oil, vinegar, Dijon mustard and garlic in a small bowl. Stir in the onion and pepper. Pour over the green beans and toss to coat. Serve at room temperature or chill, covered, in the refrigerator until ready to serve. Add the cheese and toss to coat just before serving.

Great Women, Great Food
Junior League of Kankakee County, Kankakee, Illinois

Country Green Beans

Serves 4

1 pound fresh green beans
1 teaspoon low-sodium beef bouillon
1 teaspoon Worcestershire sauce

1 onion, sliced
1 teaspoon olive oil
Liquid smoke (optional)

Wash beans; trim ends and remove strings. Place in saucepan with remaining ingredients; cover with water. Cook, covered, until beans are tender and liquid is absorbed.

A Taste of the Good Life: From the Heart of Tennessee
Saint Thomas Hospital, Nashville, Tennessee

Emerald Green Beans

Serves 6 to 8

2 pounds green beans, trimmed
Salt to taste
2 1/2 teaspoons grated fresh ginger
3/4 cup walnuts, chopped

1/2 cup golden raisins
1/4 cup (1/2 stick) butter
1/4 cup fresh lemon juice
Freshly ground pepper to taste

Cook the green beans in enough boiling salted water to cover in a saucepan for 5 minutes or until tender-crisp; drain. Submerge the green beans in an ice water bath immediately until cool; drain. Sauté the ginger, walnuts and raisins in the butter in a skillet over medium-high heat for 2 to 3 minutes. Add the green beans and lemon juice. Lower the heat and cook until the beans are heated through, stirring frequently. Season with salt and pepper.

The Cook's Canvas 2
Cameron Art Museum, Wilmington, North Carolina

Green Bean Bundles

2 (16-ounce) cans whole green beans, drained
Bacon slices, cut into halves
1/2 cup (1 stick) butter

1/2 cup packed brown sugar
1 tablespoon soy sauce
1/4 teaspoon garlic powder

Bundle 10 to 12 green beans and wrap with bacon; secure with a wooden pick. Repeat the process with the remaining green beans. Arrange the bundles in a single layer in a baking dish.

Combine the butter, brown sugar, soy sauce and garlic powder in a saucepan. Bring to a boil, stirring occasionally. Pour the butter mixture over the green bean bundles. Marinate, covered, in the refrigerator for 4 to 10 hours. Bake at 375 degrees for 45 minutes.

MariThyme Treasures
Texas Maritime Museum, Houston, Texas

Green Beans with Shiitake Mushrooms

2 pounds French green beans or thin
   green beans, trimmed
3 tablespoons butter
8 ounces shiitake mushrooms, stemmed and sliced

2 tablespoons butter
2 shallots, minced
2 garlic cloves, minced
Salt and pepper to taste

Cook the green beans in a saucepan of boiling water for 3 to 5 minutes or until tender-crisp. Remove to a colander and rinse under cold water; drain. Melt 3 tablespoons butter in a large skillet over medium-high heat. Add the mushrooms and sauté for 5 minutes. Remove to a bowl. This may all be prepared 1 to 2 hours in advance.

Add 2 tablespoons butter to the skillet. Add the shallots and garlic and sauté for 2 minutes. Add the green beans and mushrooms. Cook until heated through, tossing frequently. Season with salt and pepper.

Recipes of Note
Greensboro Symphony Guild, Greensboro, North Carolina

Haricots Verts with Roasted Garlic Butter

Makes 6 (4 ounces beans with 2 teaspoons sauce) servings

1 head garlic
2 tablespoons finely chopped shallots
1/4 teaspoon salt
4 teaspoons butter, softened

2 teaspoons chopped fresh rosemary
1 1/2 pounds haricots verts
1 tablespoon salt

Preheat the oven to 350 degrees. Remove the white papery skin from the garlic head; do not peel or separate the cloves. Wrap the garlic head in foil and bake for 1 hour. Cool for 10 minutes and separate the cloves. Squeeze to extract the garlic pulp and discard the skins.

Combine the garlic pulp, shallots, 1/4 teaspoon salt, butter and rosemary in a bowl and mix well. Add the beans and 1 tablespoon salt to enough boiling water to cover in a medium saucepan and cook for 2 minutes or until tender-crisp. Drain and toss the hot beans with the butter mixture. If these tiny French green beans are not available, substitute with fresh green beans and cook for 2 to 3 minutes longer or until tender-crisp.

Tables of Content
Junior League of Birmingham, Inc., Birmingham, Alabama

Baked Heirloom Beets with Balsamic Vinegar

Serves 4

1 pound (golf ball-size) beets of various colors, leaves and stems trimmed
10 garlic cloves, pressed
1/4 cup fresh marjoram or oregano

Salt and pepper to taste
3/4 cup balsamic vinegar
1/3 cup olive oil

Preheat the oven to 400 degrees. Arrange the beets, garlic and marjoram on a sheet of foil large enough to enclose. Season generously with salt and pepper and bring the sides of the foil up. Pour a mixture of the vinegar and olive oil over the beet mixture and seal the foil.

Bake for 1 hour or until the beets are tender. Let stand until cool enough to handle. Peel and slice or chop the beets, reserving the juices. Serve the beets with the reserved juices over watercress or mixed salad greens or as a side to grilled meats. Serve at room temperature if desired.

California Mosaic
The Junior League of Pasadena, Pasadena, California

Ripley's Exceptional Brussels Sprouts

Serves 4 to 6

2 pints Brussels sprouts
2 large yellow onions or Vidalia onions
4 garlic cloves, minced
1/4 cup (1/2 stick) butter

1/2 cup water
2 tablespoons curry powder
1 tablespoon minced fresh thyme, or 1 teaspoon
    dried thyme

Trim the ends of the brussels sprouts and cut the sprouts into halves. Cut the onions into bite-size squares. Combine the brussels sprouts, onions, garlic, butter, water, curry powder and thyme in a large saucepan. Cook, covered, over high heat for 10 minutes, stirring occasionally. Reduce the heat to low and simmer for 12 to 15 minutes longer or until the brussels sprouts are tender. Serve immediately.

Savor the Moment
Junior League of Boca Raton, Boca Raton, Florida

Grilled Cabbage

Serves 4

1 head cabbage
Garlic powder (to taste)
Salt and pepper (to taste)

Cayenne pepper (to taste)
2 tablespoons butter
1/2 (12-ounce) can light beer

Cut out the core of the cabbage, making a lid with the core. Season the center of the cabbage with garlic powder, salt, black pepper and cayenne pepper. Add the butter to the center. Pour the beer into the center and replace the core lid. Wrap completely in several layers of foil and place on a grill rack. Grill over medium heat for 1 hour.

Now Serving
Junior League of Wichita Falls, Wichita Falls, Texas

Carrot Soufflé

Serves 6

1 pound carrots, peeled and sliced
½ cup butter or margarine, softened
3 eggs
1 cup sugar

3 tablespoons flour
1 teaspoon baking powder
1 ½ teaspoons vanilla extract

Cook carrots in boiling water to cover in a saucepan until tender; drain. Place the carrots and butter in a blender or food processor and process until smooth. Add the eggs, sugar, flour, baking powder and vanilla. Process until smooth. Spoon into a greased 1-quart soufflé dish. Bake at 350 degrees for 45 minutes or until set.

A Sunsational Encore
Junior League of Greater Orlando, Orlando, Florida

Grilled Corn with Lime Butter

Serves 12

¼ cup (½ stick) butter, melted
Juice of 2 limes
1 teaspoon salt

½ teaspoon pepper
1 dozen ears Silver Queen corn, husked

Mix the butter, lime juice, salt and pepper in a shallow dish. Roll the ears of corn in the butter mixture or brush it on the corn. Grill the corn over a hot fire for 5 to 10 minutes or until lightly browned on all sides, turning occasionally. Remove to a platter and let cool to room temperature before serving.

Par 3: Tea-Time at the Masters®
The Junior League of Augusta, Augusta, Georgia

Corn Casserole

Serves 6 to 8

1 (8-ounce) package yellow rice
1 (11-ounce) can Mexicorn
1 (10-ounce) can cream of mushroom soup

1 cup sour cream
Shredded cheese for sprinkling

Cook the rice using the package directions. Add the Mexicorn, soup and sour cream and mix well. Spoon into a baking dish. Sprinkle with cheese. Bake at 400 degrees for 20 minutes.

Down Home: Treasured Recipes from our House to Yours
West Point Junior Auxiliary, West Point, Mississippi

Corn Pudding

Serves 6 to 8

4 tablespoons bacon drippings
1 large onion, chopped
1/4 bell pepper, chopped
One 16-ounce can cream-style corn
2/3 cup yellow cornmeal
1 can milk (measure in corn can)

1 egg
1 teaspoon salt
Tabasco sauce
1 teaspoon sugar (optional)
1 teaspoon Worcestershire sauce (optional)
One can French fried onion rings or paprika

In bacon drippings, sauté onions and pepper. Add corn and cornmeal. Stir in milk and egg that have been beaten together. Bring to a boil, stirring constantly. Add salt and Tabasco sauce and optional ingredients if desired. Pour into greased 2-quart casserole and bake, uncovered, at 300 degrees for 50 minutes. Cover with can of onion rings or paprika just before serving.

River Road Recipes II: Second Helping
Junior League of Baton Rouge, Baton Rouge, Louisiana

Best Ever Corn Pudding

Serves 6 to 8

6 ears fresh corn
6 tablespoons (3/4 stick) butter
2 tablespoons sugar
2 tablespoons (scant) flour
1/2 cup light cream

4 eggs, beaten
1 1/2 teaspoons baking powder
2 tablespoons brown sugar
1/4 teaspoon cinnamon
2 tablespoons butter or margarine, melted

Cut the corn from the ears and measure 4 cups and set aside. Melt 6 tablespoons butter with the sugar in a saucepan. Stir in the flour and cook until bubbly; remove from the heat. Add the cream gradually. Stir in the eggs and baking powder and mix well. Mix in the corn. Spoon into a buttered 1 1/2-quart baking dish. Bake at 350 degrees for 45 minutes or until a knife inserted in the center comes out clean. Mix the brown sugar and cinnamon in a small bowl. Drizzle 2 tablespoons melted butter over the pudding and sprinkle with the brown sugar mixture. Bake for 5 minutes longer. You may substitute two drained 12-ounce cans of yellow or white corn kernels for the fresh corn if you prefer.

Oh My Stars!
Junior League of Roanoke Valley, Roanoke, Virginia

Company Corn Pudding

Serves 6

1 tablespoon butter
1 1/2 tablespoons all-purpose flour
2 cups fresh corn kernels (from about 4 ears)
1 3/4 cups half-and-half

3 eggs
1 tablespoon sugar
1 teaspoon salt
2 cups heavy cream or whipping cream

Preheat the oven to 325 degrees. Coat a 2-quart soufflé dish with the butter and sprinkle with the flour, tilting the dish to ensure even coverage. Combine 1 cup of the corn and the half-and-half in a blender and process until smooth. Add the eggs, sugar and salt and pulse just to combine.

Mix the corn mixture, remaining 1 cup corn and the cream in a bowl. Pour into the prepared soufflé dish and bake for 70 minutes or until the center of the pudding barely moves when the pan is lightly touched. Let stand for 10 minutes before serving.

Tables of Content
Junior League of Birmingham, Inc., Birmingham, Alabama

Southern Indiana Corn Pudding

Serves 9

1 1/2 cups cream-style corn
1 cup yellow cornmeal
2 medium onions, chopped
1/4 cup buttermilk
1/2 cup (1 stick) butter, melted

2 eggs, beaten
1/2 teaspoon baking soda
1 1/2 to 2 cups (6 to 8 ounces) shredded sharp
    Cheddar cheese
1 (4-ounce) can diced green chiles

Combine the cream-style corn, cornmeal, onions, buttermilk, butter, eggs and baking soda in a large bowl and mix well. Pour 1/2 of the batter into a greased 9-inch square baking pan. Layer with 1/2 of the cheese, the green chiles and the remaining cheese and batter. Bake at 350 degrees for 1 hour. Cool in the pan for 15 minutes before cutting into squares.

Note: May be prepared ahead and chilled. Bring to room temperature before baking.

Once Upon A Time
Junior League of Evansville, Evansville, Indiana

Wild West Corn

Serves 6 to 8

8-ounce package cream cheese
1/2 cup milk
4-ounce can green chilies, diced

1 teaspoon salt
2-ounce jar pimientos, drained
2 cans whole kernel corn, drained

Melt cream cheese and milk, stirring constantly. Add remaining ingredients. Pour into buttered 1 1/2-quart casserole. Bake at 350 degrees for 30 minutes uncovered. Variation: Shoe-peg corn can be used in place of whole kernel corn.

Stir Ups
Junior Welfare League of Enid, Enid, Oklahoma

We originally published *Stir Ups* with the goal of creating a first-rate cookbook that would serve as a permanent money making project for our organization. Indeed, twenty-five years later our dream, *Stir Ups*, has sold more than 100,000 copies, inspired the vision for a second cookbook, *Cooking by the Bootstraps*, and stirred up memories for countless people whose roots are in Oklahoma.

Eggplant Patrice

Serves 6

1 small eggplant
2 medium tomatoes, sliced
1 medium onion, chopped

1 green bell pepper, chopped
Salt, pepper and garlic salt
1 1/2 cups grated sharp Cheddar cheese

Slice unpeeled eggplant 1/4 inch thick; parboil slices until partially tender. In a casserole dish, layer eggplant, sliced tomatoes, chopped onion and green bell pepper. Sprinkle with salt, pepper, garlic salt and 1/2 of the grated cheese. Repeat layers, ending with cheese. Cover and bake in a preheated oven at 400 degrees until mixture is steaming. Remove cover, reduce heat to 350 degrees and bake for 30 to 45 minutes or until eggplant is tender and sauce is thick and golden brown.

A Southern Collection Then and Now
Junior League of Columbus, Columbus, Georgia

Fried Okra

Serves 4 to 5

1 pound fresh or frozen okra (4 cups)
1/4 cup all-purpose flour
1/4 cup milk

1 cup cornmeal
Salt and pepper to taste
Vegetable oil for frying

Cut the okra into 1/2-inch pieces. Place the okra in a 1-gallon sealable plastic bag and add the flour. Seal tightly and toss to coat. Pour the milk into the bag and seal tightly. Turn the bag until the okra is completely coated. Remove the okra to another 1-gallon sealable plastic bag and add the cornmeal. Seal tightly and toss to coat. Season to taste with salt and pepper. Preheat oil in a deep skillet and add the okra. Fry until medium brown in color and drain on paper towels. Serve immediately.

Tables of Content
Junior League of Birmingham, Inc., Birmingham, Alabama

Onion Patties

Vegetable oil
3/4 cup all-purpose flour
2 tablespoons minced fresh parsley
1 tablespoon yellow cornmeal
1 tablespoon sugar
2 teaspoons baking powder

2 teaspoons dried sage
1 teaspoon salt
3/4 cup milk
3 drops of Tabasco sauce
2 1/2 cups finely chopped onions

Pour enough oil into a skillet to measure about 1 inch and heat to 360 to 380 degrees. Combine the flour, parsley, cornmeal, sugar, baking powder, sage and salt in a bowl. Stir in the milk, Tabasco sauce and onions. Drop the onion mixture by tablespoonfuls into the hot oil and press lightly. Cook until brown on both sides, turning once; drain. You may prepare in advance and keep warm in a 225-degree oven for up to 1 hour.

Compliments of
The Woman's Exchange of Memphis, Memphis, Tennessee

Blue Cheese Vidalia Onions

2 large Vidalia onions, sliced
6 ounces blue cheese, crumbled
2 tablespoons butter, softened

2 teaspoons Worcestershire sauce
1/2 teaspoon dill weed
Pepper to taste

Arrange the onions in a 9×13-inch baking pan. Combine the cheese, butter, Worcestershire sauce, dill weed and pepper in a bowl and mix well. Spread over the onions. Bake, uncovered, at 425 degrees for 20 minutes. Broil until the cheese mixture is brown.

Home Again, Home Again
Junior League of Owensboro, Owensboro, Kentucky

Vidalia Onion Torte

Serves 15 to 20

4 cups chopped Vidalia onions
24 ounces cream cheese, softened

2 cups freshly grated Parmesan cheese
1/2 cup mayonnaise

Pat the onions with paper towels to remove excess moisture. Combine the onions, cream cheese, Parmesan cheese and mayonnaise in a bowl and mix well. Spoon into a pie plate or quiche pan. Bake at 425 degrees for 15 minutes or until golden brown.

Downtown Savannah Style
Junior League of Savannah, Savannah, Georgia

Roasted Red Potato Bites

Makes 24

12 small red potatoes
1 tablespoon olive oil
4 ounces cream cheese, softened
1/2 cup (2 ounces) shredded sharp Cheddar cheese

1/2 cup (2 ounces) shredded Swiss cheese
8 ounces bacon, crisp-cooked and crumbled
1/2 cup minced green onions
1 teaspoon thyme

Rub the potatoes with olive oil and place on a baking sheet. Bake at 400 degrees for 45 minutes or until tender; cool. Cut each potato into halves. If needed, cut a small slice off the bottom of each half for a base so the potatoes can sit level. Scoop the potato pulp into a large mixing bowl, leaving 1/4-inch-thick shells. Set the shells aside. Add the cream cheese, Cheddar cheese, Swiss cheese, bacon, green onions and thyme to the potato pulp and mix well. Spoon or pipe the cheese mixture into the potato shells. Place on a lightly greased baking sheet. Broil 6 inches from the heat source for 3 to 5 minutes or until lightly browned. Garnish with sliced green onions.

Note: The potatoes may be refrigerated, covered, up to 2 days before broiling. Bring them to room temperature before broiling.

Toast of the Coast
The Junior League of Jacksonville, Jacksonville, Florida

Scalloped Potato Casserole

1 (2-pound) sack frozen hash brown
   potatoes, thawed
1 teaspoon salt
1/4 teaspoon pepper
1/2 cup chopped onion

1 (103/4-ounce) can cream of chicken soup
1 pint sour cream
2 cups grated Cheddar cheese
1/4 to 1/2 cup melted butter or margarine
2 cups crushed corn flakes

Combine all ingredients except butter and corn flakes. Place in a 2-quart greased casserole. Pour butter over top. Sprinkle corn flakes all over. Bake at 350 degrees for 45 minutes. For smaller servings, bake in two (1-quart) casseroles. Serve one and freeze the other for later.

A Taste of Georgia
Newnan Junior Service League, Newnan, Georgia

Roasted New Potatoes with Garlic and Rosemary

Serves 8 to 10

3 pounds small red potatoes, quartered
1/4 cup olive oil
1/2 teaspoon salt
1/2 teaspoon freshly ground pepper

3 large garlic cloves, thinly sliced
2 teaspoons dried rosemary
2 tablespoons minced fresh parsley
2 tablespoons minced fresh chives

In a large roasting pan, combine oil, salt, pepper, garlic and rosemary. Stir in potatoes until well coated. Roast, uncovered, at 375 degrees for 1 hour or until potatoes are tender, turning them 2 to 3 times. Remove from the oven. Before serving, toss with parsley and chives.

For Goodness Taste
Junior League of Rochester, Inc., Rochester, New York

Rosemary Potatoes

Serves 12

3/4 stick of butter
1 medium white or yellow onion, sliced
2 cloves garlic, minced
1 teaspoon Creole seasoning

1 tablespoon dried rosemary
1/2 teaspoon pepper
5 medium russet potatoes, peeled and sliced
1/2 cup grated Parmesan cheese

Melt butter in a medium skillet over medium-high heat. Add onion and cook until transparent, about 5 minutes. Lower the heat to medium, and add garlic, Creole seasoning, rosemary and pepper. Cook for 2 minutes. Spread half of the sliced potatoes in a 2-quart or larger baking dish. Add half of the butter mixture and stir to coat the potatoes. Add the second half of the potatoes and the second half of the butter. Stir to coat. Cover with lid or aluminum foil and bake at 375 degrees for 45 minutes. Remove cover and sprinkle the top with cheese. Bake, uncovered, for at least 15 minutes until the cheese melts. Can also be topped with Cheddar or Asiago cheese.

Add Another Place Setting
Junior League of Northwest Arkansas, Springdale, Arkansas

Pecan-Topped Sweet Potatoes

Serves 8 to 10

4 pounds sweet potatoes, peeled, cooked, mashed
3/4 cup sugar
2 eggs, beaten
1/2 cup (1 stick) butter, softened
1 tablespoon vanilla extract

1 cup packed brown sugar
1/3 cup flour
1/3 cup butter, softened
1 cup pecans, chopped

Combine the sweet potatoes, sugar, eggs, 1/2 cup butter and vanilla in a bowl and mix until blended. Spoon the mixture into a 9×13-inch baking dish. Combine the brown sugar, flour and 1/3 cup butter in a bowl and mix with a fork until crumbly. Stir in the pecans. Sprinkle the crumb mixture over the sweet potatoes. Bake at 350 degrees for 30 minutes. Serve warm. Double the topping mixture for an extra-sweet and crunchy treat.

Cooking by the Bootstraps
Junior Welfare League of Enid, Enid, Oklahoma

Floribbean Sweet Potato Timbales

3 pounds sweet potatoes or yams, peeled,
   cut into chunks
1/4 cup freshly squeezed Florida orange juice
1/4 cup packed light brown sugar
1/4 cup butter or margarine
1 1/2 tablespoons Grand Marnier
1 tablespoon finely grated fresh orange peel

1/2 teaspoon cinnamon
1/4 teaspoon nutmeg
1/8 teaspoon ginger
2 eggs, lightly beaten
1/4 cup freshly grated coconut
Tropical Fruit Salsa

Combine the sweet potatoes with enough boiling water to cover in a saucepan. Cook for 20 to 30 minutes or until tender; drain.

Combine the sweet potatoes, orange juice, brown sugar, butter, liqueur, orange peel, cinnamon, nutmeg and ginger in a bowl. Mash until smooth. Add the eggs, stirring until blended. Spoon into a greased 2-quart square baking dish. Bake at 350 degrees for 45 minutes.

Make the timbales by oiling a small deep cup. Spoon the warm sweet potato mixture into the cup and press lightly; smooth the top. Run a small knife around the inside of the cup and invert onto individual plates or a platter. (If one of the timbales falls apart, return the mixture to the cup and try again.) Garnish top and sides of timbales with the coconut and Tropical Fruit Salsa.

TROPICAL FRUIT SALSA
1 ripe mango, chopped
1 ripe papaya, chopped

1 ripe plum or nectarine, chopped
2 kiwifruit, chopped
2 tablespoons freshly squeezed Florida orange juice

Mix the mango, papaya, plum, kiwifruit and orange juice in a bowl.

Made in the Shade
The Junior League of Greater Fort Lauderdale, Fort Lauderdale, Florida

"I've always thought of myself as a domestic feminist. I've spent time at home rearing four daughters, and volunteering was a way I could continue to work, yet maintain control of my time when family needed to come first. Whenever the girls were young and faced a difficult situation, I would always ask, 'Are we girls, or are we women?!' in a rousing, 'Coach Mom' voice. The answer would come back, in young, sweet voices I can still hear, 'We are women!'

At less than twenty years old, our Junior League is very young in the realm of Junior Leagues, and compiling a cookbook is somewhat of a coming-of-age project. By taking on our cookbook project, the Junior League of Northwest Arkansas figuratively asked its members the same question I would ask my daughters. Our membership responded in a united, strong voice. 'Not only are we women, we're women who can cook!'"

Susan Fountain Hui
Junior League of Northwest Arkansas

Superior Steakhouse's Whipped Sweet Potatoes

Serves 4

8 sweet potatoes
1 cup heavy cream
½ cup (1 stick) butter
2 cups maple syrup
1 cup packed brown sugar
½ cup granulated sugar

Juice of 2 oranges
1 tablespoon vanilla extract
1 tablespoon ground cinnamon
1 ½ teaspoons ground nutmeg
Marshmallows (optional)

Arrange the sweet potatoes on a baking sheet and bake at 400 degrees for 1 hour or until tender. Cool slightly and peel the sweet potatoes. Place the pulp in a large bowl.

Heat the heavy cream and butter in a saucepan until the butter melts. Add the butter mixture, maple syrup, brown sugar, granulated sugar, orange juice, vanilla, cinnamon and nutmeg to the sweet potato pulp and whip with an electric mixer until blended and fluffy. Spoon into a baking dish and top with marshmallows. Broil until the marshmallows are brown.

Mardi Gras to Mistletoe
Junior League of Shreveport-Bossier, Shreveport, Louisiana

Simple Artichoke-Spinach Soufflé

Serves 6

2 (12-ounce) packages frozen spinach soufflé, partially thawed
1 (14-ounce) can artichoke hearts, drained and sliced
1 (8-ounce) package cream cheese, softened

Preheat oven to 350 degrees. Place soufflé and artichokes in a buttered 2-quart baking dish. Add cream cheese which has been cut into small cubes. Place in oven for about 5 minutes or until ingredients have melted enough to be combined. Stir until cheese is well incorporated and return to oven for 50 to 60 minutes.

Magic
Junior League of Birmingham, Inc., Birmingham, Alabama

Sautéed Spinach with Raisins and Pine Nuts

Serves 4 to 6

1/2 cup golden or dark raisins
3/4 cup warm water
1 tablespoon olive oil
2 garlic cloves, thinly sliced or crushed
1/3 cup pine nuts

2 bunches fresh spinach
 (about 1 1/2 to 2 pounds), trimmed
Salt and pepper to taste
Balsamic vinegar (optional)

Plump the raisins in the warm water in a small bowl; drain. Heat the olive oil in a 6-quart Dutch oven over medium-high heat. Sauté the garlic in the hot oil for 1 minute. Stir in the pine nuts. Cook until golden brown, stirring constantly. Stir in the raisins. Add the spinach and season with salt and pepper. Cook for 3 to 5 minutes or until the spinach wilts, stirring constantly. Drizzle with a small amount of balsamic vinegar and serve immediately.

An Occasion to Gather
Junior League of Milwaukee, Milwaukee, Wisconsin

Spinach Madeleine

Serves 5 to 6

2 packages frozen chopped spinach
4 tablespoons butter
2 tablespoons flour
2 tablespoons chopped onion
1/2 cup evaporated milk
1/2 cup vegetable liquor
1/2 teaspoon black pepper

3/4 teaspoon celery salt
3/4 teaspoon garlic salt
Salt to taste
6-ounce roll of jalapeño cheese
1 teaspoon Worcestershire sauce
Red pepper to taste

Cook spinach according to directions on package. Drain and reserve liquor. Melt butter in saucepan over low heat. Add flour, stirring until blended and smooth, but not brown. Add onion and cook until soft but not brown. Add liquid slowly, stirring constantly to avoid lumps. Cook until smooth and thick; continue stirring. Add seasonings and cheese which has been cut into small pieces. Stir until melted. Combine with cooked spinach. This may be served immediately or put into a casserole and topped with buttered bread crumbs. The flavor is improved if the latter is done and kept in refrigerator overnight. This may also be frozen.

River Road Recipes: The Textbook of Louisiana Cuisine
Junior League of Baton Rouge, Baton Rouge, Louisiana

Spinach Phyllo Pie

Serves 6

1 tablespoon olive oil or vegetable oil
1/2 cup chopped onion
1 cup chopped red bell pepper
1 garlic clove, minced
2 (9-ounce) packages frozen chopped spinach, thawed and squeezed dry
8 ounces cream cheese, softened
1/2 cup crumbled feta cheese or Gorgonzola cheese

2 eggs
1 tablespoon chopped fresh dill weed, or 1 teaspoon dried dill weed
1/2 teaspoon salt
1/2 teaspoon pepper
8 (9×14-inch) sheets phyllo dough, thawed
2 tablespoons butter or margarine, melted

Heat the olive oil in a skillet over medium-high heat. Add the onion, bell pepper and garlic and sauté until tender-crisp. Remove from the heat and stir in the spinach, cream cheese, feta cheese, eggs, dill weed, salt and pepper. Trim the phyllo dough on a work surface to a 9×12-inch stack and discard the trimmed dough. Cover the dough with waxed paper and then a damp kitchen towel to prevent drying. Remove four sheets of dough and brush each with melted butter. Layer the buttered phyllo dough into a greased 9-inch pie plate, gently pressing into the pie plate and allowing the excess dough to hang over the edge. Spread the spinach mixture evenly over the buttered phyllo dough. Fold the overhanging phyllo dough over the filling. Brush the remaining sheets of phyllo dough with melted butter and layer over the top of the spinach mixture. Tuck the overhanging phyllo dough gently into the pie plate. Cut the pie into six wedges with a sharp knife. Bake in a preheated 375-degree oven until heated through and golden brown. Let stand for 10 minutes before serving.

Marshes to Mansions
Junior League of Lake Charles, LA, Lake Charles, Louisiana

Church Street Squash

Serves 6

2 pounds yellow or zucchini squash
1 medium onion, chopped
4 tablespoons butter, divided
3/4 cup sharp Cheddar cheese, grated
1 cup sour cream

1 teaspoon salt
1/2 teaspoon pepper
1 egg, whisked
1/2 cup Pepperidge Farm stuffing mix, plain
1 tablespoon paprika

Cook squash until tender. Mash with fork after draining. Let stand until cool. Sauté onion in 2 tablespoons butter until yellow, not brown. Mix squash, onion, cheese, sour cream, salt, pepper and egg. Gently pour into greased casserole. Sprinkle stuffing mix on top and dot with 2 tablespoons butter. Sprinkle paprika on top. Cook, uncovered, 30 minutes at 350 degrees or until bubbly. It does freeze well after cooking and covered.

Charleston Receipts Repeats
Junior League of Charleston, Charleston, South Carolina

Butternut Squash Risotto

Serves 4 to 6

1 medium butternut squash
6 cups chicken stock, divided
2 tablespoons unsalted butter, divided
1 tablespoon olive oil
4 shallots, peeled and minced
2 cups Arborio rice

½ cup dry white wine
1 tablespoon fresh rosemary, chopped
Freshly grated nutmeg
Salt and freshly ground pepper to taste
½ cup Parmesan cheese, grated, divided
Rosemary sprigs for garnish

Cut squash into eighths; discard seeds. Steam squash for 10 to 11 minutes or until tender. Scoop flesh from skin and mash lightly. In a 2-quart saucepan, heat stock to a simmer and set aside. In a large, heavy saucepan over medium heat, melt 1 tablespoon butter. Add oil and shallots; cook for 2 minutes. Add rice; cook, stirring for 5 minutes. Add wine to rice; cook, stirring, until wine is nearly absorbed. Stir in squash and 1 cup stock; cook at a steady simmer until liquid is nearly absorbed. Stir in remaining stock, 1 cup at a time, until rice is creamy and firm, but not hard in the center, 15 to 20 minutes. Add chopped rosemary and nutmeg; salt and pepper. Stir in remaining butter and most of the Parmesan, reserving some for garnish. Serve in shallow bowls garnished with cheese and rosemary sprigs.

The Bess Collection
Junior Service League of Independence, Independence, Missouri

Squash Casserole 1

Serves 6 to 8

2 to 3 cups cooked squash
1 egg, slightly beaten
½ stick margarine, sliced
½ cup mayonnaise
1 tablespoon sugar

1 cup grated Cheddar cheese, divided
1 to 1½ cups cracker crumbs, divided
Dash cayenne pepper
Salt and pepper
Herbs (optional)

Put well-drained, hot squash in large mixing bowl. Add eggs, margarine, mayonnaise, sugar, half the cheese, and half the cracker crumbs. Season with cayenne pepper, salt, pepper, and herbs (oregano is especially good in this dish). Mix all ingredients well. Put into buttered 1½-quart casserole dish and top with remaining cheese and crumbs. Bake at 350 degrees for 20 minutes. Crookneck squash or a mixture of crookneck and zucchini may be used.

A Taste of Georgia
Newnan Junior Service League, Newnan, Georgia

Squash Medley

1 butternut squash, peeled, seeded and cubed
1 acorn squash, peeled and cubed
2 cups (1-inch pieces) unpeeled zucchini
2 tomatoes, cut into 1-inch pieces
1/2 cup (1 stick) butter, melted
1/4 cup chopped onion

2 teaspoons sugar
1 teaspoon salt
1/2 teaspoon pepper
1/8 teaspoon oregano
4 to 5 tablespoons grated Parmesan cheese

Toss the butternut squash, acorn squash, zucchini and tomatoes in a bowl. Add the butter, onion, sugar, salt, pepper and oregano and mix gently. Spoon the squash mixture into an 8-cup baking dish and sprinkle with the cheese. Bake, covered, at 350 degrees for 1 hour.

An Occasion to Gather
Junior League of Milwaukee, Milwaukee, Wisconsin

Squash Rockefeller

3 large yellow summer squash or mirliton,
    cut into halves and seeded
Salt to taste
1 pound fresh spinach, stems removed
3 tablespoons oyster liquor or clam juice
3 tablespoons anisette
1/2 cup (2 ounces) grated Parmesan cheese

1 teaspoon chopped fresh tarragon
1/2 teaspoon chopped fresh basil
Coarsely ground black pepper to taste
Cayenne pepper to taste
1 cup seasoned bread crumbs
1/2 cup (2 ounces) grated Parmesan cheese

Cook the squash in boiling salted water in a saucepan for 5 minutes or until tender; drain. Cook the spinach in boiling water in a saucepan for 3 minutes or until tender-crisp; drain. Press the excess moisture from the spinach and finely chop. Combine the spinach, oyster liquor, liqueur, 1/2 cup cheese, tarragon, basil, black pepper, cayenne pepper and salt in a bowl and mix well. Add the bread crumbs gradually, stirring until the mixture has the consistency of a stuffing and is firm enough to adhere. Arrange the squash halves cut side up on a baking sheet. Stuff the squash halves with equal portions of the spinach mixture and sprinkle with 1/2 cup cheese. Bake at 350 degrees for 10 to 12 minutes or until heated through.

River Road Recipes IV: Warm Welcomes
Junior League of Baton Rouge, Baton Rouge, Louisiana

Sweet-and-Sour Tomatoes and Peppers

Serves 8

4 ripe tomatoes, cut into eighths
¼ cup peanut oil or canola oil
4 green bell peppers, cut into 1-inch cubes
½ cup white vinegar

¼ cup sugar
Soy sauce to taste
1 teaspoon cornstarch
2 tablespoons water

Place the tomatoes in a serving bowl and chill, covered, in the refrigerator. Heat a large heavy skillet until very hot and add the peanut oil. Heat until smoking and add the bell peppers. Cook until the bell peppers are covered with gray spots, stirring constantly. Add a mixture of the vinegar and sugar and cook until bubbly, stirring frequently. Season to taste with soy sauce. Dissolve the cornstarch in the water in a small bowl and stir into the bell pepper mixture. Cook until thickened, stirring constantly. Pour the bell pepper mixture over the chilled tomatoes and toss to mix. Serve immediately.

Compliments of
The Woman's Exchange of Memphis, Memphis, Tennessee

Tally Ho Tomato Pudding

Serves 6

2 cups bread cubes, crusts trimmed
½ cup (1 stick) butter, melted
1 cup packed brown sugar
1 cup tomato purée
¼ cup water

Preheat the oven to 350 degrees. Spread the bread cubes in a medium baking dish. Drizzle with the butter. Combine the brown sugar, tomato purée and water in a saucepan and mix well. Cook for 5 minutes, stirring frequently. Spoon over the bread cubes. Bake for 50 minutes. Serve warm.

Note: This recipe is a Toledo tradition.

Art Fare
Toledo Museum of Art Aides, Toledo, Ohio

Tomato Basil Tart

Serves 8

1 unbaked (9-inch) pie shell
1 cup fresh basil
4 garlic cloves
1/2 cup (2 ounces) shredded mozzarella cheese
5 or 6 plum tomatoes, seeded and
  cut into 1/4-inch slices

1 cup (4 ounces) shredded mozzarella cheese
1/2 cup mayonnaise
1/4 cup (1 ounce) grated Parmesan cheese
1/8 teaspoon pepper

Line the pie shell with foil and bake at 450 degrees for 5 minutes. Remove the foil and bake for 8 minutes longer. Reduce the oven temperature to 350 degrees. Process the basil and garlic in a food processor until chopped. Sprinkle 1/2 cup mozzarella cheese over the bottom of the baked pie shell. Layer the tomatoes over the cheese and sprinkle with the basil mixture. Mix 1 cup mozzarella cheese, the mayonnaise, Parmesan cheese and pepper in a bowl and spread over the tomatoes. Bake for 20 minutes or until golden brown. Cool slightly and cut into wedges.

Worth Tasting
Junior League of the Palm Beaches, West Palm Beach, Florida

Tomatoes Stuffed with Orzo

Serves 6

1 cup orzo
6 large tomatoes
1 (14- to 15-ounce) jar spaghetti sauce
1 small onion, finely chopped
2 tablespoons olive oil
1 (10-ounce) package frozen chopped spinach,
  thawed and squeezed dry

1 cup (4 ounces) shredded Cheddar cheese
1 cup (4 ounces) shredded mozzarella cheese
1/4 teaspoon salt
1/4 teaspoon pepper

Cook the orzo using the package directions until al dente, omitting the salt; drain and place in a large bowl. Cut a thin slice off the tops of the tomatoes. Scoop out and dice the pulp, reserving the tomato shells. Spread the tomato pulp in an 8×12-inch glass or ceramic baking dish. Add the spaghetti sauce and mix well. Sauté the onion in the olive oil in a small skillet until slightly brown. Add the onion, spinach, Cheddar cheese, mozzarella cheese, salt and pepper to the orzo and mix well. Mound the orzo mixture into the reserved tomato shells. Place the tomato shells in the sauce. Cover with a foil tent. Bake at 375 degrees for 1 hour or until the sauce is hot and the orzo is heated through.

Between the Lakes
The Junior League of Saginaw Valley, Saginaw, Michigan

Vegetable Gâteau

Serves 6 to 8

CRÊPES
²/₃ cup milk
²/₃ cup water
3 large eggs

¹/₄ teaspoon salt
1 cup flour
3 tablespoons butter, melted
1 ¹/₂ tablespoons vegetable oil

CUSTARD
1 cup cream cheese, softened
1 cup heavy cream

6 eggs
¹/₈ teaspoon nutmeg
Salt and pepper to taste

VEGETABLES AND CHEESE
1 bunch broccoli, trimmed, separated into florets
6 tablespoons butter, softened
1 pound carrots, peeled, julienned
¹/₂ teaspoon dried dillweed, or 1 tablespoon
    chopped fresh dillweed

Salt and pepper to taste
1 pound mushrooms, finely minced
¹/₄ cup minced shallots or scallions
2 cups coarsely shredded Swiss cheese

For the crêpes, combine the milk, water, eggs and salt in a food processor container. Add the flour and butter. Process for 1 minute. Chill, covered, for 1 hour or longer. Coat a 6¹/₂- or 7-inch cast-iron skillet with the oil. Heat just until the skillet begins to smoke. Pour about ¹/₄ cup of the batter into the middle of the skillet, tilting the skillet to cover the bottom. Cook for about 1 minute; turn. Cook for 30 seconds longer or until brown. Repeat the process with the remaining batter, stacking the crêpes between sheets of waxed paper.

For the custard, process the cream cheese, heavy cream, eggs, nutmeg, salt and pepper in a food processor until smooth.

For the vegetables and cheese, blanch the broccoli in a small amount of water in a saucepan for 3 minutes; drain. Add 2 tablespoons of the butter and toss to coat. Sauté the carrots in 2 tablespoons of the butter in a skillet. Season with the dillweed, salt and pepper. Sauté the mushrooms and shallots in the remaining 2 tablespoons butter in a skillet. Season with salt and pepper.

To assemble, preheat the oven to 350 degrees. Line a buttered 8-inch springform pan with some of the crêpes, allowing an overhang. Layer with another layer of crêpes. Sprinkle ¹/₄ of the Swiss cheese over the bottom of the pan. Layer with the carrots. Sprinkle with ¹/₄ of the remaining Swiss cheese. Add enough of the custard to come up to the level of the carrots. Cover with more of the crêpes. Spread with the mushrooms and shallots. Add enough of the custard to cover the mushrooms. Arrange additional crêpes over the mushroom layer to cover. Sprinkle with ¹/₂ of the remaining Swiss cheese. Top with the broccoli, remaining Swiss cheese and remaining custard. Fold over the crêpe overhang. Layer with enough crêpes to cover the filling.

Place a sheet of buttered waxed paper over the top. Cover with foil. Bake on the lower middle rack for 1³/₄ hours. Remove from oven. Let stand at room temperature for 10 to 15 minutes. Remove to a platter. Cut into wedges and serve with hollandaise sauce or a light tomato sauce.

Art Fare
Toledo Museum of Art Aides, Toledo, Ohio

Ratatouille

2 pounds zucchini	2 pounds tomatoes
2 pounds eggplant, peeled	Salt and pepper
1/3 cup butter	Basil
3 green peppers, thinly sliced	Thyme
2 onions, sliced	Bay leaf
3 cloves garlic	

Cut the unpeeled zucchini and eggplant into 1/2-inch slices and sauté in the butter a few at a time, several minutes on each side. Remove and drain. In the same skillet, stir the green peppers, onions and garlic. Cook for 10 minutes. Remove and discard garlic. Add the tomatoes that have been peeled, seeded and sliced. Layer the eggplant, zucchini and half of the tomato mixture, season with salt, pepper and herbs. Repeat, ending with tomato mixture and seasonings. Bake, covered, for about 1 hour in a 350-degree oven. This is a great hot vegetable or serve cold as a salad or hors d'oeuvre.

The Cotton Country Collection
The Junior League of Monroe, Inc., Monroe, Louisiana

Oven-Roasted Vegetables

Serves 8

4 white, red or new potatoes, cut into quarters	1/2 teaspoon freshly ground pepper
12 small carrots, peeled	1 teaspoon finely chopped fresh rosemary, or 1/2
12 small boiling onions	teaspoon dried rosemary
2 tablespoons extra-virgin olive oil	4 to 6 Roma tomatoes, cut into halves and seeded
2 garlic cloves, minced or crushed	Extra-virgin olive oil
1 teaspoon herbes de Provence	Salt and freshly ground pepper to taste
1 teaspoon seasoned salt	

Place the potatoes, carrots and onions in a large sealable plastic bag. Combine 2 tablespoons olive oil with the garlic, herbes de Provence, seasoned salt, 1/2 teaspoon pepper and rosemary in a bowl and mix well. Pour over the vegetables, seal the bag and mix gently. Marinate in the refrigerator for up to 2 hours.

Preheat the oven to 425 degrees. Remove the vegetables to two large baking sheets lined with foil; do not crowd to ensure even browning. Roast for 5 minutes.

Arrange the tomatoes on a baking sheet. Drizzle with additional olive oil and season with salt and pepper to taste. Place in the oven. Roast the potato mixture and the tomatoes together for 15 minutes longer or until evenly brown. Remove to a heated platter and serve with roasted meat or fowl.

The Bells are Ringing: A Call to Table
Mission San Juan Capistrano Women's Guild, San Juan Capistrano, California

Bulgur with Garden Vegetables

1 1/4 cups water
1 cup bulgur
1/2 teaspoon salt
1 red bell pepper, cut into 1/4- to 1/3-inch pieces
1 zucchini, cut into 1/4- to 1/3-inch pieces
1 yellow squash, cut into 1/4- to 1/3-inch pieces
1/4 red onion, coarsely chopped

1/3 cup toasted pine nuts
1/4 cup olive oil
Juice of 1 lime
1/4 cup minced fresh dillweed, or
    4 teaspoons dried dillweed
1/2 teaspoon salt
1/4 teaspoon pepper

Bring the water to a boil in a small saucepan. Stir in the bulgur and 1/2 teaspoon salt. Boil for 1 minute. Remove from the heat. Let stand, covered, for 15 minutes. Pour the bulgur into a large salad bowl and let cool. Stir in the bell pepper, zucchini, yellow squash, onion and pine nuts. Whisk the olive oil, lime juice, dillweed, 1/2 teaspoon salt and pepper together in a small bowl. Pour over the salad and toss to combine. Serve cold or at room temperature.

Tastes, Tales and Traditions
Palo Alto Auxiliary for Children, Palo Alto, California

Vegetable Spoon Bread

Serves 8

1 (10-ounce) package frozen chopped spinach,
    thawed, drained
1 (8-ounce) can creamed corn
2 eggs, lightly beaten

1 cup sour cream
1/2 cup butter, melted
1/4 teaspoon salt
1 (8-ounce) package corn muffin mix

Preheat the oven to 350 degrees; grease an 8-inch round baking dish. Combine the spinach, corn, eggs, sour cream, butter and salt in a large bowl; mix well. Add the corn muffin mix and stir until thoroughly combined. Pour the batter into the baking dish. Bake for 30 to 45 minutes or until a toothpick inserted in the center comes out clean. Let cool on a wire rack.

A Thyme to Remember
The Dallas County Medical Society Alliance, Dallas, Texas

Crawfish Cornbread Dressing

Serves 12

1 cup chopped onion
1 toe garlic, chopped
1/4 cup chopped green onion tops
1/4 cup chopped fresh parsley
1 tablespoon margarine
1 teaspoon corn oil
1 pound crawfish tails, lightly rinsed and drained
1/3 cup water
1/3 cup white wine
Two 8-ounce packages cornbread mix

1 egg
2 egg whites
2/3 cup low-fat or skim milk
One 14-ounce can defatted chicken broth, less salt
1 large chopped onion
1 cup chopped celery
1 green bell pepper, chopped
2 toes garlic, minced
2 tablespoons poultry seasoning
1/4 cup water

Sauté onion, garlic, onion tops, and parsley on low heat in margarine and oil until margarine rises to the top (about 30 minutes). Do not burn. Add crawfish. Add water and wine to the pot. Bring mixture to a boil and then simmer for 10 minutes. Prepare cornbread similar to the package, but use only a total of 1 egg and replace other eggs with 2 egg whites (egg substitute may also be used), and use low-fat or skim milk. Cool and crumble into a large bowl. Use 1/4 to 1/3 cup of the chicken broth to sauté the remaining vegetables. Add to cornbread, plus the rest of ingredients, reserving the crawfish mixture. Put in a 9×13-inch pan. Lightly mix 1/2 of crawfish mixture into cornbread mixture. Cover with foil. Bake for 30 minutes at 350 degrees. Use rest of crawfish mixture as a sauce.

River Road Recipes III: A Healthy Collection
Junior League of Baton Rouge, Baton Rouge, Louisiana

Barley and Mushroom Casserole

Serves 6

1/2 cup (1 stick) butter or margarine
1 cup quick-cooking barley
1 onion, chopped
2 cups chicken broth
1/2 cup slivered almonds

1 (2-ounce) envelope onion soup mix
1 (3-ounce) can sliced mushrooms, or 1 cup sliced
    fresh mushrooms
Butter to taste
1 (5-ounce) can sliced water chestnuts

Preheat the oven to 350 degrees. Melt 1/2 cup butter in a saucepan and stir in the barley and onion. Sauté until light golden brown. Remove from the heat and stir in the broth, almonds and soup mix. Drain the canned mushrooms, reserving the liquid. Sauté the mushrooms in butter in a skillet until tender. Stir the reserved mushroom liquid, sautéed mushrooms and water chestnuts into the barley mixture. Pour into a 2-quart baking dish and bake, covered, for 1 hour, adding additional liquid if needed. You may prepare one to two days in advance and store, covered, in the refrigerator. Bake just before serving. You may freeze leftovers for future use.

Simply Sarasota
Junior League of Sarasota, Sarasota, Florida

RECIPES WORTH SHARING

Mrs. Truman's Cheese Soufflé

4 tablespoons butter
2 tablespoons flour
1 cup scalded milk or tomato juice
1/2 teaspoon salt

Few grains cayenne
1/2 cup grated cheese
4 egg yolks (beaten light)
4 egg whites (beaten stiff)

Melt butter, add flour. Gradually add the scalded milk or tomato juice, and stir until thick and smooth. Add salt, cayenne and cheese. Stir until smooth. Remove from fire, add yolks. Cool, cut and fold in whites. Pour into buttered baking dish or ramekins. Set in pan of hot water. If desired firm, bake 30 to 45 minutes in a moderately slow oven (325 degrees). If desired soft, bake 20 minutes in moderately hot oven (375 degrees). Serve at once.

The Bess Collection
Junior Service League of Independence, Independence, Missouri

Baked Manchego Cheese with Pear Compote and Sliced Pears

Serves 8

PEAR COMPOTE
4 teaspoons vegetable oil
2 tablespoons finely chopped red bell pepper
1/4 teaspoon dry mustard
Pinch of salt
4 pears, peeled, cored and chopped

Pinch of ground allspice
Pinch of ginger
Pinch of ground cloves
1 tablespoon (heaping) golden raisins
1/4 cup apple cider vinegar
1/4 cup packed light brown sugar

CHEESE
1/2 cup unblanched whole almonds, ground
1/2 cup panko (Japanese bread crumbs)
1/2 teaspoon salt
1 egg

16 ounces Manchego cheese, rind removed and cheese cut into 16 equal wedges
Sliced almonds
2 pears, cored and thinly sliced

For the compote, heat the oil in a small skillet. Add the bell pepper, dry mustard and salt and sauté for 5 minutes. Add the pears, allspice, ginger and cloves and sauté for 1 to 2 minutes. Stir in the raisins, vinegar and brown sugar. Bring to a boil. Cook until the pears have softened and the mixture is the texture of chunky applesauce. Chill, covered, until cold.

For the cheese, combine the almonds, panko and salt in a flat shallow dish. Beat the egg in a flat shallow dish.

Dip each cheese wedge in the egg and then coat in the panko mixture. Place in a Silpat-lined or baking parchment-lined 10×15-inch baking pan. Spray each wedge with nonstick cooking spray. Bake at 400 degrees for 5 to 7 minutes or just until the cheese is softened. Place two cheese wedges at a right angle on each of eight dessert plates. Top each with about 1 tablespoon of the compote and sprinkle with sliced almonds. Arrange pear slices next to the cheese. Serve with water biscuits or baguette slices.

Popovers to Panache
The Village Club, Bloomfield Hills, Michigan

VEGETABLES & SIDES

227

Oriental Chick Peas

Serves 6 to 8

3 cups desi chick peas
4 cups water
2 (14-ounce) cans of chicken broth
1 small onion, chopped
1/2 cup finely chopped celery

1/2 cup finely chopped carrots
2 tablespoons butter
2 tablespoons seasoned rice vinegar
Salt and pepper to taste

Cook chick peas in the water and one can of the chicken broth at a low boil in a large saucepan for 35 to 40 minutes or until tender; drain. Sauté the onion, celery and carrots in the butter in a large skillet until tender. Stir in the chick peas, vinegar, salt, pepper and the remaining can of broth. Cook over medium-low heat for about 15 minutes or until most of the broth has cooked away to allow the flavors to blend. Spoon into a serving dish using a slotted spoon.

Be Present At Our Table
Germantown United Methodist Women, Germantown, Tennessee

Awesome Layered Grits

Serves 8 to 10

4 cups water
1 cup grits
1 teaspoon salt
1 (6-ounce) roll garlic cheese, chopped
1/2 cup (1 stick) butter
2 eggs, lightly beaten

1/4 cup milk
2 to 3 tomatoes, sliced
1 cup chopped fresh basil
1 large sweet onion, finely chopped
2 cups shredded Monterey Jack cheese
2 cups shredded Cheddar cheese

Bring the water to a boil in a saucepan. Stir in the grits and salt. Reduce the heat and cover. Simmer for 20 minutes or until thick. Remove from the heat and stir in the garlic cheese, butter, eggs and milk. Pour into a 2 1/2-quart baking dish. Bake at 350 degrees for 45 to 50 minutes. Remove to a wire rack and let cool. (May be made ahead up to this point and refrigerated.) Arrange the tomato slices on the grits. Sprinkle with the basil, onion, Monterey Jack cheese and Cheddar cheese. Bake at 350 degrees for 20 minutes or until hot. Cut into squares. Excellent with ham.

A League of Our Own: From Blue Jeans to Ball Gowns
Rockwall Women's League, Rockwall, Texas

Gourmet Cheese Grits

1 quart milk
1/2 cup butter
1 cup uncooked grits
1 teaspoon salt
1/2 teaspoon ground white pepper

1 egg
1/3 cup butter
4 ounces Gruyère cheese, grated
1/2 cup grated fresh Parmesan cheese

Bring milk to a boil over medium heat, stirring often. Add 1/2 cup butter and grits. Cook, stirring constantly, until mixture is the consistency of oatmeal (about 5 minutes). Remove grits from heat. Add salt, pepper, and egg, beating until well combined. Add 1/3 cup butter and Gruyère cheese. Pour into a greased 2-quart casserole dish. Sprinkle with Parmesan cheese. Bake at 350 degrees for 1 hour.

Food for Thought
Junior League of Birmingham, Inc., Birmingham, Alabama

Jalapeño Grits

1 cup stone-ground grits
4 cups water
1 teaspoon salt
2 cups (8 ounces) shredded Pepper Jack cheese

1/2 cup (1 stick) butter, chopped
3 eggs, beaten
1 tablespoon finely chopped jalapeño chile
Salt and pepper to taste

Combine the grits with cold water to cover in a bowl. Skim off the chaff; drain. Bring 4 cups water and 1 teaspoon salt to a boil in a medium saucepan. Add the grits gradually, stirring constantly. Reduce the heat and simmer for 30 minutes or until thick and creamy, stirring frequently. Remove from the heat. Add the cheese to the grits and mix well. Add the butter and beat until smooth. Stir in the eggs and jalapeño chile. Season with salt and pepper to taste. Spoon into a greased 2-quart baking dish. Bake at 350 degrees for 35 minutes or until the grits are firm and the top is slightly brown.

From Grouper to Grits
The Junior League of Clearwater-Dunedin, Clearwater, Florida

Cashew Rice

1 cup chopped onion
8 ounces mushrooms, sliced
1/2 cup cashews
1/2 cup sliced celery
5 tablespoons butter
2 cups water

1 cup white rice
2 chicken bouillon cubes
1/2 teaspoon salt
1/4 teaspoon freshly ground pepper
1/2 teaspoon thyme

Sauté the onion, mushrooms, cashews and celery in 2 tablespoons of the butter in a skillet for 5 minutes. Stir in the remaining 3 tablespoons butter, water, rice, bouillon cubes, salt, pepper and thyme. Bring to a boil, cooking until the bouillon cubes dissolve, stirring occasionally; reduce heat. Simmer, covered, for 15 minutes or until the rice is tender and the liquid is absorbed.

Texas Ties
Junior League of North Harris and South Montgomery Counties, Inc., Spring, Texas

Ginger and Shiitake Mushroom Fried Rice

Serves 4 to 6

1 egg
1 tablespoon water
6 teaspoons (about) canola oil
6 to 8 scallions, white and green parts
    chopped separately
1 1/2 teaspoons minced fresh gingerroot

1/4 teaspoon kosher salt or sea salt
8 ounces fresh shiitake mushrooms, stems
    discarded, caps thinly sliced
3 cups cooked rice
1 tablespoon sesame oil

Beat the egg with the water in a bowl. Warm a wok or large nonstick skillet over medium heat until hot. Add 1 teaspoon of the canola oil and swirl to coat the pan. Add 1/2 of the egg mixture and swirl to coat the bottom of the pan with a thin layer. Cook for about 1 minute or until the egg is set. Remove the round of cooked egg from the pan. Add another teaspoon of the canola oil to the pan. Add the remaining egg mixture and repeat the cooking process. Stack the egg rounds and roll up like a cylinder. Cut the cylinder crosswise into small strips; set aside.

Heat the remaining 4 teaspoons canola oil in the wok over medium heat, adding more oil if needed to coat the pan. Add the white scallion parts, ginger and salt. Stir-fry for about 30 seconds. Add the mushrooms. Stir-fry for 3 to 5 minutes or until tender. Add the rice. Stir-fry for about 10 minutes or until the rice is light brown. Remove from the heat. Add the green scallion parts, egg strips and sesame oil and toss to mix. Taste and adjust the flavors by adding small amounts of salt and sesame oil.

Once Upon A Time
Junior League of Evansville, Evansville, Indiana

Wild Rice Dressing

1 (6-ounce) package wild rice
4 cups water
1 1/2 cups chopped pecans
1 cup chopped onion

1 cup chopped celery
1/2 cup (1 stick) butter
8 ounces mushrooms, sliced
Salt and pepper to taste

Rinse and drain the wild rice. Combine with the water in a 3-quart saucepan and bring to a boil. Reduce the heat and simmer; loosely covered, for 45 to 60 minutes or until the rice is tender; drain any remaining water. Sprinkle the pecans into a skillet and cook over low heat until toasted. Sauté the onion and celery in the butter in a large saucepan until tender. Add the mushrooms, salt and pepper and sauté for 5 minutes longer. Stir in the wild rice and pecans. Spoon into a baking dish and bake at 350 degrees for 20 minutes or until heated through. You should serve this dish within 2 hours of preparing it to preserve the crunchiness of the pecans.

Notably Nashville
Junior League of Nashville, Nashville, Tennessee

Four-Cheese Risotto

Serves 6

1 large sweet onion, chopped
3 tablespoons olive oil
2 garlic cloves, crushed
1 pound arborio rice
1 cup dry white wine
8 cups chicken broth, heated

1/4 cup (1 ounce) shredded Parmesan cheese
1/4 cup crumbled blue cheese
1/4 cup (1 ounce) shredded smoked Gouda cheese
1/4 cup (1 ounce) shredded Pepper Jack cheese
2 tablespoons butter
1 teaspoon salt

Sweat the onion in the olive oil in a medium saucepan for 3 minutes, stirring constantly. Stir in the garlic and sweat for 2 minutes longer, stirring constantly. Reduce the heat to medium and stir in the rice. Cook for 3 minutes, stirring constantly. Add the wine and cook until the wine is absorbed.

Stir 1 cup of the broth into the rice mixture and cook until the broth is absorbed. Add the remaining broth 1 cup at a time, cooking until the broth is absorbed after each addition. Remove from the heat and stir in the Parmesan cheese, blue cheese, Gouda cheese, Pepper Jack cheese, butter and salt.

Note: To sweat onions, cook until the onions are softened but not brown, stirring constantly and adjusting the heat as needed to prevent browning.

Starfish Café: Changing Live One Recipe at a Time . . .
Union Mission/Starfish Café, Savannah, Georgia

Gourmet Mac 'n' Cheese

Serves 4 to 6

3 tablespoons unsalted butter, plus more for dish
2 shallots, diced
1/4 cup all-purpose flour
2 3/4 cups milk (use whole milk for best results)
1 cup grated Parmesan cheese, divided
3/4 cup grated Gruyère cheese
3/4 cup grated fontina cheese
3/4 cup crumbled Gorgonzola or other blue cheese

3 ounces thinly sliced prosciutto,
    cut into 1/2-inch pieces
Pinch cayenne pepper, more to taste
Salt and freshly ground black pepper
12 ounces dry gemelli or other spiral pasta
1/2 cup fresh or dried bread crumbs
3 tablespoons finely chopped fresh parsley

Preheat the oven to 375 degrees. Butter an 8-inch square baking dish.

Melt the butter in a large saucepan over medium heat. Add the shallots and sauté until tender and aromatic, about 5 minutes. While the butter is still bubbling, add the flour and cook, whisking constantly, for 1 minute. Slowly whisk in the milk and continue cooking, whisking constantly, until the mixture bubbles and becomes thick, 3 to 5 minutes. Take the pan from the heat and add 3/4 cup of the Parmesan with the Gruyère, fontina, and Gorgonzola, whisking to help the cheese melt gently into the sauce. Stir in the prosciutto and cayenne with salt and pepper to taste; set aside.

Bring a large pot of salted water to a boil. Add the pasta, and cook until the pasta is tender outside but still uncooked in the center, about 5 to 7 minutes. Drain the pasta in a colander, rinse under cold running water to stop the cooking, and drain well. Stir the pasta into the cheese sauce and pour into the prepared dish.

Stir together the bread crumbs, parsley, and remaining 1/4 cup of the Parmesan cheese and sprinkle the mixture over the pasta. Bake until the pasta is heated through and browned on top, about 30 minutes. If the top is not turning golden brown, put it under the broiler for a few minutes, watching carefully. Transfer the dish to a wire cooling rack and let cool 5 minutes before servings.

Celebrate the Rain
The Junior League of Seattle, Seattle, Washington

Cakes, Pies and Cookies

"When readers look at the beautiful food photographs in magazines or cookbooks, they likely have no idea what went into getting just one shot—we sure didn't until Labor Day weekend 2005.

Preparations began well ahead of time. As with most nonprofits and community cookbooks, we were operating on a tight budget. We raided our homes for furniture, dishes, and accessories to enhance the Mission photos, and we stormed the grocery stores to amass supplies of food for our shots. On Saturday, we met with the food stylist at the Mission to go through our checklist for the next day. But no amount of planning could fully prepare us for the frenzied pace of the actual shoot.

Sunday morning, we all arrived at the Mission very early to begin food prep for each photo: Pans were clanging, knives chopping, and blenders whirring. The food stylist-turned-art director went about the Mission grounds at a mad pace deciding the best site for each image. The photographer arrived. His demeanor was focused and calm, a direct contrast to the rest of us who were buzzing about in a state of low-grade chaos. Nevertheless, the mix worked well and by the end of the day we were almost half way through the work at hand. We were all surprised by the amount of time required to shoot a single vignette.

It truly turned out to be a 'labor' day weekend. Monday brought temperatures near 100 degrees. We were hard pressed to keep our frostings from melting and our lettuces from wilting. The temperature, coupled with the fact that we were carting all our food and props a great distance in small wagons, made the Mission grounds seem much more expansive than they really are. By the end of the day we were all exhausted, but happily so. Everything went according to plan and the collaboration of experts and amateurs was a huge success. Leafing through our cookbook will quickly confirm that!"

Joy Horsch

Mary Smith
Mission San Juan Capistrano Women's Guild, California

Almond Pound Cake

2 1/2 cups flour
1 cup sugar
1/2 teaspoon salt
1/2 teaspoon baking soda
1/4 cup canola oil

2 teaspoons almond extract
1 cup nonfat plain yogurt
1/2 cup egg substitute
1/4 cup low-fat buttermilk
1 teaspoon vanilla

Preheat oven to 350 degrees. Combine ingredients in large bowl and beat for 3 minutes at medium to high speed with electric mixer. Pour batter into 10-inch nonstick bundt pan sprayed with nonstick cooking spray. Bake for 60 to 70 minutes or until cake is springy and lightly brown. Let cool upright for at least 15 minutes. Invert pan and turn out cake. Let cool completely on rack. Cut into 1-inch slices.

A Taste of the Good Life: From the Heart of Tennessee
Saint Thomas Hospital, Nashville, Tennessee

Virginia Apple Walnut Cake

4 large (about 2 1/2 pounds) Granny Smith apples
1/3 cup honey
1 tablespoon ground cinnamon
3 cups flour
1 tablespoon baking powder
2 cups sugar
1 teaspoon salt

1 cup vegetable oil
4 eggs
1/3 cup orange juice
2 teaspoons vanilla extract
1/2 cup chopped walnuts
1/2 cup walnut halves

Line a 10-inch tube pan with baking parchment or coat with shortening or nonstick cooking spray. Peel the apples and slice 1/4 inch thick. Toss with the honey and cinnamon in a bowl.

Mix the flour, baking powder, sugar and salt in a mixing bowl. Add the oil, eggs, orange juice and vanilla and beat at low speed to mix. Beat at medium-high speed for 2 minutes or until smooth.

Spread 1/3 of the batter in the prepared tube pan. Drain the apples, reserving any juice. Arrange 1/3 of the apple slices in a spoke design over the batter and sprinkle with the chopped walnuts. Repeat the process to use the remaining ingredients.

Pour the reserved juices over the top and arrange the walnut halves around the outer edge. Place on a baking sheet with a rim. Bake at 350 degrees on the center oven rack for 1 hour and 20 minutes to 1 1/2 hours or until a wooden pick or skewer inserted into the center comes out clean; cover loosely with foil if necessary to prevent overbrowning.

Cool in the pan for 10 minutes. Loosen the cake from the side of the pan with a knife and remove to a wire rack to cool completely. Loosen the cake from the tube and bottom of the pan with a knife and remove to a serving plate with a spatula.

Oh My Stars!
Junior League of Roanoke Valley, Roanoke, Virginia

Fresh Apple Cake with Caramel Glaze

Serves 16

2 cups sugar
1 1/2 cups vegetable oil
3 eggs
2 teaspoons vanilla extract
3 cups flour
2 teaspoons cinnamon
1 teaspoon baking soda
1/2 teaspoon mace
1/2 teaspoon salt
3 cups diced apples
Juice of 1 lemon
1 cup chopped walnuts
Caramel Glaze (see below)

Beat the sugar and oil in a mixing bowl until smooth. Add the eggs 1 at a time, beating well after each addition. Add the vanilla. Stir the flour, cinnamon, baking soda, mace and salt together in a bowl. Gradually add to the egg mixture, beating constantly. Place the apples in a bowl and sprinkle with lemon juice. Fold the apples into the batter. Add the walnuts. The batter will be very thick. Spoon into a well greased and floured bundt pan. Bake at 325 degrees for 1 1/4 hours. Remove from the oven and cool on a wire rack for 15 minutes. Invert onto a serving plate and cool on the rack. Spoon the Caramel Glaze over the cooled cake.

CARAMEL GLAZE
6 tablespoons butter
6 tablespoons brown sugar
1/4 cup heavy cream
1 teaspoon vanilla extract

Melt the butter in a small saucepan. Add the brown sugar, cream and vanilla. Bring to a rolling boil. Boil rapidly for 3 to 4 minutes or until the mixture sheets off a spoon. Cool slightly.

Between the Lakes
The Junior League of Saginaw Valley, Saginaw, Michigan

The proceeds from the sale of *Oh My Stars! Recipes that Shine* support programs designed to help women and children in and around the Roanoke Valley.

Deluxe Carrot Cake

Makes 1 cake

Carrot Cake
2 cups flour
2 cups sugar
2 teaspoons baking soda
1 teaspoon salt

2 teaspoons cinnamon
4 eggs
1 cup cooking oil
4 cups grated raw carrots (about 1 pound)
3/4 cup chopped nuts

Coconut Cream Cheese Frosting
4 tablespoons butter or margarine
2 cups coconut
8 ounces cream cheese

2 teaspoons milk
3 1/2 cups confectioners' sugar, sifted
1/2 teaspoon vanilla

Carrot Cake
Mix flour, sugar, baking soda, salt, and cinnamon together. Set aside. In a large bowl, beat eggs until foamy. Slowly beat in oil. Add flour mixture slowly, beating until smooth. Mix in carrots and nuts. Pour into 3 greased and floured 9-inch round cake pans. Bake at 350 degrees for 25 minutes. Test for doneness. Allow to cool for 10 minutes before removing from pans. Then cool completely on racks.

Coconut Cream Cheese Frosting
Melt 2 tablespoons of the butter in a skillet. Add coconut, stirring constantly over low heat until golden brown. Spread on absorbent paper to cool. Cream remaining butter with the cream cheese. Add milk and sugar alternately, beating well. Add vanilla, and stir in 1 3/4 cups of the coconut. (Remaining coconut will be used as a garnish.) Frost between cooled cake layers and on top. Sprinkle with reserved coconut.

Applehood & Motherpie
Junior League of Rochester, Inc., Rochester, New York

Chocolate Chocolate Chip Cake

Serves 16

2 cups sour cream
2 eggs
1/2 cup Kahlúa
1 (2-layer) package devil's food or other cake mix
   without pudding

1 (4-ounce) package chocolate pudding mix
1/4 cup vegetable oil
2 cups (12 ounces) semisweet chocolate chips
Confectioners' sugar for sprinkling

Combine the sour cream, eggs, Kahlúa, cake mix, pudding mix and oil in a large mixing bowl and mix well. Stir in the chocolate chips. Pour into a bundt pan. Bake at 350 degrees for 45 to 50 minutes or until the cake springs back when lightly touched. Cool in the pan. Invert onto a serving plate and sprinkle with the confectioners' sugar.

Between the Lakes
The Junior League of Saginaw Valley, Saginaw, Michigan

Eat-the-Whole-Thing Chocolate Chip Bundt Cake

Serves 16 to 20

1 (2-layer) package butter-recipe cake mix
1 (6-ounce) package chocolate instant pudding mix
1 cup sour cream
1/2 cup vegetable oil
1/ cup water

4 eggs
2 cups (12 ounces) milk chocolate chips
1 cup confectioners' sugar
1/4 cup evaporated milk

Preheat the oven to 350 degrees. Combine the cake mix, pudding mix, sour cream, oil, water and eggs in a mixing bowl and beat until blended. Stir in the chocolate chips. Spoon the batter into a greased and floured bundt pan and bake for 55 to 60 minutes or until the cake tests done. Invert onto a cake plate and cool for 10 to 15 minutes. Whisk the confectioners' sugar and evaporated milk in a bowl until of a glaze consistency and drizzle over the cake.

Simply Sarasota
Junior League of Sarasota, Sarasota, Florida

Chocolate Kahlúa Cake

Serves 10 to 12

1 (2-layer) package pudding-recipe chocolate
   cake mix
2 cups sour cream
4 eggs

3/4 cup vegetable oil
1/2 cup Kahlúa
1 cup chocolate chips

Combine the cake mix, sour cream and eggs in a bowl and mix well. Stir in the oil and Kahlúa. Fold in the chocolate chips. Spoon into a greased and floured bundt pan. Bake at 350 degrees for 55 to 60 minutes or until the cake tests done. Cool in pan on a wire rack for 10 minutes. Remove to a wire rack to cool completely.

Made in the Shade
Junior League of Greater Fort Lauderdale, Fort Lauderdale, Florida

Kahlúa Cake

1 (2-layer) package yellow cake mix
1 (3.4-ounce) package chocolate instant pudding mix
4 eggs
1 cup vegetable oil
1/3 cup Kahlúa

1/3 cup vodka
1/2 cup sugar
3/4 cup water
1/4 cup Kahlúa
1/2 cup confectioners' sugar

For the cake, preheat the oven to 350 degrees. Combine the cake mix, pudding mix, eggs and oil in a mixer bowl and beat until smooth. Add 1/3 cup Kahlúa, vodka, sugar and water and mix well; batter will be thin. Spoon into a greased and floured bundt pan. Bake for 50 minutes or until a wooden pick inserted in the center comes out clean. Cool in the pan for several minutes. Remove to a serving plate.

For the glaze, mix 1/4 cup Kahlúa and confectioners' sugar in a bowl. Spoon over the warm cake. Let stand until cool.

Apron Strings
Junior League of Little Rock, Little Rock, Arkansas

Hummingbird Cake

CAKE
3 cups flour
2 cups sugar
1 teaspoon salt
1 teaspoon baking soda
1 teaspoon cinnamon

3 eggs, beaten
1 cup vegetable oil
1 1/2 teaspoons vanilla extract
1 (8-ounce) can crushed pineapple
2 cups mashed bananas
2 cups pecans, chopped

CREAM CHEESE FROSTING
16 ounces cream cheese, softened
1 cup (2 sticks) margarine, softened

1 (1-pound) package confectioners' sugar
2 teaspoons vanilla extract

For the cake, preheat the oven to 350 degrees. Mix the flour, sugar, salt, baking soda and cinnamon in a large bowl. Add the eggs and oil and stir just until moistened. Add the vanilla, undrained pineapple, bananas and pecans and mix well. Spoon into 3 greased and floured 9-inch cake pans. Bake for 25 to 30 minutes or until the layers test done. Cool in the pans for 5 minutes. Invert onto wire racks to cool completely.

For the frosting, beat the cream cheese and margarine in a mixing bowl until smooth. Add the confectioners' sugar and beat until fluffy. Beat in the vanilla.

To assemble, spread the frosting between the layers and over the top and side of the cake. Prepare the cake the day before serving to enhance the flavor.

Creating Comfort
Genesis Women's Shelter, Dallas, Texas

RECIPES WORTH SHARING

Cranberry Gingerbread

GINGERBREAD
2 cups fresh cranberries, chopped or ground
2 tablespoons (heaping) flour
1 tablespoon (heaping) sugar
1 cup (2 sticks) butter
1 cup sugar
1 egg

3 tablespoons (heaping) molasses
1 cup buttermilk
2 cups all-purpose flour
1 teaspoon baking soda
1/2 teaspoon each ginger and salt
2 teaspoons cinnamon
3 tablespoons (heaping) sugar

BROWN SUGAR WHIPPED CREAM
1 cup whipping cream
1/3 cup sour cream

1/3 cup brown sugar
1 1/2 teaspoons vanilla extract

To prepare the gingerbread, mix the cranberries, 2 tablespoons flour and 1 tablespoon sugar in a small bowl. Melt the butter in a 9×13-inch baking pan and swirl to coat the sides. Pour the butter into a mixing bowl and combine with 1 cup sugar, the egg and molasses. Beat until smooth. Stir in the buttermilk. Add 2 cups flour, the baking soda, ginger, salt and 1 teaspoon of the cinnamon; beat for 3 minutes. Gently stir in one-half of the cranberry mixture. Pour into prepared pan. Sprinkle with remaining cranberry mixture and pat lightly into the batter. Mix 3 tablespoons sugar and the remaining 1 teaspoon cinnamon in a small bowl; sprinkle over the cranberries. Bake at 350 degrees for 40 to 45 minutes or until the gingerbread tests done. Cut into squares to serve.

To prepare the whipped cream, combine cream, sour cream, brown sugar and vanilla in a mixing bowl. Beat until peaks form. The whipped cream can be prepared a few hours before serving. Spoon over gingerbread.

Be Present At Our Table
Germantown United Methodist Women,
Germantown, Tennessee

The birthing of the charity cookbook is a wonderful story about women who used their ingenuity to redefine a book form to address society's unfinished business. The movement spread like wildfire, with thousands and thousands of titles in every shape and fashion soon to be independently published by women's groups.

Now the story has new chapters, but the message is the same. . . . women transforming communities by using a cookbook to carry a socially conscious message into another's home. The story is still being written today with the evolution of new recipe collections benefiting charitable causes of all descriptions. It's truly a chain reaction that raises millions of dollars annually for nonprofit organizations.

Ellen Rolfes

Tontitown Cream Cake

Serves 12 to 16

1/2 cup vegetable shortening
1 stick of butter
2 cups sugar
5 egg yolks
2 cups flour
1 teaspoon baking soda

1 cup buttermilk
1 teaspoon vanilla extract
1 (7-ounce) can of coconut
1 cup chopped pecans
5 egg whites, stiffly beaten

ICING:
1/2 stick of butter, softened
8 ounces cream cheese, softened

3 3/4 cups powdered sugar
1 teaspoon vanilla extract
Toasted coconut, optional

Cream shortening with butter in a large mixing bowl. Add sugar and beat until mixture is smooth. Add egg yolks and beat well. Combine flour and baking soda and add to butter mixture alternately with buttermilk. Add vanilla extract, coconut and pecans. Fold in egg whites. Place in three 9-inch round greased and floured cake pans and bake at 350 degrees for 25 minutes. Cool layers on a rack before icing the cake.

For the icing, cream the butter and cream cheese. Add powdered sugar and vanilla extract. Mix until smooth. Spread icing between cake layers and on top of cake. Sprinkle top of cake with toasted coconut, if desired.

Add Another Place Setting
Junior League of Northwest Arkansas, Springdale, Arkansas

Potato Mocha Pound Cake

Serves 16

1 tablespoon instant coffee powder
2 tablespoons hot water
1 1/2 cups low-fat milk
2 cups flour
2 cups sugar
1 cup instant potato flakes

4 teaspoons baking powder
1/2 teaspoon salt
1 (4-ounce) package chocolate instant
  pudding mix
1 cup butter, softened
4 eggs

Combine the coffee powder and hot water in a cup, stirring until the coffee powder is dissolved. Mix with the milk in a small bowl. Combine the flour, sugar, potato flakes, baking powder, salt, pudding mix, butter and eggs in a large mixer bowl. Beat at low speed until mixed. Beat in the milk mixture. Beat at medium speed for 4 minutes. Pour into a greased and floured 10-inch bundt pan. Bake at 350 degrees for 50 to 55 minutes or until a wooden pick inserted near the center comes out clean. Cool in the pan for 30 minutes. Invert onto a serving platter. Top with ice cream, Kahlúa or with a chocolate glaze.

Note: Be sure to grease and flour the bundt pan, even if it has a nonstick lining.

Beyond Burlap
Junior League of Boise, Boise, Idaho

Texas Peach Bellini Cake

2 1/2 cups flour
2 1/4 teaspoons baking powder
1/2 teaspoon salt
2 cups sugar
4 eggs

1 cup vegetable oil
1/2 cup champagne
1/2 cup peach schnapps
1 teaspoon almond extract
Peaches and Cream Frosting (below)

Preheat the oven to 350 degrees; butter and flour two 9-inch round cake pans. Sift the flour, baking powder and salt into a medium bowl. Beat the sugar and eggs in the large mixer bowl of an electric mixer at medium speed until well combined. Stir in the oil, champagne, peach schnapps, almond extract and flour mixture. Beat at low speed for 1 minute. Pour the batter into the prepared cake pans.

Bake for 35 to 40 minutes or until a cake tester inserted into the center comes out clean. Cool in the pans on wire racks for 10 minutes. Remove from the pans and let cool completely on the racks.

Place 1 cake player on a serving plate; spread the top with half the Peaches and Cream Frosting. Top with the remaining layer; spread the remaining Peaches and Cream Frosting on the top, leaving the side unfrosted.

PEACHES AND CREAM FROSTING
2 1/4 cups sour cream
2 tablespoons whipping cream

1 teaspoon almond extract
6 cups sliced fresh peaches
1 cup confectioners' sugar

Combine the sour cream, whipping cream, almond extract and peaches in a bowl; mix well. Add the confectioners' sugar and stir until well combined.

A Thyme to Remember
The Dallas County Medical Society Alliance, Dallas, Texas

After the Civil War, women's clubs organized cookbook projects to benefit widows, veterans, and orphans. By 1915, as many as 6,000 community cookbooks had been published in the United States, and women were raising money to fund kindergartens and promote temperance and other political causes.

Raspberry Cordial Cake

6 ounces frozen whole raspberries
1/4 cup raspberry gelatin powder
1 (2-layer) package white cake mix
1 (4-ounce) package vanilla instant pudding mix
3/4 cup plus 2 tablespoons water

1/2 cup canola oil
4 eggs
Raspberry Glaze (below)

Heat the raspberries in a saucepan over low heat until beginning to boil. Stir in the gelatin. Boil for a few minutes. Remove from the heat and let cool. Combine the cake mix, pudding mix, water, oil and eggs in a large bowl. Beat with an electric mixer at low speed for 2 minutes. Scrape the bottom and side of the bowl. Beat at medium speed for 1 minute. Remove 1/2 cup batter and stir into the cooled raspberry mixture. Pour 1/2 of the plain batter into a greased and floured bundt pan. Drizzle 3 tablespoons of the raspberry mixture on top. Swirl with a knife. Add the remaining plain batter. Drizzle the remaining raspberry mixture and swirl with a knife. Bake at 350 degrees for 50 minutes or until a wooden pick inserted in the center comes out clean. Remove to a wire rack and let cool slightly. Poke holes in the top of the cake with a fork. Pour the Raspberry Glaze over the warm cake. Let stand for 15 minutes. Remove to a serving plate. Store in an airtight container in the refrigerator.

RASPBERRY GLAZE
1/2 cup (1 stick) butter
1 cup sugar
1/4 cup water

1/2 teaspoon raspberry gelatin powder
1/4 cup brandy
1/4 cup raspberry schnapps

Mix the butter, sugar and water in a saucepan. Bring to a boil and boil for 3 minutes. Stir in the gelatin and remove from the heat. Let cool slightly and stir in the brandy and raspberry schnapps.

A League of Our Own: From Blue Jeans to Ball Gowns
Rockwall Women's League, Rockwall, Texas

A League of Our Own has united active and past members in a common bond that reflects our organization's commitment to one another and to our community.

Rum Cake

CAKE
1 (2-layer) package yellow cake mix
1 (4-ounce) package vanilla instant pudding mix

4 eggs
1/2 cup canola oil
1 cup dark rum

RUM GLAZE
1/2 cup (1 stick) butter or margarine
1/4 cup water

1 cup sugar
1/2 cup rum

To prepare the cake, combine the cake mix, pudding mix, eggs, oil and rum in a mixing bowl and beat until smooth. Pour into a greased and floured bundt pan or tube pan. Bake at 325 degrees for 1 hour. Cool in the pan for 10 minutes. Invert onto a cake plate to cool completely.

To prepare the glaze, melt the butter in a saucepan. Stir in the water and sugar. Bring to a boil and boil for 5 minutes, stirring constantly. Stir in the rum. Drizzle over the cake.

Great Women, Great Food
Junior League of Kankakee County, Kankakee, Illinois

Crunchy Caramel Apple Pie

Serves 8

1 unbaked (9-inch) deep-dish pie shell
1/4 cup sugar
3 tablespoons flour
1 teaspoon cinnamon
1/8 teaspoon salt
5 1/2 cups sliced peeled apples

1/2 cup packed brown sugar
1/2 cup (1 stick) butter
1/2 cup flour
1/2 cup quick-cooking oats
1/2 cup chopped pecans
1/3 cup caramel or butterscotch ice cream topping

Crimp the edges of the pie shell. Combine the sugar, 3 tablespoons flour, cinnamon and salt in a bowl. Stir in the apples. Spoon into the pie shell. Mix the brown sugar, butter, 1/2 cup flour and oats in a bowl with a pastry blender until crumbly. Sprinkle over the apples. Bake at 375 degrees for 20 to 30 minutes. Cover the pie with foil. Bake for 20 minutes. Uncover the pie. Sprinkle with the pecans and drizzle with the caramel topping. Cool on a wire rack. Serve with ice cream.

Note: This recipes works especially well with Granny Smith or another tart apple.

Once Upon A Time
Junior League of Evansville, Evansville, Illinois

Topsy-Turvy Apple Pie

Serves 8

5 tablespoons butter, divided
1/2 cup pecan halves
1/2 cup light brown sugar, firmly packed
2 (9-inch) unbaked pie crusts
8 medium apples, peeled, cored, and sliced
2 tablespoons lemon juice
1 tablespoon flour

1 cup granulated sugar
1/2 cup dark brown sugar, firmly packed
1 teaspoon cinnamon
1/2 teaspoon nutmeg
1 teaspoon vanilla
1 tablespoon cornstarch

Melt 4 tablespoons butter in 9-inch deep-dish pie plate; tilt and swirl to coat sides. Place pecans on bottom of pie plate in a pattern, rounded side down. Pat light brown sugar evenly over pecans and butter. Cover with one pastry layer. Mix apple slices, lemon juice, flour, granulated sugar, dark brown sugar, cinnamon, nutmeg, vanilla, and cornstarch; spoon into pie plate. Dot with remaining tablespoon butter. Fit top pastry over filling; flute edges, and cut slits in top to vent steam. Moisten the edges slightly with water. Bake at 350 degrees for 45 to 50 minutes. Remove from oven. Cool on a wire rack for 5 to 10 minutes before turning pie out onto a large plate.

The Bess Collection
Junior Service League of Independence, Independence, Missouri

Berry Pie

Serves 8

2 1/2 to 3 cups fresh berries, such as raspberries,
    strawberries, blueberries and blackberries
1 baked pie shell
1 cup mashed berries
1 cup sugar

2 1/2 tablespoons cornstarch
1/2 cup water
1 tablespoon lemon juice
1 tablespoon butter

Place the fresh berries in the pie shell. Cook the mashed berries, sugar, cornstarch and water in a saucepan over medium heat until the sauce is clear, stirring frequently. Add the lemon juice and butter. Stir until the butter is melted. Pour over the berries in the pie shell. Chill, covered, in the refrigerator.

Life is Delicious
Hinsdale Junior Woman's Club, Hinsdale, Illinois

Old-Fashioned Buttermilk Pie

Serves 8 to 10

1/2 cup (1 stick) salted butter, softened
1 2/3 cups sugar
3 eggs
1 teaspoon vanilla extract

1 cup buttermilk
2 tablespoons flour
Dash of freshly ground nutmeg
1 unbaked (9-inch) pie shell

Preheat the oven to 350 degrees. Cream the butter and sugar in a mixing bowl until light and fluffy. Add the eggs and mix well. Add the vanilla, buttermilk, flour and nutmeg and mix well. Pour into the pie shell. Bake for 50 to 55 minutes or until golden brown and a knife inserted near the center comes out clean. Cool on a wire rack before serving.

Creating Comfort
Genesis Women's Shelter, Dallas, Texas

Pear Pie

Serves 6 to 8

1 (29-ounce) can, or 2 (15-ounce) cans pear
   halves, drained
1 baked (9-inch) deep-dish pie shell
1 cup sugar
1/4 cup (1/2 stick) butter, softened

1/4 cup all-purpose flour
2 eggs
1 teaspoon vanilla extract
3 tablespoons minced crystallized ginger (optional)

Preheat the oven to 350 degrees. Spread the drained pears on a paper towel to dry. Arrange the pears pinwheel fashion in the pie shell cut side down. Combine the sugar, butter and flour in a bowl and blend well. Add the eggs and vanilla and beat until light and fluffy. Stir in the crystallized ginger. Pour over the pears, spreading evenly. Bake on the bottom shelf of the oven for 1 hour or until the filling has set. Serve warm with whipped cream.

Note: Do not substitute fresh pears in this quick-and-easy recipe. Can be made ahead and frozen. To freeze, cool baked pie to room temperature and freeze uncovered. When frozen, cover tightly. To serve, defrost and heat to warm.

Tastes, Tales and Traditions
Palo Alto Auxiliary for Children, Palo Alto, California

Raspberry Cream Pie

Serves 6

1 cup sugar
1/3 cup flour
2 large eggs, lightly beaten
1 1/3 cups sour cream
1 teaspoon vanilla extract
3 cups fresh raspberries or frozen
   raspberries, thawed

1 unbaked (9-inch) pie shell
1/3 cup flour
1/3 cup packed brown sugar
1/3 cup chopped pecans
3 tablespoons butter, softened

GARNISH
Whipped cream
Fresh raspberries

Combine 1 cup sugar, 1/3 cup flour, eggs, sour cream and vanilla in a large bowl and mix well. Fold in the raspberries gradually. Spoon into the pie shell. Bake a 400 degrees for 30 to 35 minutes or until the center is set. Mix 1/3 cup flour, brown sugar, pecans and butter in a small bowl. Sprinkle over the hot pie. Bake for 10 minutes longer or until golden brown. Cool on a wire rack. Garnish with whipped cream and fresh raspberries.

Savor the Moment
Junior League of Boca Raton, Boca Raton, Florida

Sweet Potato Pie

Serves 6 to 8

1 pound unpeeled sweet potatoes
1/2 cup (1 stick) butter, softened
3/4 cup sugar
1/4 cup cream
2 eggs

1 tablespoon vanilla extract
1/2 teaspoon nutmeg
1/2 teaspoon cinnamon
1 unbaked (9-inch) pie shell

Scrub the sweet potatoes. Boil in water to cover in a large saucepan until tender; drain. Let cool until cool enough to handle. Peel the sweet potatoes. Place in a mixing bowl and break into large chunks with a spoon. Add the butter and beat with an electric mixer until blended. Add the sugar, cream, eggs, vanilla, nutmeg and cinnamon. Beat at medium speed until smooth. Pour into the pie shell. Bake at 350 degrees for 55 to 60 minutes or until a knife inserted in the center comes out clean.

Be Present At Our Table
Germantown United Methodist Women, Germantown, Tennessee

Chocolate Chip Cookie Pie

Serves 8

2 eggs
1/2 cup flour
1/2 cup sugar
1/2 cup packed brown sugar

1/2 cup (1 stick) butter, softened
1 cup semisweet chocolate chips
1 cup pecans, chopped
1 unbaked (9-inch) pie shell

Beat the eggs in a mixing bowl at high speed for 3 minutes or until frothy. Add the flour, sugar and brown sugar and beat until blended. Beat in the butter. Stir in the chocolate chips and pecans. Spoon the chocolate mixture into the pie shell. Bake at 325 degrees for 55 to 60 minutes or until the center is set. Let stand until cool.

Cooking by the Bootstraps
Junior Welfare League of Enid, Enid, Oklahoma

Fudge Pie

Serves 6 to 8

2 (1-ounce) squares unsweetened chocolate, melted
1 stick butter, melted
2 eggs
1/4 cup flour

1 cup sugar
1 teaspoon vanilla
1/2 cup chopped pecans

Combine chocolate, butter and eggs. Stir until creamy. Add flour, sugar, vanilla and pecans. Pour ingredients into a buttered pie plate. Bake at 375 degrees for 25 minutes. Serve warm with vanilla or mocha ice cream or serve cool with whipped cream. May also be baked in a pie shell.

Magic
Junior League of Birmingham, Inc., Birmingham, Alabama

Bodacious Brownies, AKA "Big Booty Brownies"

Makes 1 dozen

1 (2-layer) package chocolate cake mix
2 cups chopped walnuts
1 egg
1/2 cup (1 stick) butter, melted

8 ounces cream cheese, softened
3 eggs
1 (1-pound) package confectioners' sugar

Mix the cake mix, walnuts, 1 egg and butter in a bowl. (The batter will be stiff.) Press into a buttered 9×13-inch baking pan. Beat the cream cheese, 3 eggs and the confectioners' sugar in a mixing bowl until smooth. Spread in the prepared pan. Bake at 350 degrees for 45 minutes. Cool in the pan before serving.

Roux To Do
Junior League of Greater Covington, Covington, Louisiana

Never Fail Brownies

Makes 2 dozen

1 cup vegetable oil
2 cups sugar
4 large eggs
1 cup all-purpose flour

2/3 cup unsweetened cocoa
1/2 teaspoon salt
1 teaspoon vanilla extract
1 cup chopped nuts

Preheat oven to 350 degrees. In a large bowl, combine all ingredients except nuts and mix well. Fold in nuts (or reserve to sprinkle on top of batter before baking). Spread in greased 13×9×2-inch baking dish. Bake 25 minutes. (Do not overbake.)

Very Virginia
The Junior League of Hampton Roads, Hampton Roads, Virginia

Oatmeal Brownies

OAT CRUST
1 cup quick-cooking oats
1/2 cup all-purpose flour
1/2 cup packed brown sugar

1/4 teaspoon baking soda
1/4 teaspoon salt
1/2 cup (1 stick) butter, melted

BROWNIES
1 cup sugar
3/4 cup all-purpose flour
1/3 cup butter, melted

2 ounces unsweetened chocolate, melted
2 eggs
1 teaspoon vanilla extract

COCOA ICING
1 3/4 cups confectioners' sugar
1/4 cup (1/2 stick) butter, softened

1/4 cup baking cocoa
2 tablespoons milk
1 teaspoon vanilla extract

For the crust, preheat the oven to 350 degrees. Combine the oats, flour, brown sugar, baking soda and salt in a bowl and mix well. Stir in the butter. Spread the oat mixture over the bottom of a greased 9×9-inch baking pan and bake for 10 minutes. Maintain the oven temperature.

For the brownies, combine the sugar, flour, butter, chocolate, eggs and vanilla in a mixing bowl and beat until blended. Spread the chocolate mixture over the baked layer and bake for 25 minutes. Cool in the pan on a wire rack.

For the icing, combine the confectioners' sugar, butter, baking cocoa, milk and vanilla in a bowl and stir until of a spreading consistency. Spread over the top of the cooled brownies. Let stand until set and cut into bars.

Tables of Content
Junior League of Birmingham, Inc., Birmingham, Alabama

*A*fter the devastation of Louisiana by Hurricane Katrina in August 2005, the Junior League of Greater Covington was trying to recover like everyone else in this area. Our recipe for Fais Do-Do Drunken Shrimp found its way to the *Today Show*, thanks to the 2005 cookbook chairpersons. When Willard Scott highlighted the recipe as one of his favorites, *Roux to Do* sales went through the roof and in some way brought a little hope and encouragement to the League to help the recovery and rebuilding efforts.

The Junior League of Greater Covington partnered with the American Red Cross to assist in recovery efforts in St. Tammany Parish. Since 1977, our league has donated approximately $1,000,000 and more than 250,000 volunteer hours to our community through various projects focusing on women and children.

Shelley Attales Roberts
Junior League of Greater Covington, Covington, Louisiana

Saucepan Brownies

1/2 cup all-purpose flour
1 teaspoon baking powder
1/8 teaspoon salt
2 ounces unsweetened chocolate, chopped
1/2 cup (1 stick) butter

1 cup sugar
2 eggs, lightly beaten
1/2 teaspoon vanilla extract
1/2 cup chopped pecans (optional)

Preheat the oven to 350 degrees. Mix the flour, baking powder and salt together. Melt the chocolate and butter in a saucepan over medium-low heat, stirring occasionally. Remove from the heat and stir in the flour mixture, sugar, eggs, vanilla and pecans. Spoon the batter into a greased and floured 8×8-inch baking pan and bake for 25 minutes. Cool in the pan on a wire rack and cut into bars.

Tables of Content
Junior League of Birmingham, Inc., Birmingham, Alabama

Turtle Brownies

2 1/4 cups all-purpose flour, sifted
2 1/2 cups sugar
1 teaspoon salt
1 1/2 cups (3 sticks) unsalted butter, softened
3 cups (18 ounces) chocolate chips

6 eggs, at room temperature
1 tablespoon vanilla
1 1/2 cups walnuts, chopped
1 jar caramel sauce

Lightly butter and flour a 9×13-inch baking dish and line with waxed paper. Mix the flour, sugar and salt with a fork in a bowl. Place the butter and chocolate chips in a microwave-safe bowl. Microwave on High at 30-second intervals until melted, stirring after each interval. Whisk in the eggs one at a time. Stir in the flour mixture and vanilla. Fold in the walnuts. Pour into the prepared baking dish and spread evenly. Bake at 350 degrees for 30 to 45 minutes or until a wooden pick inserted in the center comes out almost completely clean. Cool completely in the pan on a wire rack.

To serve, cut into squares and place on a dessert plate. Drizzle with the caramel sauce.

Starfish Café: Changing Lives One Recipe at a Time . . .
Union Mission/Starfish Café, Savannah, Georgia

Blondies with Pecans and Chocolate Chips

Makes 2 dozen

2 cups flour
1 teaspoon baking powder
3/4 teaspoon salt
1/4 teaspoon baking soda
10 tablespoons unsalted butter

2 cups packed light brown sugar
2 eggs
2 teaspoons vanilla extract
3/4 cup (4 1/2 ounces) semisweet chocolate chips
3/4 cup chopped pecans (about 3 ounces)

Mix the flour, baking powder, salt and baking soda in a medium bowl. Melt the butter in a large saucepan over low heat. Remove from the heat. Add the brown sugar and whisk to blend. Whisk in the eggs and vanilla. Stir in the flour mixture gradually. The batter will be thick. Spread the batter into a buttered and floured 9×13-inch pan. Sprinkle with the chocolate chips and pecans. Bake at 350 degrees for 25 minutes or until a tester inserted into the center comes out with moist crumbs attached. Cool in the pan on a wire rack. Cut into squares.

Down Home: Treasured Recipes from our House to Yours
West Point Junior Auxiliary, West Point, Mississippi

No-Bake Chocolate Bars

Makes 7 to 8 dozen bars

2 cups fine graham cracker crumbs
2 1/4 cups confectioners' sugar
1 cup (2 sticks) butter, melted
1 (18-ounce) jar extra-crunchy peanut butter

1 1/2 cups (9 ounces) semisweet chocolate morsels
1 1/2 cups (9 ounces) white chocolate morsels
1/2 cup (1 stick) butter

Mix the graham cracker crumbs and confectioners' sugar in a bowl. Combine 1 cup melted butter and the peanut butter in a bowl and mix until creamy. Add the crumb mixture and mix well. Press the crumb mixture over the bottom of a greased 11×17-inch baking sheet with sides. Heat the chocolate morsels, white chocolate morsels and 1/2 cup butter in a saucepan over low heat until blended, stirring occasionally. Pour the chocolate mixture over the prepared layer and chill for 1 hour or until set. Cut into bars.

Tables of Content
Junior League of Birmingham, Inc., Birmingham, Alabama

Chocolate Caramel Bars

Makes 6 dozen small bars

1 (14-ounce) bag caramels
2/3 cup evaporated milk, divided
1 (18 1/2-ounce) package regular German Chocolate cake mix or Duncan Hines Swiss Chocolate Deluxe II cake mix

1 1/2 sticks butter or margarine, melted
1 (6-ounce) package semi-sweet chocolate chips
1 cup chopped nuts

Preheat oven to 350 degrees. In top of double boiler over medium heat, combine caramels and 1/3 cup of evaporated milk, stirring constantly until melted and smooth. Remove from heat. Combine cake mix, melted butter, and remaining milk in mixer until well blended. Press half of cake mixture into a greased 9×13-inch pan. Bake 6 minutes. Sprinkle chocolate chips and nuts over crust. Pour caramel mixture evenly over chips and nuts. Dollop rest of cake mixture over caramel. Return to oven and bake another 15 to 18 minutes. Cool, then chill 30 minutes. Cut into small bars. Store at room temperature or freeze.

Magic
Junior League of Birmingham, Inc., Birmingham, Alabama

Key Lime Bars

Makes 2 dozen bars

1 cup flour
1/4 cup confectioners' sugar
1/2 cup butter, softened
2 eggs, lightly beaten

1 cup sugar
2 tablespoons flour
1/3 cup Key lime juice
2 tablespoons sifted confectioners' sugar

Combine 1 cup flour and 1/4 cup confectioners' sugar in a bowl and mix well. Add the butter, stirring or processing in a food processor until the mixture forms a ball. Pat the dough with lightly floured fingers over the bottom of a greased 8×8-inch baking pan. Bake at 350 degrees for 15 to 20 minutes.

Mix the eggs and sugar in a bowl. Stir in 2 tablespoons flour. Add the Key lime juice and mix well. Spread over the warm baked layer. Bake for 20 to 25 minutes. Cool in the pan on a wire rack. Sprinkle with 2 tablespoons sifted confectioners' sugar. Cut into bars.

Note: If Key lime juice is not available, use regular lime juice.

Made in the Shade
Junior League of Greater Fort Lauderdale, Fort Lauderdale, Florida

Lemon Bars

CRUST
1 cup (2 sticks) unsalted butter
$^1\!/_4$ teaspoon salt
$^1\!/_2$ cup confectioners' sugar
2 cups flour, sifted

FILLING
4 eggs, lightly beaten
$^1\!/_4$ cup fresh lemon juice
2 cups sugar
$^1\!/_4$ cup flour
Grated zest of 1 lemon
Confectioners' sugar for sprinkling

For the crust, preheat the oven to 350 degrees. Process the butter, salt, confectioners' sugar and flour $^1\!/_2$ at a time in a food processor. Press into a greased 9×13-inch baking dish with a fork. Bake for 20 to 30 minutes or until golden brown.

For the filling and assembly, reduce the oven temperature to 325 degrees. Combine the eggs, lemon juice, sugar, flour and lemon zest in a bowl and mix well by hand. Pour the filling over the prepared crust. Bake for 20 to 30 minutes or until firm. Let stand until cool and sprinkle with confectioners' sugar. Cut into bars and store in the refrigerator. This recipe freezes well.

Creating Comfort
Genesis Women's Shelter, Dallas, Texas

Mexican-Style Pecan Chocolate Squares

Makes 32 squares

CRUST
3/4 cup (1 1/2 sticks) chilled unsalted butter,
     cut into 1/2-inch pieces
2 cups all-purpose flour
1/2 cup packed light brown sugar

2 teaspoons ground cinnamon
1/2 teaspoon salt
2 ounces grated bittersweet chocolate
     (scant 1/2 cup)

TOPPING
1/2 cup (1 stick) unsalted butter
1 cup packed dark brown sugar
2 tablespoons heavy cream or fat-free
     half-and-half

1/3 cup honey
1/2 teaspoon salt
3 cups (10 ounces) toasted pecans, coarsely
     chopped in a food processor

For the crust, combine the butter, flour, brown sugar, cinnamon and salt in a food processor. Pulse about 20 times or until well mixed. Pat into a nonstick 9×9-inch baking pan. Bake at 350 degrees for 25 minutes or until firm and light brown. Sprinkle the chocolate evenly over the baked crust and set aside.

For the topping, melt the butter in a saucepan. Stir in the brown sugar, cream, honey and salt. Simmer for 1 minute, stirring occasionally. Stir in the pecans. Pour over the crust and spread evenly. Bake at 350 degrees for 16 to 20 minutes or until bubbly. Remove to a wire rack to cool completely. Cut into 1-inch squares. Tightly covered bars will keep for 5 days or they may be frozen.

Recipes of Note
Greensboro Symphony Guild, Greensboro, North Carolina

With recipes as diverse as the Greensboro Symphony Guild's membership itself, our cookbook, *Recipes of Note*, represents a variety of cooking styles from gourmet to down-home fare and provides the gift of continued support for our region's crown jewel—the Greensboro Symphony Orchestra.

Paul's Pumpkin Bars

4 eggs
1 2/3 cups sugar
1 cup cooking oil
1 (16-ounce) can pumpkin
2 cups flour

2 teaspoons baking powder
2 teaspoons cinnamon
1 teaspoon salt
1 teaspoon baking soda

FROSTING
1 (3-ounce) package softened cream cheese
1/2 cup margarine, softened

1 teaspoon vanilla
2 cups sifted confectioners' sugar

Beat eggs, sugar, oil and pumpkin in bowl until light and fluffy. Combine flour, baking powder, cinnamon, salt, and soda. Add to pumpkin mixture, and mix thoroughly. Spread batter in an ungreased 15×10×1-inch jelly roll pan. Bake, cool, and frost.

FROSTING
Cream cheese and margarine. Stir in vanilla. Slowly add sugar, beating until mixture is smooth. Frost cooled bars.

Applehood & Motherpie
Junior League of Rochester, Inc., Rochester, New York

Red Raspberry and White Bars

1 cup butter
1 (10-ounce) package plus 1 cup vanilla milk chips
4 eggs
1 cup sugar

2 cups flour
1 1/2 teaspoons almond extract
1 cup raspberry jam or spreadable fruit
1/2 cup sliced almonds, toasted

Heat the butter in a small saucepan over low heat until melted. Remove from heat. Add the package of vanilla milk chips; do not stir. Beat the eggs in a mixer bowl until foamy. Beat in the sugar gradually at high speed until mixture is pale yellow. Add the flour and mix well. Stir in the butter mixture. Stir in the almond extract. Spread half the batter in a greased and floured 9×13-inch baking pan.

Bake in a preheated 325-degree oven for 15 to 20 minutes or until golden brown. Melt the jam in a saucepan over low heat. Spread over the warm baked layer. Stir the remaining chips into the remaining batter. Drop by teaspoonfuls over the jam. Sprinkle with almonds. Bake for 25 to 30 minutes or until a wooden pick inserted in the center comes out clean. Cool completely. Cut into bars.

If You Can't Stand the Heat, Get Out of the Kitchen
Junior Service League of Independence, Independence, Missouri

Milk Chocolate Macadamia Nut Cookies

Makes 3 to 5 dozen cookies

1 cup (2 sticks) unsalted butter, softened
1 cup packed brown sugar
1 cup sugar
2 eggs
2 teaspoons vanilla extract

2 1/2 cups flour
1 teaspoon baking soda
1 teaspoon salt
8 ounces milk chocolate, coarsely chopped
1 cup coarsely chopped macadamia nuts

Preheat the oven to 325 degrees. Cream the butter, brown sugar and sugar in a large bowl until light and fluffy. Add the eggs and vanilla and mix well. Combine the flour, baking soda and salt in a bowl. Add to the creamed mixture and mix well. Stir in the chocolate and macadamia nuts. Drop by 1/4 cups 2 inches apart onto a parchment paper-lined cookie sheet. Bake for 17 to 18 minutes or until light brown and set in the center. Remove to a wire rack to cool completely.

You may prepare the cookie dough in advance and refrigerate for several hours. Spoon 1/4 cups of the dough in single layers into resealable freezer bags and freeze until ready to bake. To bake, increase the baking time by 2 to 3 minutes.

For a chocolate and white chocolate chunk version, add 3 ounces melted semisweet chocolate to the creamed mixture and 1/4 cup cocoa to the dry ingredients and substitute 8 ounces semisweet chocolate chunks for the milk chocolate and 8 ounces chopped white chocolate for the macadamia nuts.

Every Day Feasts
The Junior League of Tampa, Tampa, Florida

Chocolate Chocolate Chip Cookies

Makes 4 dozen cookies

1 cup (2 sticks) butter, softened
1 1/2 cups sugar
2 eggs
1 teaspoon vanilla
1 tablespoon coffee-flavored liqueur

2 cups flour
2/3 cup baking cocoa
1/4 teaspoon baking soda
1/2 teaspoon salt
2 cups chocolate chips

Preheat oven to 350 degrees. Cream butter, sugar, eggs, vanilla and liqueur. Combine flour, baking cocoa, baking soda and salt. Blend into creamed mixture. Add chips. Drop by teaspoonfuls 2 inches apart on baking sheets. Bake 8 minutes. Leave on sheets to cool 2 minutes before removing.

An Occasion to Gather
Junior League of Milwaukee, Milwaukee, Wisconsin

Chocolate Truffle Cookies

1/2 cup all-purpose flour
1/2 teaspoon baking powder
1/4 cup (1/2 stick) unsalted butter
1 cup (6 ounces) semisweet chocolate chips
4 ounces unsweetened chocolate
4 eggs

1 1/2 cups sugar
1 teaspoon vanilla extract
4 teaspoons freeze-dried coffee granules
4 1/2 cups ground walnuts
1 cup (6 ounces) semisweet chocolate chips

Mix the flour and baking powder together. Combine the butter and 1 cup chocolate chips in the top of a double boiler. Cook over simmering water until melted and smooth, stirring occasionally. Add the unsweetened chocolate. Cook until melted; do not stir. Remove from the heat. Combine the eggs, sugar, vanilla and coffee granules in a bowl and beat well.

Stir in the melted chocolate mixture gradually. Add the dry ingredients and mix well. Stir in the walnuts and 1 cup chocolate chips. Shape by teaspoonfuls into ovals on a greased cookie sheet. Bake at 350 degrees for 5 minutes or until the tops are slightly cracked. Cool on the cookie sheet for 5 minutes. Remove to a wire rack to cool completely.

Popovers to Panache
The Village Club, Bloomfield Hills, Michigan

Hillary Clinton's Cookies

1 cup shortening
1/2 cup sugar
1 cup packed light brown sugar
1 teaspoon vanilla extract
2 eggs

1 1/2 cups flour
1 teaspoon baking soda
1 teaspoon salt
2 cups rolled oats
2 cups semisweet chocolate chips

Preheat the oven to 350 degrees. Cream the shortening, sugar, brown sugar and vanilla in a large bowl until light and fluffy. Add the eggs and beat until smooth. Mix the flour, baking soda and salt together. Add to the creamed mixture gradually and mix well. Stir in the oats and chocolate chips. Drop by rounded teaspoonfuls onto greased cookie sheets. Bake for 8 to 10 minutes or until golden brown. Cool on the cookie sheets for 2 minutes. Remove to a wire rack to cool completely.

Apron Strings
Junior League of Little Rock, Little Rock, Arkansas

Chocolate-Tipped Butter Cookies

Makes 4 dozen cookies

1 cup butter, softened
1/2 cup confectioners' sugar, sifted
1 teaspoon vanilla extract
2 cups flour

1 cup semisweet chocolate chips
1 tablespoon shortening
1/2 cup finely chopped pecans

Cream the butter in a mixer bowl. Add the confectioners' sugar gradually, beating until light and fluffy. Add the vanilla. Add the flour gradually, beating constantly. Chill, covered, for 1 to 2 hours. Shape the dough into 1/2×2-inch logs. Place on a nonstick cookie sheet. Flatten 3/4 of each log lengthwise with the tines of a fork. Bake at 350 degrees for 12 to 14 minutes or until golden brown. Remove to wire racks to cool. Melt the chocolate chips and shortening in a saucepan over low heat, stirring constantly. Dip the unflattened tips of the cookies in the chocolate mixture and roll the coated tips in the pecans. Place on a surface lined with waxed paper. Let stand until the chocolate is firm.

A Sunsational Encore
Junior League of Greater Orlando, Orlando, Florida

White Chocolate Granola Cookies

Makes 3 dozen cookies

1/2 cup chopped dried apricots
1 cup chopped dried cherries
1 cup hot water
2 cups all-purpose flour
3/4 teaspoon baking soda
3/4 teaspoon cinnamon
1 cup (2 sticks) butter, at room temperature

2 1/4 cups packed brown sugar
2/3 cup granulated sugar
2 eggs
1 1/2 teaspoons vanilla extract
2 1/4 cups old-fashioned oats
2 cups white chocolate chunks
1 cup crumbled granola

Place the apricots and cherries in a medium bowl. Cover with hot water and let stand for 15 minutes; drain. Whisk the flour, baking soda and cinnamon together. Cream the butter, brown sugar and granulated sugar in a mixing bowl until light and fluffy. Beat in the eggs and vanilla. Add the dry ingredients and mix well. Stir in the oats, chocolate chunks, granola, apricots and cherries. Drop by spoonfuls onto a cookie sheet. Bake at 325 degrees for 15 minutes. Remove to a wire rack to cool.

Life is Delicious
Hinsdale Junior Woman's Club, Hinsdale, Illinois

Ginger Cookies

4 cups White Lily flour
4 teaspoons baking soda
2 teaspoons cinnamon
1 teaspoon ginger
1 teaspoon ground cloves

1 ½ cups (3 sticks) margarine
½ cup molasses
2 cups sugar
2 eggs
Sugar

Sift the flour, baking soda, cinnamon, ginger and cloves together. Melt the margarine in a saucepan and combine with the molasses, 2 cups sugar and eggs in a mixing bowl; beat until smooth. Add the sifted dry ingredients and mix well to form a dough. Chill, covered, for several hours. Shape the dough into small balls and roll in additional sugar. Place on cookie sheets and bake at 350 degrees for 8 to 10 minutes or until firm and golden brown. Cool on the cookie sheets for 5 minutes and remove to wire racks to cool completely. You may increase the recipe, shaping the chilled dough into a roll 1 inch in diameter. Cut into 3/4-inch pieces, dip the cut side into the sugar and bake as above.

Note: A recipe rumored to have come from the kitchen of the boyhood home of General Robert E. Lee.

Notably Nashville
Junior League of Nashville, Nashville, Tennessee

Soft Gingersnap Cookies

5 cups flour, sifted
4 teaspoons baking soda
4 teaspoons cinnamon
2 teaspoons ground cloves
2 teaspoons ginger

2 cups packed brown sugar
1 ½ cups (3 sticks) butter, softened
½ cup dark molasses
2 eggs
Sugar to taste

Mix the flour, baking soda, cinnamon, cloves and ginger in a bowl. Beat the brown sugar, butter, molasses and eggs in a mixing bowl until light and fluffy. Add the flour mixture to the creamed mixture gradually, beating constantly until blended. Shape the dough into 1-inch balls and roll in sugar. Arrange the balls on a cookie sheet. Bake at 350 degrees for 10 minutes. Cool on the cookie sheet for 2 minutes. Remove to a wire rack to cool completely.

Note: To easily measure molasses, honey or syrup, dip the measuring cup or spoon in hot water, and brush with oil or spray with nonstick cooking spray before measuring the ingredient.

An Occasion to Gather
Junior League of Milwaukee, Inc., Milwaukee, Wisconsin

Lemon Gingersnaps

Cookies

4 cups all-purpose flour

2 teaspoons baking soda

1 teaspoon ground cinnamon

1 teaspoon ground cloves

1 teaspoon ground ginger

1 1/2 cups shortening or butter, softened

2 cups sugar

1/2 cup molasses

2 eggs, beaten

1/2 cup sugar

Lemon Glaze

1 (1-pound) package confectioners' sugar

1/3 cup fresh lemon juice

2 teaspoons grated lemon zest (about 1 large lemon)

For the cookies, preheat the oven to 375 degrees. Mix the flour, baking soda, cinnamon, cloves and ginger together. Beat the shortening and 2 cups sugar in a mixing bowl at medium speed until light and fluffy. Add the molasses and eggs to the creamed mixture and beat until smooth. Add the flour mixture and beat until blended.

Shape the dough into 1-inch balls and coat with 1/2 cup sugar. Arrange the balls on a greased cookie sheet and flatten slightly with the bottom of a glass. Bake for 8 to 10 minutes or until golden brown. Cool on the cookie sheet for 2 minutes and remove to a wire rack.

For the glaze, combine the confectioners' sugar, lemon juice and lemon zest in a bowl and mix until smooth. Spread the glaze over the slightly warm cookies. Let stand until cool and store in an airtight container.

Tables of Content

Junior League of Birmingham, Inc., Birmingham, Alabama

Lemon Sour Cream Cookies

Makes 4 dozen cookies

1/2 cup butter
1/3 cup shortening
1 cup sugar
3/4 teaspoon baking powder
1/2 teaspoon mace
1/4 teaspoon baking soda

Dash of salt
1/3 cup sour cream
1 egg
1 teaspoon vanilla extract
2 1/2 cups flour
2 teaspoons finely shredded lemon peel

Beat the butter and shortening at medium to high speed in a large mixer bowl for 30 seconds. Add the sugar, baking powder, mace, baking soda and salt and beat well, scraping the side of the bowl occasionally. Beat in the sour cream, egg and vanilla. Beat in as much flour as possible. Stir in the remaining flour and lemon peel using a wooden spoon. Divide the dough into 2 equal portions. Chill, covered, for 1 to 2 hours or until the dough is easy to handle. Roll each portion 1/8 to 1/4 inch thick on a floured surface. Cut into desired shapes with floured 2- to 2 1/2-inch cookie cutters. Place 1/2 inch apart on ungreased cookie sheets. Bake at 375 degrees for 7 to 8 minutes or until the edges are firm. Cool on wire racks. Decorate as desired.

Note: Do not substitute margarine for butter in this recipe.

A Sunsational Encore
Junior League of Greater Orlando, Orlando, Florida

Macaroons

Makes 25 cookies

2 eggs
2/3 cup sugar
4 or 5 tablespoons all-purpose flour

1/2 teaspoon almond extract or vanilla extract
8 ounces flaked coconut

Beat the eggs lightly in a mixing bowl. Add the sugar, flour and almond extract and blend until smooth. Add the coconut and mix well. Drop by spoonfuls onto a well-greased cookie sheet. Bake at 350 degrees for 12 minutes or until light brown. Remove immediately to a wire rack to cook completely. Store in an airtight container.

Note: If the cookies cool on the cookie sheet they will stick.

Shall We Gather
Trinity Episcopal Church, Wetumpka, Alabama

Crispy Oat Cookies

Makes 10 dozen cookies

1 cup (2 sticks) butter, softened
1 cup sugar
1 cup packed brown sugar
1 egg
1 cup vegetable oil
1 teaspoon vanilla extract
3 1/2 cups flour

1 teaspoon baking soda
1/2 teaspoon salt
1 cup rolled oats
1 cup cornflakes, crushed
1/2 cup flaked coconut
1/2 cup pecans, chopped

Cream the butter in a large mixing bowl until light and fluffy. Beat in the sugar and brown sugar until blended. Beat in the egg. Add the oil and vanilla and beat to mix well. Mix the flour, baking soda and salt in a bowl. Add to the butter mixture and stir to mix well. Stir in the oats, cornflakes, coconut and pecans. Shape into 1-inch balls and place on ungreased cookie sheets. Flatten with a fork. Bake at 325 degrees for 15 minutes. Remove the cookies to a wire rack to cool.

For Such A Time As This: A Cookbook
Park Cities Baptist Church, Dallas, Texas

Santa Fe Chief Sugar Cookies

Makes 130 to 150 cookies

4 1/4 cups sifted flour
1 teaspoon baking soda
1 teaspoon cream of tartar
1/2 teaspoon salt
1 cup (2 sticks) butter, softened
1 cup sugar

2 eggs, beaten
1 teaspoon vanilla extract
1 cup confectioners' sugar, sifted
1 cup vegetable oil
Sugar to taste

Sift the flour, baking soda, cream of tartar and salt into a bowl and mix well. Beat the butter and 1 cup sugar in a mixing bowl until light and fluffy. Beat in the eggs and vanilla until blended. Add the confectioners' sugar 1 tablespoon at a time, mixing well after each addition. Add the oil gradually and beat until blended. Beat in the flour mixture.

Shape the dough into 1-inch balls. Roll in sugar to taste. Arrange the balls 2 inches apart on an ungreased cookie sheet. Flatten the balls to 1/4 inch thick with a glass dipped in sugar. Bake at 375 degrees for 10 to 12 minutes or until light brown. Cool on cookie sheet for 2 minutes. Remove to a wire rack to cool completely. Store in an airtight container. May store, covered, in the refrigerator for several weeks. Do not freeze.

A Taste of Enchantment
Junior League of Albuquerque, Albuquerque, New Mexico

Desserts

"I received my copy of *Stir Ups* by the Junior Welfare League of Enid, Oklahoma, when I got married. I used it occasionally, but mostly it served as a fond memory of time shared in the kitchen with my mom and grandma. When *Cooking by the Bootstraps* came out, I knew I wanted to add it to my collection. This was not my mom's cookbook. Instead, it was fresh and exciting, created by my contemporaries in my hometown.

When I later joined the Junior Women's League of Enid, I felt this would be a way for me to give back to the community that raised me. It would also be a way for me to grow.

Lucky for me, I was assigned to the cookbook office. I served as packer, cookbook co-chair, chair, and cookbook office steering. These jobs challenged me to dust off skills that I once used and inspired me to embrace other talents I didn't even know I had. Tackling a project, setting deadlines, and meeting them have given me the strength to raise my family according to my rules, not the societal norm. Meeting new people and going new places have fueled my sense of adventure. Watching those behind me learn and grow in their roles has given me great joy. All of these things have brought peace to my life and those around me.

The cookbook office is not one of the most visible areas in our League. In highlighting community involvement, other committees get the spotlight. However, the money raised by the cookbooks is used to support these other committees. Simply put, without our support, our community presence would be curtailed. I am proud to serve my League and my community by being part of the JWL cookbook office. Yes, the hours are long and the praise is sometimes scarce, but the rewards are many!"

Melissa Atwood
Junior Welfare League of Enid, Enid, Oklahoma

Almond Torte

3/4 cup (1 1/2 sticks) butter, softened
1 1/2 cups sugar
2 eggs
1 1/2 cups all-purpose flour

2 teaspoons almond extract
Pinch of salt
1/2 cup sliced almonds
2 tablespoons sugar

Beat the butter, 1 1/2 cups sugar and the eggs in a bowl until light and fluffy. Beat in the flour, almond extract and salt. Pour into a greased 9- or 10-inch springform pan and smooth the top of the batter. Sprinkle with the almonds and 2 tablespoons sugar. Bake at 350 degrees for 30 to 40 minutes or until golden brown. Remove to a wire rack to cool completely. Loosen from the side of the pan with a sharp knife and remove the side. Cut into small wedges and serve. Drizzle with chocolate sauce and top with red raspberries. Use colored sugar instead of plain sugar on the top for holidays and special occasions.

Recipes of Note
Greensboro Symphony Guild, Greensboro, North Carolina

Chocolate Torte

2 cups (12 ounces) chocolate chips
1 cup (2 sticks) butter
5 eggs

1 1/4 cups sugar
5 tablespoons all-purpose flour
1 1/2 teaspoons baking powder

Preheat the oven to 325 degrees. Melt the chocolate chips with the butter in a saucepan, stirring to blend well. Let stand until cool. Beat the eggs with the sugar, flour and baking powder in a mixing bowl. Add the chocolate mixture and mix well. Spread evenly in a buttered and floured cake pan. Bake for 30 minutes. Cover with foil and bake for 10 minutes longer or until the cake tests done but is still very moist. Chill in the refrigerator. Serve with ice cream and warm chocolate sauce.

Note: You may frost with your favorite chocolate frosting and garnish with almonds.

The Bells Are Ringing: A Call to Table
Mission San Juan Capistrano Women's Guild, San Juan Capistrano, California

Espresso Chocolate Torte

2 1/2 cups (5 sticks) unsalted butter, cut into pieces
2 1/4 cups sugar
3 cups (18 ounces) semisweet chocolate chips
1 cup plus 2 tablespoons strong brewed coffee

1/4 teaspoon vanilla extract
9 eggs, beaten
Whipped cream

Combine the butter, sugar, chocolate chips, coffee and vanilla in a 3-quart saucepan. Cook until the chocolate is melted and the mixture is very hot, stirring constantly. Add to the eggs gradually, beating constantly until combined. Pour into a large greased springform pan. Bake at 250 degrees for 2 hours. Refrigerate, covered, until the cake is set. Remove the side of the springform pan. Let stand until room temperature. Serve with whipped cream.

Shall We Gather

Trinity Episcopal Church, Wetumpka, Alabama

Huguenot Torte

4 eggs
3 cups sugar
8 tablespoons flour
5 teaspoons baking powder

1/2 teaspoon salt
2 cups chopped tart cooking apples
2 cups chopped pecans or walnuts
2 teaspoons vanilla

Beat whole eggs in electric mixer or with rotary beater until very frothy and lemon-colored. Add other ingredients in above order. Pour into two well-buttered baking pans about 8 by 12 inches. Bake in 325-degree oven about 45 minutes or until crusty and brown. To serve, scoop up with pancake turner (keeping crusty part on top), pile on large plate and cover with whipped cream and a sprinkling of the chopped nuts, or make 16 individual servings.

Charleston Receipts

Junior League of Charleston, Charleston, South Carolina

Fruit Tart

PASTRY
3/4 cup (1 1/2 sticks) butter, softened

1/2 cup confectioners' sugar
1 1/2 cups flour

CREAMY FILLING
10 ounces (1 2/3 cups) white chocolate chips or
    vanilla chips

1/4 cup heavy cream
8 ounces cream cheese, softened

TOPPING
Sliced bananas, strawberries, blueberries,
    raspberries, sliced kiwifruit, sliced peaches
    and/or blackberries

GLAZE
1/4 cup sugar
1 tablespoon cornstarch

1/2 cup pineapple juice
1/ teaspoon lemon juice

For the pastry, beat the butter and confectioners' sugar in a bowl until blended. Add the flour and beat until smooth, scraping the bowl occasionally. Press the pastry over the bottom and up the side of a 12-inch tart pan. Bake at 300 degrees for 20 to 25 minutes or until light brown. Cool in the pan on a wire rack.

For the filling, combine the white chocolate chips and heavy cream in a microwave-safe bowl. Microwave for 2 minutes and stir. Add the cream cheese and beat until blended. Spoon the filling over the baked layer.

For the topping, arrange the desired fruit in a decorative pattern over the top of the filling.

For the glaze, combine the sugar and cornstarch in a small saucepan and mix well. Stir in the pineapple juice and lemon juice. Cook over medium heat until thickened, stirring constantly. Drizzle the glaze over all the fruit to prevent browning. Chill, covered, in the refrigerator.

An Occasion to Gather
Junior League of Milwaukee, Milwaukee, Wisconsin

Chocolate Pecan Tarts

Makes 16 tarts

1/2 cup pecans, chopped
2 tablespoons plus 1 teaspoon bourbon
16 unbaked tart shells
1/2 cup (3 ounces) semisweet chocolate chips
3 eggs, well beaten

1 cup sugar
3/4 cup light corn syrup
1/4 cup (1/2 stick) butter or margarine, melted
1/4 teaspoon salt
1 teaspoon vanilla extract

Mix the pecans and bourbon in a small bowl. Place the tart shells on a baking sheet. Cover the bottom of the shells with the chocolate chips. Beat the eggs, sugar, corn syrup, butter, salt and vanilla in a mixing bowl until smooth. Stir in the pecan mixture. Pour 1/2 cup of the pecan filling into each prepared tart shell. Bake at 375 degrees for 20 minutes or until set.

Roux To Do
Junior League of Greater Covington, Covington, Louisiana

Pecan Cups

Makes 60

SHELL:
1 cup margarine or butter
1 (8-ounce) package cream cheese

Dash of salt
2 cups flour, sifted

FILLING:
2 eggs, beaten
1 1/2 cups brown sugar, packed

2 tablespoons melted butter
1 1/2 cups pecans, chopped
1/2 teaspoon vanilla

To make shells, beat butter, cream cheese, and salt until fluffy. Add flour and continue to mix. Put dough in refrigerator until firm enough to handle. After chilling, form dough into little balls and press into bottom and sides of small lightly buttered muffin tins.

For filling, mix all ingredients and pour into shells. Bake at 350 degrees for 30 minutes.

Note: Tiny muffin tins make dainty bite-sized pieces.

Stir Ups
Junior Welfare League of Enid, Enid, Oklahoma

Hazelnut Raspberry Cheesecake

Serves 12

HAZELNUT CRUST
1 cup hazelnuts, finely ground
1 cup flour

1/4 cup packed brown sugar
1/2 cup (1 stick) butter, softened

CREAM CHEESE FILLING
24 ounces cream cheese, softened
1 cup sugar

4 eggs, at room temperature
1 teaspoon vanilla extract

TOPPINGS
1 cup sour cream
2 tablespoons sugar
1/2 teaspoon vanilla extract

1 pint fresh raspberries
3/4 cup raspberry preserves
2 tablespoons raspberry liqueur or water

For the crust, combine the hazelnuts, flour and brown sugar in a bowl and mix well. Add the butter and stir until combined. Pat over the bottom of a 10-inch springform pan. Bake at 400 degrees for 10 to 15 minutes or until light brown. Reduce the oven temperature to 350 degrees.

For the filling, combine the cream cheese, sugar, eggs and vanilla in a mixing bowl and beat at high speed for 5 minutes or until smooth, scraping the bowl occasionally. Spoon the filling over the baked crust and bake for 40 minutes or until set. Cool in the pan on a wire rack for 10 minutes. Maintain the oven temperature.

For the toppings, combine the sour cream, sugar and vanilla in a bowl and mix well. Spread the sour cream mixture over the top of the cheesecake. Bake for 5 minutes. Cool in the pan on a wire rack.

Arrange the raspberries in circles over the top of the cheesecake, starting from the middle. Combine the preserves and liqueur in a small saucepan and mix well. Simmer until the preserves melt, stirring occasionally. Drizzle the preserves mixture over the top of the cheesecake and chill, covered, until serving time.

From Grouper to Grits
The Junior League of Clearwater-Dunedin, Clearwater, Florida

Orange Cheesecake Flan

ORANGE GLAZE

1/2 cup sugar

3 tablespoons orange marmalade

Juice of 1/2 orange

CHEESECAKE FLAN

8 ounces cream cheese, softened

1/2 cup sugar

1 teaspoon vanilla extract

1 tablespoon grated orange zest

6 eggs, at room temperature

2 cups milk, at room temperature

Fresh orange segments

For the glaze, butter a 9-inch round baking pan. Combine the sugar, orange marmalade and orange juice in a small saucepan over medium heat. Bring to a boil and simmer for 5 to 6 minutes or until the mixture thickens slightly, stirring occasionally. Pour 1/2 of the glaze into the prepared cake pan, tilting to coat the bottom evenly. Chill until the glaze hardens. Reserve the remaining glaze for the garnish.

For the flan, preheat the oven to 350 degrees. Beat the cream cheese in the large bowl of an electric mixer until light and fluffy. Beat in the sugar, vanilla and orange zest. Add the eggs 1 at a time, beating at medium speed after each addition until smooth. Beat in the milk at very low speed. Pour the cream cheese mixture over the orange glaze in the pan. Place the pan in a larger baking pan. Add water to the larger pan to a depth of 1 inch. Bake for 1 hour and 10 minutes or until the center is set and a knife inserted in the center comes out clean. Cool on a wire rack. Chill for at least 5 hours. Loosen the custard from the pan edge with a knife, and invert onto a rimmed serving dish. Reheat the reserved orange glaze. Dip orange segments in the glaze and arrange in a circle over the middle of the cake.

Tastes, Tales and Traditions
Palo Alto Auxiliary for Children, Palo Alto, California

Apple Dew Delight

2 (8-count) cans refrigerator crescent rolls
2 large Granny Smith apples, peeled, cored and
    cut into eighths
1 cup (2 sticks) margarine, melted

1 ½ cups sugar
1 ½ teaspoons cinnamon
1 (12-ounce) can Mountain Dew soda

Separate each can of crescent rolls into eight pieces on a work surface. Roll one apple slice in each crescent dough piece, starting at the wide end. Arrange the apple rolls in a 9×13-inch baking dish. Combine the melted margarine, sugar and cinnamon in a bowl and mix well. Pour the margarine mixture evenly over the apple rolls. Pour the soda around the edges of the apple rolls but not over the top. Bake in a preheated 350-degree oven for 45 minutes.

Marshes to Mansions
Junior League of Lake Charles, LA, Lake Charles, Louisiana

Berrylicious Angel Food

Serves 4 to 6

8 ounces light whipped topping
3/4 (8-ounce) container lemon chiffon light yogurt
1 angel food cake

Sliced fresh strawberries
Fresh blueberries
Fresh raspberries

Combine the whipped topping and yogurt in a serving bowl and mix well. Break the angel food cake into bite-size pieces and fold into the whipped topping mixture. Add the strawberries, blueberries and raspberries and mix gently. Chill, covered, for 30 to 60 minutes and spoon into dessert bowls.

Worth Tasting
Junior League of the Palm Beaches, West Palm Beach, Florida

Raspberry Meringue Angel Cake

MERINGUE
4 egg whites
1/2 teaspoon cream of tartar

1 1/4 cups granulated sugar
2 teaspoons almond flavoring

In an electric mixer, beat egg whites and cream of tartar until stiff. Add sugar slowly with mixer still on. Fold in almond flavoring. Draw two 10-inch circles on a piece of parchment. Using a pastry bag, squeeze meringue to line the circle, filling it in with a coil-like design. Bake in a 200-degree oven for 1 hour or until firm. Or place in 350-degree oven overnight turning off the oven when the meringues are placed in it.

FILLING
One 12-ounce package raspberries with sugar
1/3 cup granulated sugar

2 tablespoons cornstarch
1 to 2 tablespoons Framboise
   (raspberry liqueur or Kirsch)

Cook raspberries with sugar and cornstarch until slightly thickened. Add Framboise. Remove from heat and cool in the refrigerator.

TOPPING
One 24-ounce carton light whipped topping

2 tablespoons Framboise
One 10-inch (16-ounce) angel food cake

To whipped topping, fold in Framboise. Slice angel food cake into two layers. Place one layer on a platter, top with half of raspberry filling. Place meringue on top and one cup of the whipped topping. Repeat cake, filling, and meringue and cover entire cake with remaining whipped topping. Refrigerate overnight.

River Road Recipes III: A Healthy Collection
Junior League of Baton Rouge, Baton Rouge, Louisiana

Lemon Chiffon Ring with Fresh Fruit

Serves 8

4 teaspoons unflavored gelatin
1/2 cup cold water
2/3 cup sugar
2/3 cup lemon juice
6 egg yolks
1/8 teaspoon salt
2 teaspoons grated lemon zest

6 egg whites
1/3 cup sugar
1 cup seedless grapes
2 cups fresh strawberries
1 cup whipped cream (optional)
Mint leaves

Sprinkle the gelatin over the cold water in a bowl. Let stand until softened. Combine 2/3 cup sugar and the lemon juice in a bowl and mix well. Beat the egg yolks and salt at high speed in a heatproof mixing bowl until pale yellow and thick. Add the lemon mixture to the egg yolk mixture gradually, beating constantly until blended. Place the bowl over hot water in a double boiler. Cook the mixture, stirring constantly, until thick enough to coat the back of a spoon. Remove from the heat. Add the gelatin and mix until dissolved. Stir in the lemon zest. Chill, covered, until the mixture begins to thicken. Beat the egg whites in a mixing bowl until soft peaks form. Add 1/3 cup sugar, 1 tablespoon at a time, beating well after each addition. Beat until stiff peaks form. Fold the egg white mixture into the gelatin mixture. Spoon into a large ring mold. Chill, covered, until firm. Invert onto a serving plate. Fill the center with the grapes and strawberries. Frost with whipped cream and garnish with mint leaves.

The Cook's Canvas 2
Cameron Art Museum, Wilmington, North Carolina

Simple Blackberry Cobbler

Serves 6

5 cups fresh blackberries
1 cup all-purpose flour
1 cup sugar
1 teaspoon baking powder

3/4 teaspoon salt
1 egg, beaten
1/2 cup (1 stick) butter, melted
1/4 teaspoon ground cinnamon

Preheat the oven to 350 degrees. Spread the blackberries in a 2-quart baking dish. Combine the flour, sugar, baking powder and salt in a bowl and mix well. Stir in the egg and crumble the mixture over the berries. Drizzle with the butter and sprinkle with the cinnamon. Bake for 45 minutes. Serve warm in dessert bowls topped with vanilla ice cream.

Note: Substitute fresh peaches, blueberries or raspberries for the blackberries, if desired.

Tables of Content
Junior League of Birmingham, Inc., Birmingham, Alabama

Simple Peach Cobbler

6 to 8 peaches, peeled and diced
1/4 cup sugar
1/4 cup water
1 cup flour
2 teaspoons baking powder

1/2 teaspoon salt
1 cup sugar
1 egg, beaten
1/2 cup butter

Place peaches in 13-inch Pyrex baking dish. Sprinkle with 1/4 cup sugar and 1/4 cup water. Mix flour, baking powder, salt, 1 cup sugar and egg until crumbly. Sprinkle over top of peaches and add 1/2 cup butter in thin slices over top of peaches. Bake at 350 degrees for 35 to 40 minutes. Serve plain or with ice cream.

Note: You can substitute canned peaches if fresh are not available.

Stir Ups
Junior Welfare League of Enid, Enid, Oklahoma

Peach Crisp

Serves 6

2 pounds firm fresh peaches (8 to 10 medium sized)
1 tablespoon sugar
1 tablespoon lemon juice
1/2 cup brown sugar

6 tablespoons butter, softened
1/2 cup all-purpose flour
3/4 cup quick-cooking rolled oats
Vanilla ice cream

Preheat oven to 350 degrees. Peel and slice peaches. Place in 8-inch pie pan and sprinkle with sugar and lemon juice. Cream brown sugar and butter and add flour and oats. Mix well. Spread mixture over peaches. Bake for 30 minutes until top is brown and crisp. Serve warm with ice cream. When fresh peaches are not available, use 29-ounce can peaches, and omit white sugar and lemon juice.

Charleston Receipts Repeats
Junior League of Charleston, Charleston, South Carolina

Fresh Peach Crisp

1 cup flour
1/2 cup sugar
1/2 cup light brown sugar, firmly packed
1/4 teaspoon salt
1/2 teaspoon ground cinnamon

1/2 cup margarine
4 cups fresh peaches, sliced
1 tablespoon lemon juice
2 tablespoons water

Combine flour, sugar, brown sugar, salt and cinnamon; cut in margarine with 2 knives or pastry blender until mixture resembles coarse cornmeal. Combine peaches, lemon juice and water; spoon into a greased 9×9×1 3/4-inch baking dish. Sprinkle flour mixture over peaches. Bake, covered, at 350 degrees for 15 minutes. Remove cover and bake 35 to 45 minutes longer.

Savannah Style
Junior League of Savannah, Savannah, Georgia

Bread Pudding with Whiskey Sauce

PUDDING:
2 cups stale bread cubes (French bread is best)
4 cups milk, scalded
3/4 cup sugar
1 tablespoon butter

1/4 teaspoon salt
4 eggs, slightly beaten
1 teaspoon vanilla
1/2 to 1 cup coarsely chopped pecans (optional)

Soak bread in milk 5 minutes. Add sugar, butter, salt, eggs, and vanilla. Mix well. Stir in pecans. Pour into 1 1/2-quart baking dish. Bake in pan of hot water for one hour at 350 degrees.

WHISKEY SAUCE:
1/2 cup sugar
1/4 cup water

2 tablespoons butter
1 or 2 jiggers bourbon whiskey

Cook first three ingredients until dissolved. Remove from heat and add whiskey. Serve over bread pudding. Best served warm.

River Road Recipes II: A Second Helping
Junior League of Baton Rouge, Baton Rouge, Louisiana

Our Famous Bread-and-Butter Pudding

PUDDING:
1 loaf sliced white bread, torn into
 small cubes
1 quart heavy cream
3 tablespoons unsalted butter, melted
1 tablespoon vanilla extract
1/2 cup water

1 cup golden raisins
1/2 cup raisins
3 eggs
1 1/2 cups sugar

CRÈME ANGLAISE:
2/3 cup heavy cream
1/3 cup sugar

2 egg yolks
1 tablespoon vanilla extract

To prepare the pudding, mix the bread, cream, butter and vanilla in a large mixing bowl. Let stand for 10 minutes. Bring the water to a boil in a saucepan. Pour over the raisins in a medium heatproof bowl. Beat the eggs and sugar at medium-high speed in a mixing bowl for 5 minutes or until thick. Add to the bread mixture and stir to mix. Stir in the raisins. Pour into a 9×13-inch baking pan sprayed with nonstick cooking spray. Bake at 350 degrees for 45 to 60 minutes or until the pudding is golden brown and slightly set. Remove from the oven and cool on a wire rack. Chill in the refrigerator for 24 hours before serving.

To prepare the crème anglaise, bring the cream just to a boil in a saucepan over medium heat. (This usually takes 3 to 5 minutes.) Remove from the heat. Beat the sugar and egg yolks at medium-high speed in a mixing bowl for 3 minutes or until thick. Add the cream gradually, beating constantly at low speed. Return the mixture to the saucepan. Cook over medium heat for 5 to 7 minutes or until the mixture begins to thicken and coat the back of a spoon, stirring constantly. Cool in the refrigerator for 1 hour. Stir in the vanilla and return to the refrigerator until ready to serve.

To serve, warm the bread pudding in the oven or microwave. Cut into squares and drizzle with the crème anglaise.

Note: This recipe received BEST DESSERT IN SAVANNAH at the Taste of Savannah 2002.

Starfish Café: Changing Lives One Recipe at a Time...
Union Mission/Starfish Café, Savannah, Georgia

White Chocolate Blueberry Bread Pudding

Serves 24

12 to 18 miniature croissants
12 eggs
2 cups sugar
1 cup sweetened condensed milk
1/4 cup vanilla extract

4 cups fresh blueberries
1/2 cup pecans
1 cup (2 sticks) butter
5 1/3 cups white chocolate chips
6 tablespoons whiskey

Tear the croissants into pieces and spread over the bottom of a greased 9×13-inch baking dish. Combine the eggs, sugar, sweetened condensed milk and vanilla in a bowl and mix well. Pour evenly over the croissants. Sprinkle the blueberries and pecans over the top. Bake in a preheated 350-degree oven for 50 minutes. Remove to a wire rack. Combine the butter and white chocolate chips in the top of double boiler over simmering water. Cook until the mixture is melted and smooth, whisking constantly. Stir in the whiskey just before serving. Serve the bread pudding with the sauce over the top or on the side.

Marshes to Mansions
Junior League of Lake Charles, LA, Lake Charles, Louisiana

Bananas Foster

Serves 6

2 tablespoons butter
4 tablespoons brown sugar
2 bananas
Pinch cinnamon

1 tablespoon banana liqueur
1 ounce rum or brandy
Ice cream

Mix butter and brown sugar in saucepan. Cook over medium heat until it is caramelized. Cut bananas in quarters. Add and cook until tender. Add cinnamon and liqueur; stir. Add rum or brandy to top of mixture. Do not stir. Light. Spoon over vanilla ice cream while flaming.

River Road Recipes: The Textbook of Louisiana Cuisine
Junior League of Baton Rouge, Baton Rouge, Louisiana

Easy King Cake

2 (8-count) cans refrigerator cinnamon rolls
Yellow, green and purple sprinkles
1 plastic baby doll

1/4 cup confectioners' sugar (optional)
1 tablespoon milk (optional)

Arrange the cinnamon rolls in a circle with sides touching on a baking sheet. Bake using the package directions. Immediately spread with the icing that accompanied the cinnamon rolls and sprinkle with the colored sprinkles. Push the plastic baby doll into the cake from the bottom so that it is not visible from the top. If additional icing is required, spread with a mixture of the confectioners' sugar and milk.

Mardi Gras to Mistletoe
Junior League of Shreveport-Bossier, Shreveport, Louisiana

Brown Sugar Ice Cream

6 egg yolks
1 1/2 cups packed light brown sugar
1 1/2 cups whipping cream
4 1/2 cups half-and-half or light cream
2 1/4 teaspoons vanilla extract

Cook the egg yolks and brown sugar in a heavy saucepan over low heat until thick and well blended, whisking constantly. Combine the whipping cream and half-and-half in another saucepan; stir to mix well. Bring just to a boil over medium-high heat.

Stir a small amount of the hot cream mixture into the egg yolk mixture; stir the egg yolk mixture into the hot cream mixture. Cook over low heat for 6 minutes or until the mixture coats the back of a spoon, stirring constantly. Do not boil. Strain the mixture into a bowl. Stir in the vanilla. Let cool for 30 minutes or to room temperature, stirring occasionally.

Chill, covered, in the refrigerator for 5 hours or until very cold. Pour into the bowl of an ice cream freezer and process according to the manufacturer's directions.

A Thyme to Remember
The Dallas County Medical Society Alliance, Dallas, Texas

Lemon Ice Cream

6 to 8 lemons
3 cups sugar
2 quarts half-and-half

Slice 2 of the lemons in thin slices. Combine slices with the juice of the remaining lemons and pour over sugar. Let stand several hours. Put half-and-half in ice cream churn and freeze until semi-stiff. Remove cover and add lemon and sugar mixture and finish freezing.

A Southern Collection Then and Now
Junior League of Columbus, Columbus, Georgia

Chocolate Sauce

Makes 3 cups

2 ounces unsweetened chocolate
6 tablespoons margarine
1 1/2 cups sugar
1/4 teaspoon salt

Pinch of cream of tartar
1 cup evaporated milk
1 teaspoon vanilla extract

Place the chocolate and margarine in the top of a double boiler. Cook over simmering water until melted. Stir in the sugar gradually. Add the salt and cream of tartar. Stir in the evaporated milk gradually. Add the vanilla and stir to mix. Cook, covered, for 30 minutes. Do not overcook. Pour into a bowl and let cool. Cover and chill until ready to serve. Pour over ice cream.

For Such A Time As This: A Cookbook
Park Cities Baptist Church, Dallas, Texas

Chocolate Pâte

Makes 2 3/4 cups

6 tablespoons butter, cut into small pieces
2 3/4 cups chopped semisweet chocolate
3/4 cup whipping cream

Melt the butter and chocolate in a double boiler over hot water. Bring the whipping cream to a boil in a small saucepan. Pour over the chocolate mixture and stir until blended and smooth. Store, covered, in the refrigerator for up to 6 weeks. Use as a spread for shortbread for dessert.
Note: The chocolate mixture can be poured into any mold, such as a star, heart, tree, and so forth, to make serving more festive.

Shortbread

Mix 1 cup plus 3 tablespoons unbleached all-purpose flour and 1/3 cup cornstarch together. Beat 10 tablespoons unsalted butter, softened, 1/4 cup confectioners' sugar, 1 1/3 tablespoons granulated sugar and 1/4 teaspoon salt in a mixing bowl until fluffy. Sift the flour mixture gradually into the creamed mixture, beating constantly after each addition. Press the dough firmly into an 8×8-inch baking pan until smooth. Pierce the dough lightly with a fork into patterns of your choice. Bake at 300 degrees for 45 to 50 minutes or until the edges are slightly darker than the center. Remove the pan to a wire rack. Cool slightly and cut into the desired shapes.

Now Serving
Junior League of Wichita Falls, Wichita Falls, Texas

Potato Fudge

2 ounces unsweetened chocolate
3 tablespoons butter
1/3 cup mashed cooked potato

1/8 teaspoon salt
1 teaspoon vanilla extract
1 (16-ounce) package confectioners' sugar

Melt the chocolate and butter in a double boiler over hot water. Add the potato, salt and vanilla and mix gently. Blend in the confectioners' sugar. Knead or mix until smooth. Press into a buttered 8-inch pan. Let cool. Cut into squares and remove from the pan.

Beyond Burlap
Junior League of Boise, Boise, Idaho

Michigan Nut and Berry Bark

1 pound bittersweet chocolate, finely chopped
1 cup nuts, toasted (such as almonds, walnuts or macadamia)
1 cup dried cranberries, apricots or cherries
1/4 cup flaked coconut, toasted

1/2 cup dried cranberries, apricots or cherries
1/2 cup nuts, toasted
1/4 cup flaked coconut, toasted
4 ounces white chocolate, melted

Melt bittersweet chocolate in the top of a double boiler over simmering water. Stir in 1 cup nuts, 1 cup dried cranberries and 1/4 cup coconut. Pour onto a parchment- or foil-lined 10×15-inch baking pan. Spread the chocolate mixture over the parchment to a 10×14-inch rectangle with a rubber spatula. Sprinkle with 1/2 cup dried cranberries, 1/2 cup nuts and 1/4 cup coconut. Cover with plastic wrap and gently pat down. Remove the plastic wrap and drizzle with the white chocolate. Chill, covered, until the bark is hard. Break into large pieces. Store in an airtight container for a week or freeze in sealable plastic bags.

Between the Lakes
The Junior League of Saginaw Valley, Saginaw, Michigan

Microwave Pralines

Pralines are a chewy sweet confection made from a mixture of pecans, cream, and brown sugar. Many Louisiana cooks make them from old family recipes, as evidenced by the fact that four different praline recipes can be found in River Road Recipes I *and five recipes appear in* River Road Recipes II. *This recipe is unique because even people who swear that they cannot make candy will have success making these super-easy pralines.*

1 (16-ounce) package light brown sugar
1 cup heavy cream
1/4 cup (1/2 stick) butter

2 cups pecan pieces
1 tablespoon vanilla extract

Combine the brown sugar and heavy cream in a microwave-safe bowl and mix well. Microwave on High for 7 minutes; stir. Add the butter. Microwave on High for 7 minutes longer and stir vigorously. Stir in the pecans and vanilla. Drop by teaspoonfuls onto a baking sheet lined with waxed paper. Let stand until set.

Note: Saying "PEE-kans" is a sure way to become the center of a joke in Louisiana. The only acceptable pronunciation is "pih-KAWNS." Similarly, the correct pronunciation for our delectable pih-KAWN candy is "PRAW-leens," not "PRAY-leens."

River Road Recipes IV: Warm Welcomes
Junior League of Baton Rouge, Baton Rouge, Louisiana

Bess' Signature Coconut Balls

Makes 18 balls

2/3 cup sweetened condensed milk
1/8 teaspoon salt
1 teaspoon vanilla extract

1/4 teaspoon almond extract
1 1/2 cups coconut

Combine the condensed milk, salt, vanilla and almond extracts in a bowl and mix well. Stir in the coconut. Shape into 18 balls. Place 2 inches apart on a greased cookie sheet. Bake at 350 degrees for 15 minutes or until lightly browned.

If You Can't Stand the Heat, Get Out of the Kitchen
Junior Service League of Independence, Independence, Missouri

Creole Porcupines

3 tablespoons butter (no substitute)
1 cup brown sugar, firmly packed
2 eggs, well beaten

1 1/2 cups chopped pecans
1 cup chopped dates
3 cups shredded coconut

Melt butter and stir into sugar. Beat in eggs. Add pecans, dates, and 1 cup of the coconut. Form into small balls and roll in the remaining 2 cups of coconut. Place on greased baking sheet and bake at 300 degrees until cookies just begin to brown lightly, or about 25 minutes.

A Taste of Georgia
Newnan Junior Service League, Newnan, Georgia

Oreo Balls

8 ounces cream cheese, softened
1 package Oreos, finely crushed

1 cup (6 ounces) semisweet chocolate chips
1 1/2 cups (9 ounces) white chocolate chips

Combine the cream cheese and cookie crumbs in a bowl and mix well. (Chill if needed to shape the mixture.) Shape the cookie mixture into balls and arrange on a baking sheet lined with waxed paper. Chill for 1 hour.

Pour the semisweet chocolate chips into a microwave-safe bowl and microwave until melted. Roll the chilled balls in the chocolate and return to the baking sheet. Chill until set. Microwave the white chocolate chips in a microwave-safe bowl until melted and pour into a sealable plastic bag. Seal tightly and snip one corner of the bag. Drizzle the white chocolate over the chilled balls and chill until set.

Mardi Gras to Mistletoe
Junior League of Shreveport-Bossier, Shreveport, Louisiana

White Chocolate Peanut Butter Bites

Makes 75 to 100 pieces

4 cups crisp rice cereal
3 cups miniature marshmallows
1 cup crunchy peanut butter

1 cup dry roasted peanuts
4 cups (24 ounces) white chocolate morsels, melted

Mix the cereal, marshmallows, peanut butter and peanuts in a large bowl with a spatula. Pour the white chocolate over the cereal mixture and quickly mix to coat. Spread the cereal mixture on a sheet of waxed paper and let stand until cool and firm. Break into small pieces and store in an airtight container.

Note: Melt the white chocolate morsels in a saucepan over low heat, stirring constantly, or in the microwave on High for two minutes.

Tables of Content
Junior League of Birmingham, Inc., Birmingham, Alabama

Our Favorite Toffee

Makes 1 pound

3/4 cup finely chopped pecans
1/2 cup (1 stick) butter
1 cup sugar
1/4 cup water

1 teaspoon salt
1 cup (6 ounces) semisweet chocolate morsels
1/2 cup finely chopped pecans

Sprinkle 3/4 cup pecans over the bottom of a greased 9-inch round baking dish. Coat 2 inches of the side of a microwave-safe 2 1/2-quart glass bowl with some of the butter and place the remaining butter in the bowl. Add the sugar, water and salt; do not stir. Microwave on High for 9 to 11 minutes or until the mixture just begins to turn light brown and pour over the pecans. Sprinkle with the chocolate morsels and spread evenly with a knife. Top with 1/2 cup pecans and press lightly if needed. Chill until firm. Break into bite-size pieces and store in an airtight container.

Note: Buttering the sides of your bowl prevents the mixture from sticking when it bubbles up in the microwave.

Tables of Content
Junior League of Birmingham, Inc., Birmingham, Alabama

Kids in the Kitchen

"'MUUNKEE BREAD!' My three-year-old Robby wakes me several mornings a week with these words. It's always 'MUUNKEE BREAD!' followed by out-of-breath laughter as he skips out of the room when I say, 'Yes, Monkey Bread time.' I am guaranteed to then hear the pitter-patter of his feet as he races down the stairs to the kitchen, pulling out the pan, sugar, butter, cinnamon, and dough to make his favorite breakfast.

Many people wonder why I spend so much time on the Junior League cookbook. I can sum it up in those two words, MUUNKEE BREAD, Robby's favorite recipe from our Junior League cookbook, *Worth Tasting*. I love what we do at the Junior League, helping our community, namely the children.

My sons see all the work we do to help others, and I am proud that they have started asking me if they can help, too. Robby now does his own volunteering when he comes with me. Community outreach programs like the Junior League not only provide for those in need, they benefit all of us. Our children may actually benefit the most, as they learn to love others and make this world a better place by caring for the community. I know I learned to love volunteering through my mother, who spent numerous sleepless nights volunteering throughout my childhood for many different organizations and still does.

Those of us making community cookbooks are really making a shared community of our families, our friends, our coworkers, our members, and, most importantly, those we strive to serve. MUUNKEE BREAD reminds me every morning that my son is volunteering in his own way and is learning about the family of our community."

Jennifer Eastridge Morrison
The Junior League of the Palm Beaches, Florida

Crawford's Hillbilly Bruschetta

Serves 6

2 cups (8 ounces) shredded Cheddar cheese
3/4 cup mayonnaise
1/3 cup crumbled bacon
1 loaf French bread

Mix the cheese, mayonnaise and bacon in a bowl. Cut the bread into slices 1/2 inch thick. Spread the cheese mixture on each bread slice and place on a baking sheet. Bake at 425 degrees for 8 to 10 minutes or until golden brown and bubbly.

Great Women, Great Food
Junior League of Kankakee County, Kankakee, Illinois

Easy Nonfat Yogurt Vegetable Dip

Makes 8 (2-tablespoon) servings

1/2 cup plain nonfat yogurt
1/2 cup nonfat ranch salad dressing

1/2 teaspoon dried dillweed
1/4 teaspoon black pepper

Combine the yogurt, salad dressing, dillweed and pepper in a bowl and mix well. Serve with fresh vegetables of your choice. May substitute your favorite nonfat salad dressing for the ranch salad dressing.

A Taste of the Good Life: From the Heart of Tennessee
Saint Thomas Hospital, Nashville, Tennessee

The proceeds generated by the sale of *Great Women, Great Food* help to provide needy children with winter coats through Winter Warmth, tutor children who are not at grade level through Read to Succeed, publish Kids Life, a free community resource on early childhood development, and furnish transitional housing for families moving out of homelessness through Families Moving Forward. Raising money and awareness through the sale of *Great Women, Great Food* allows us to improve our current projects and add new ones to meet our mission and commitment to our community.

Fruit Tea

2 cups water
4 tea bags
1 (12-ounce) can frozen orange juice concentrate
1 (12-ounce) can frozen lemonade concentrate

6 ounces pineapple juice
6 ounces apricot nectar or peach nectar
1 to 1 1/2 cups sugar

Bring the water to a boil in a saucepan. Remove from the heat. Add the tea bags and steep for 5 minutes. Remove the tea bags and pour into a 1-gallon pitcher. Stir in the orange juice concentrate, lemonade concentrate, pineapple juice, apricot nectar and sugar to taste. Add enough additional water to make 1 gallon. Stir and serve.

Once Upon A Time
Junior League of Evansville, Evansville, Indiana

Banana Nut Bread

Makes 1 loaf

1/2 cup margarine
1 1/2 cups sugar
2 beaten eggs
1 teaspoon vanilla
2 cups cake flour, measured after sifting

1/2 teaspoon salt
1/2 teaspoon baking soda
1/4 cup milk
3 small or 2 large bananas, mashed to a pulp
1 cup chopped pecans

Cream margarine and sugar. Add eggs and vanilla. Beat until fluffy. Add sifted dry ingredients alternately with milk, bananas and nuts. Beat well after each addition. Bake in waxed paper-lined 6 1/2 x 10 1/2-inch pan in a 350-degree oven for 50 minutes or until brown and an inserted toothpick comes out clean. This bread keeps well in plastic wrap and also freezes well.

River Road Recipes II: Second Helping
Junior League of Baton Rouge, Baton Rouge, Louisiana

Butterscotch Pull-Apart Bread

Serves 12 to 15

3/4 cup chopped pecans
1 (24-count) package frozen yeast rolls
1 (3-ounce) package butterscotch instant pudding mix

3/4 cup packed light brown sugar
1/2 cup (1 stick) butter or margarine, melted
1 teaspoon cinnamon

Spray a bundt pan with nonstick cooking spray. Sprinkle the pecans over the bottom of the pan. Layer the frozen rolls over the nuts. Sprinkle with the pudding mix. Combine the brown sugar, butter and cinnamon in a bowl. Pour over the rolls. Let rise, covered with waxed paper, at room temperature for 8 to 12 hours. (Rolls will double in bulk.)

Bake, uncovered, at 350 degrees for 25 to 30 minutes. (Cover with foil during the last 10 minutes of the baking time to prevent overbrowning.) Let stand for 10 minutes. Invert onto a serving plate.

Note: May be made in advance. Assemble the bread as directed above, cover and refrigerate. Remove from the refrigerator 2 hours before baking to allow the rolls to rise.

Once Upon A Time
Junior League of Evansville, Evansville, Indiana

Easter Resurrection Rolls

Serves 8

1 (8-ounce) can refrigerator crescent rolls
8 large marshmallows

1/2 cup (1 stick) butter, melted
Cinnamon-sugar

Separate the crescent rolls on a work surface and flatten. Wrap each marshmallow in a crescent roll. Dip the top of each roll in the melted butter and then in cinnamon-sugar. Place the rolls in greased muffin cups, sugar side up. Bake at 350 degrees for 10 minutes. Remove to a wire rack to cool.

Note: "These Easter treats are special as the name implies, because just like the Tomb, they are empty inside!"

A League of Our Own: From Blue Jeans to Ball Gowns
Rockwall Women's League, Rockwall, Texas

Monkey Bread

3 (10-count) cans refrigerator biscuits
1 cup granulated sugar
4 teaspoons ground cinnamon

3/4 cup (1 1/2 sticks) butter
1/2 cup packed light brown sugar

Cut the biscuits into quarters. Mix the granulated sugar and cinnamon in a large sealable plastic bag. Add the biscuit quarters to the sugar mixture and seal tightly. Shake until coated. Arrange the coated biscuit quarters in a bundt pan sprayed with nonstick cooking spray.

Heat the butter and brown sugar in a saucepan until the brown sugar dissolves, stirring occasionally. Or, microwave in a microwave-safe bowl. Pour the brown sugar mixture over the prepared layers and bake at 350 degrees for 30 minutes. Invert onto a serving platter.

Note: There are many variations of Monkey Bread—add raisins, nuts, blueberries, and/or currants, or make it savory and add garlic, herbs, and/or Parmesan cheese. This traditional Monkey Bread recipe has been popular in American cookbooks since the 1950s.

Worth Tasting
Junior League of the Palm Beaches, West Palm Beach, Florida

Chocolate Chip Scones

2 cups flour
1/3 cup sugar
2 teaspoons baking powder
1/2 teaspoon salt
1/2 cup (1 stick) unsalted butter,
  cut into 1/2-inch cubes

2 eggs
1/4 cup orange juice
1 teaspoon vanilla extract
3/4 cup semisweet chocolate chips
1 egg white (optional)
1/2 teaspoon water (optional)

Combine the flour, sugar, baking powder and salt in a large bowl. Cut in the butter until crumbly. Combine the eggs, orange juice and vanilla in a small bowl. Add to the flour mixture and stir just until mixed. Knead in the chocolate chips with lightly floured hands until evenly distributed in the dough.

Pat the dough out to a 1/2-inch-thick round on a lightly floured surface. Cut into 8 equal-size wedges. Place on a baking sheet. Combine the egg white and water in a small bowl. Brush over the tops of the scones.

Bake at 425 degrees for 20 to 25 minutes. Remove to a wire rack. Serve warm or at room temperature. Store in an airtight container.

Once Upon A Time
Junior League of Evansville, Evansville, Indiana

French Market Doughnuts

Makes 36 doughnuts

1 cup milk
1/4 cup sugar
3/4 teaspoon salt
1/2 teaspoon nutmeg
1 package active dry or cake yeast

2 tablespoons lukewarm water
2 tablespoons salad oil
1 egg
3 1/2 cups sifted all-purpose flour
Sifted confectioners' sugar

Scald milk, add granulated sugar, salt, and nutmeg. Cool to lukewarm. Sprinkle or crumble yeast into warm water (use lukewarm water for cake yeast), stirring until yeast is dissolved.

To lukewarm milk mixture, add oil, egg, dissolved yeast, blending with spoon. Add flour gradually, beating well. Cover with waxed paper, then clean towel, and let rise in warm place (about 85 degrees) until double in size.

Turn dough (it will be soft) on to well-floured surface; knead gently. Roll into 18×12-inch rectangle; cut into thirty-six 3×2-inch rectangles. Cover with clean towel and let rise 1/2 hour.

Fry a few doughnuts at a time in deep fat (375 degrees) until golden brown. Drain on crumpled paper towels. Drop doughnuts in brown paper bag, sprinkle with confectioners' sugar, and shake well until thoroughly coated. Serve piping hot.

River Road Recipes: The Textbook of Louisiana Cuisine
Junior League of Baton Rouge, Baton Rouge, Louisiana

Baked French Toast with Apples

Serves 8

1/2 cup (1 stick) butter
1 cup packed brown sugar
2 tablespoons dark corn syrup
4 Granny Smith apples, peeled, cored and sliced
1 loaf French or Italian bread,
    cut into 1/2- to 1-inch slices

6 eggs
1 1/2 cups milk
1 teaspoon vanilla extract
Pinch of nutmeg
Ground cinnamon
Butter (optional)

Combine 1/2 cup butter, the brown sugar and corn syrup in a saucepan. Bring to a boil, stirring occasionally. Pour evenly over the bottom of a 9×13-inch baking dish. Top with the apple slices in a single layer. Arrange the bread slices over the apples. Combine the eggs, milk, vanilla and nutmeg in a bowl and mix well. Pour evenly over the bread. Sprinkle with cinnamon. Chill, covered, overnight. Bake at 350 degrees for 1 hour, dotting with butter halfway through baking.

Recipes of Note
Greensboro Symphony Guild, Greensboro, North Carolina

Easy Granola for Kids in the Kitchen

Makes 9¹/₂ cups

5 cups rolled oats
1 cup wheat germ
1 cup shredded unsweetened coconut
1 cup sliced unblanched almonds

1 cup hulled raw sunflower seeds
¹/₂ cup unhulled sesame seeds
³/₄ cup vegetable oil
³/₄ cup honey

Combine the oats, wheat germ, coconut, almonds, sunflower seeds and sesame seeds in a bowl. Whisk the oil and honey in a small bowl until the oil is incorporated. Pour over the oat mixture and stir to coat. Spoon into a heavy baking pan. Bake at 325 degrees for 30 to 60 minutes or until light brown and dry, stirring every 15 minutes.

Be Present At Our Table
Germantown United Methodist Women, Germantown, Tennessee

Holiday Fruit Salad

Serves 8 to 10

3 egg yolks, lightly beaten
2 tablespoons sugar
2 tablespoons white vinegar
2 tablespoons pineapple syrup
1 tablespoon salted butter
¹/₈ teaspoon salt

1 cup whipping cream, whipped
2 cups seedless grapes, cut into halves
2 cups drained pineapple tidbits
Sections of 2 oranges, chopped
2 cups miniature marshmallows

Combine the egg yolks, sugar, vinegar, pineapple syrup, butter and salt in a double boiler. Cook just until thickened, stirring frequently. Remove from the heat and spoon into a bowl. Let stand until cool. Fold in the whipped cream, grapes, pineapple, oranges and marshmallows and chill, covered, for 24 hours.

Creating Comfort
Genesis Women's Shelter, Dallas, Texas

Strawberry Pretzel Salad

Serves 10 to 12

2 1/2 cups crushed pretzels
3 tablespoons sugar
3/4 cup (1 1/2 sticks) butter, melted
8 ounces cream cheese, softened
1 cup sugar

2 cups whipped topping
2 (3-ounce) packages strawberry gelatin
2 cups boiling water
2 (10-ounce) packages frozen strawberries

Mix the crushed pretzels, 3 tablespoons sugar and melted butter in a bowl. Press over the bottom of a 9×13-inch baking dish. Bake at 350 degrees for 10 minutes. Cool to room temperature.

Beat the cream cheese and 1 cup sugar in a mixing bowl until smooth. Add the whipped topping and mix well. Spread over the cooled pretzel layer.

Dissolve the gelatin in the boiling water in a bowl. Add the strawberries and mix gently. Spoon over the cream cheese layer. Chill until firm.

Oh My Stars!
Junior League of Roanoke Valley, Roanoke, Virginia

Italian Macaroni (Kiddie Casserole)

Serves 6

1 to 1 1/2 pounds ground beef or ground chuck
1 (48-ounce) jar meat sauce
Italian seasoning or oregano to taste
2 to 4 garlic cloves, minced, or to taste
12 to 16 ounces medium shell pasta

8 ounces medium curd cottage cheese
2 1/2 cups (10 ounces) shredded Cheddar cheese
2 1/2 cups (10 ounces) shredded mozzarella cheese
Freshly grated Parmesan cheese for topping

Preheat the oven to 350 degrees. Brown the ground beef in a skillet, stirring until crumbly; drain. Add the meat sauce and mix well. Stir in the Italian seasoning and garlic and simmer, stirring occasionally.

Cook the pasta using the package directions; drain and rinse to cool. Combine the pasta and cottage cheese in a bowl and mix well.

Spread a thin layer of the meat sauce in a 9×13-inch glass baking dish. Layer the pasta mixture, Cheddar cheese, mozzarella cheese and remaining sauce 1/2 at a time in the prepared dish. Sprinkle with Parmesan cheese. Bake for 30 to 45 minutes or until bubbly and the top is light brown.

Creating Comfort
Genesis Women's Shelter, Dallas, Texas

Barbecued Franks

Serves 12

1 cup ketchup
1/4 cup hot water
1/4 cup packed brown sugar
1/4 cup vinegar
3 tablespoons Worcestershire sauce
2 tablespoons all-purpose flour
2 teaspoons paprika
2 teaspoons chili powder or dry mustard

1/2 teaspoon salt
1/2 teaspoon freshly ground black pepper
1/8 teaspoon red pepper (optional)
2 onions, chopped
12 large frankfurters (about 3 pounds)
12 hot dog buns
Coleslaw (optional)

Combine the ketchup, hot water, brown sugar, vinegar and Worcestershire sauce in a bowl. Mix the flour, paprika, chili powder, salt, black pepper and red pepper in a bowl and stir into the ketchup mixture. Add the onions and mix well. Arrange the frankfurters in a baking pan. Pour the ketchup mixture over the top. Bake at 350 degrees for 1 hour. Serve the frankfurters in buns topped with coleslaw.

The Cook's Canvas 2
Cameron Art Museum, Wilmington, North Carolina

Chicken Alberghetti

Serves 6

3 chicken breasts, boned, skinned and cut in half
Salt and pepper to taste
2 eggs, slightly beaten
3/4 cup dry bread crumbs
1/2 cup butter
8 ounces prepared Italian Cooking Sauce

1/2 cup light cream
6 slices mozzarella cheese
6 slices Swiss cheese
Butter
Parmesan cheese, canned

Season chicken with salt and pepper. Dip in egg and roll in crumbs. Sauté in butter until browned. Dilute spaghetti sauce with light cream (reserve 2 tablespoons). Pour sauce in bottom of covered casserole. Add chicken. Top each piece with 1 slice Swiss and mozzarella cheese. Add reserved sauce. Sprinkle with butter and Parmesan. Cover and bake at 350 degrees for 45 to 60 minutes.

Stir Ups
Junior Welfare League of Enid, Enid, Oklahoma

Parmesan Chicken Strips

Serves 3 or 4

4 boneless skinless chicken breasts
$1/2$ cup grated Parmesan cheese
$1/2$ cup bread crumbs
1 tablespoon dried Italian seasoning

Salt and pepper to taste
2 eggs, lightly beaten
$1/2$ cup flour
3 to 4 tablespoons olive oil

Pound the chicken $1/2$ inch thick between sheets of waxed paper. Cut each chicken breast lengthwise into 2 or 3 strips. Combine the cheese, bread crumbs, Italian seasoning, salt and pepper in a shallow dish.

Dip the chicken strips in the eggs and then coat with the flour. Dip the chicken in the eggs again and then in the cheese mixture. Sauté the chicken in the olive oil in a skillet over medium heat for 3 minutes per side or until brown and cooked through. Serve with spaghetti sauce.

Austin Entertains
The Junior League of Austin, Austin, Texas

Poppy Seed Chicken

Serves 8 to 10

5 to 6 boneless chicken breasts, cooked
8 ounces sour cream
1 (10-ounce) can condensed cream of
   chicken soup

1 tablespoon poppy seeds
1 sleeve round buttery crackers
1 stick of butter, melted

Slice chicken into bite-size pieces. Mix chicken, sour cream, soup and poppy seeds together. Spread mixture in 9×13-inch baking dish. Crush crackers, then sprinkle on top of chicken mixture. Top with melted butter. Bake at 350 degrees for 30 minutes or until bubbly.

Add Another Place Setting
Junior League of Northwest Arkansas, Springdale, Arkansas

Quick Clean-Up Chicken

Serves 4

4 chicken breasts
Seasoned salt and pepper to taste
1 yellow squash or zucchini, sliced
4 carrots, sliced

2 potatoes, cut into chunks
4 tablespoons butter
8 tablespoons chicken broth

Cut 4 squares of foil large enough to enclose the chicken and vegetables. Place 1 chicken breast on each square. Sprinkle with seasoned salt and pepper. Layer each chicken breast with 1/4 of the vegetables, 1 tablespoon of the butter and 2 tablespoons of the broth. Seal tightly to form a packet.

Arrange the packets on a baking sheet. Bake at 350 degrees for 40 to 45 minutes or until the chicken is cooked through. Open the packets carefully to avoid the steam and drain the juices.

Cooking by the Bootstraps
Junior Welfare League of Enid, Enid, Oklahoma

Tuna Casserole

Serves 4 to 6

1 large can tuna
1 can undiluted mushroom soup
1 cup diced celery
1 small diced onion
Parsley and pimento for color

1 can mushrooms, drained
1 dozen salted crackers, crumbled
Pepper to taste
Bread crumbs

Combine all ingredients in a 1 1/2-quart casserole, saving bread crumbs for top. Bake at 325 degrees for 20 to 25 minutes. This can be made a day in advance.

River Road Recipes: The Textbook of Louisiana Cuisine
Junior League of Baton Rouge, Baton Rouge, Louisiana

Candied Carrots

16 ounces carrots
1/2 cup (1 stick) butter

1 cup sugar
Almond extract to taste

Peel the carrots and julienne or coarsely grate. Place the carrots in a large heavy saucepan. Top with the butter. Sprinkle with the sugar and drizzle with almond extract. Add just enough water to cover the carrots.

Cook, covered, over medium heat until the butter melts; remove the cover. Simmer for 2 hours or until the carrots are candied. Do not substitute margarine for the butter in this recipe. You may prepare the carrots up to 1 week in advance and store, covered, in the refrigerator. Heat for 15 minutes before serving.

Austin Entertains
The Junior League of Austin, Austin, Texas

Cheesy Potato Casserole

1 (10-ounce) can cream of chicken soup (see Note)
2 cups sour cream or low-fat sour cream
1 1/2 teaspoons salt
1/4 teaspoon pepper

3 green onions, chopped
2 cups shredded Cheddar cheese
1 (32-ounce) package frozen hash brown potatoes

TOPPING
1/4 cup melted butter or margarine
2 cups crushed cornflakes

Combine the soup, sour cream, salt, pepper, green onions and cheese in a large bowl and mix well. Add the potatoes and mix well. Spoon into a greased 9×13-inch baking pan. Top with a mixture of the butter and cornflakes. Bake at 350 degrees for 45 minutes or until bubbly around the edges. May sprinkle with 3 tablespoons sesame seeds and paprika to taste instead of topping with the cornflake mixture. Easy and delicious accompaniment to ham, turkey or chicken dinners.

Note: You may substitute cream of mushroom or cream of celery soup for a different flavor.

Beyond Burlap
Junior League of Boise, Boise, Idaho

Scrumptious Banana Pudding

Serves 8

1 (14-ounce) can sweetened condensed milk
1 (6-ounce) package vanilla instant pudding mix
2 cups milk
8 ounces cream cheese, softened

16 ounces whipped topping
1 (12-ounce) package vanilla wafers
4 or 5 bananas, sliced

Combine the sweetened condensed milk, pudding mix, milk and cream cheese in a large mixing bowl and beat until smooth. Fold in 1/2 of the whipped topping. Reserve some of the vanilla wafers to garnish the top. Layer the remaining vanilla wafers, pudding mixture and bananas in a 2-quart serving dish. Top with the remaining whipped topping. Garnish with the reserved vanilla wafers and chill in the refrigerator. For a reduced-calorie version of this recipe, use reduced-fat ingredients.

Creating Comfort
Genesis Women's Shelter, Dallas, Texas

Chocolate Chip Cheese Ball

Serves 24

1/2 cup (1 stick) butter, softened
8 ounces cream cheese, softened
1/2 teaspoon vanilla extract
3/4 cup confectioners' sugar

2 tablespoons brown sugar
3/4 cup miniature chocolate chips
Chopped pecans

Beat the butter, cream cheese and vanilla in a bowl until smooth. Mix the confectioners' sugar and brown sugar in a bowl. Add to the cream cheese mixture and mix well. Stir in the chocolate chips. Chill, covered, for 2 to 3 hours. Shape into a ball and roll in the pecans. Serve with chocolate teddy bear graham crackers. This can be served as an appetizer or dessert. Children love it.

Recipes of Note
Greensboro Symphony Guild, Greensboro, North Carolina

Picnic Cupcakes

½ cup butter
1½ ounces unsweetened chocolate
1 cup sugar
2 eggs, beaten

1 teaspoon vanilla extract
⅔ cup flour
½ cup chopped nuts (optional)

FROSTING
2 ounces semisweet chocolate
¼ cup butter

1 (1-pound) package confectioners' sugar
¼ cup milk
Vanilla extract to taste

Spray 1½ dozen paper-lined muffin cups with nonstick cooking spray. Combine ½ cup butter and unsweetened chocolate in a microwave-safe dish. Microwave for 1 to 2 minutes or until blended, stirring once or twice. Combine the sugar, eggs, 1 teaspoon vanilla and chocolate mixture in a bowl and mix well. Add the flour, stirring just until blended. Stir in the nuts. Spoon into the prepared muffin cups. Bake at 350 degrees for 12 minutes. For the frosting, combine the semisweet chocolate and ¼ cup butter in a microwave-safe dish. Microwave until blended, stirring once or twice. Add the confectioners' sugar alternately with the milk, mixing well after each addition and stirring until of spreading consistency. Blend in vanilla to taste. Spread over the warm cupcakes.

Downtown Savannah Style
Junior League of Savannah, Savannah, Georgia

"Our League and our cookbook focus on tradition and family. I was reminded of this recently during our annual cookbook fundraiser, Christmas Made in the South. As fellow member Jan Johnson and I were dishing out samples of our famous Vidalia Onion Torte, she turned to me and told me that she had an epiphany. When she was a young girl, she would work the church fish suppers with her mother, who would always look at her with a twinkle in her eye. The night of our League's fundraiser, Jan finally understood her mother's twinkle all those years ago.

The insight came from watching her own daughter, a new member of our League, as she strategically placed Fritos in sample cups and shared gracious exchanges with people passing by. Knowing that her daughter could be anywhere on a Friday night, but chose to be here, helping the League help others, Jan was overcome with a feeling of pride—likely the same feeling that overcame her mother as she watched Jan all those years ago. She loved that her daughter was carrying on a family tradition of serving her community and sharing the evening with her mother.

As an expectant mother, I hope to one day experience that same pride in my future 'Junior Leaguer' as we continue our own family and community tradition of volunteerism, just as my friend Jan has done."

Beverly Kinlaw Prickett
Junior League of Savannah, Georgia

Chocolate Play Dough

1 (1-pound) package confectioners' sugar
1 (4-ounce) package chocolate instant pudding mix
1/2 cup peanut butter

1/3 cup margarine, softened
4 to 5 tablespoons milk

Combine the confectioners' sugar and pudding mix in a bowl and mix well. Add the peanut butter, margarine and milk and stir until smooth. You can play with this until snack time and then eat your creations. Be sure to wash your hands before you begin, and play on a clean surface.

Mardi Gras to Mistletoe
Junior League of Shreveport-Bossier, Shreveport, Louisiana

Peanut Butter Play Dough

1 cup peanut butter
1 cup honey

1 cup powdered milk
1 cup oatmeal

Combine ingredients in a large bowl. Mix with spoon, then knead with hands. If mixture is too sticky, add more milk and oatmeal in equal amounts until mixture is consistency for modeling. Harden your creation in the refrigerator. Then eat it for dessert!

A Taste of Georgia, Another Serving
Newnan Junior Service League, Newnan, Georgia

Strawberries

1 cup pecans
1 cup coconut
1/2 cup condensed milk
Two 3-ounce or one 6-ounce package strawberry gelatin
1/2 teaspoon vanilla
Red and green sugar crystals

Chop nuts and coconut together in blender. Combine with all other ingredients except colored sugars. Roll into strawberry-shaped pieces. Then roll in red sugar crystals, trying not to get red sugar on "stem" end of strawberries. Dip stem end in green sugar crystals.

River Road Recipes II: Second Helping
Junior League of Baton Rouge, Baton Rouge, Louisiana

World's Fastest Strawberry Mousse

Serves 4

One 10-ounce package frozen unsweetened
   strawberries
1 cup plain nonfat yogurt

1/3 cup sugar
1 tablespoon vanilla
1 teaspoon lemon juice

Mix all ingredients in blender and freeze. Serve in sherbet glasses. Variations: Replace the strawberries with your favorite fresh or frozen fruit—raspberries, blueberries, etc.

River Road Recipes III: A Healthy Collection
Junior League of Baton Rouge, Baton Rouge, Louisiana

The proceeds from the three cookbooks published by the Junior League of Hampton Roads, Virginia, enables them to provide Dignity Kits, which include new clothes and toiletries for sexual assault survivors, and Bereavement Kits for children facing the death of a loved one so they might better understand their grief and loss.

Chunky Monkey Bars

Makes 1 dozen

1 large package brownie mix
8 ounces chocolate chips
3/4 cup chopped roasted peanuts

1/2 cup honey
1/4 cup creamy peanut butter

Preheat the oven using the brownie mix package directions. Prepare and bake the brownie mix in a greased 9×13-inch baking dish, using the directions for the cake-like brownies. Remove from the oven and sprinkle immediately with the chocolate chips and peanuts.

Combine the honey and peanut butter in a saucepan. Heat over low heat until smooth and heated through. Pour over the prepared layers and let stand until cool. Chill slightly for ease of cutting.

The Bells Are Ringing: A Call to Table
Mission San Juan Capistrano Women's Guild, San Juan Capistrano, California

Lochness Bars

Makes 60

1/2 cup margarine
1 (6-ounce) package chocolate chips
1 cup peanut butter

1 (10 1/2-ounce) package miniature marshmallows
4 1/4 cups crispy rice cereal
1 cup peanuts, optional

FROSTING:
1 (6-ounce) package chocolate chips
1 (6-ounce) package butterscotch chips

Combine margarine, chocolate chips and peanut butter in saucepan. Cook over low heat until melted, stirring until smooth. Add marshmallows and stir until melted. Blend in cereal and peanuts. Spread in 13×9×2-inch baking pan. Chill until firm. Prepare frosting by melting chocolate chips and butterscotch chips together, blending until smooth. Spread on chilled bars. Cut into 2×1-inch bars.

Children's Party Book
The Junior League of Hampton Roads, Hampton Roads, Virginia

Potato Chip Cookies

Makes 8 dozen cookies

2 cups (4 sticks) butter, softened
1 cup granulated sugar
3 cups all-purpose flour

2 teaspoons vanilla extract
1 1/2 cups crushed potato chips
Confectioners' sugar

Cream the butter and granulated sugar in a mixing bowl until light and fluffy. Add the flour and vanilla and mix well. Stir in the potato chips. Drop by teaspoonfuls onto greased cookie sheets. Bake at 350 degrees for 12 to 15 minutes or until light golden brown. Remove to wire racks to cool. Sift confectioners' sugar onto all sides of the cooled cookies.

Now Serving
Junior League of Wichita Falls, Wichita Falls, Texas

Children's Favorite Lollipops

Makes 32 lollipops

2 cups sugar
2/3 cup light corn syrup
1 cup water

1/2 teaspoon oil of peppermint
Food coloring as desired
Wooden candy sticks

Combine the sugar, corn syrup and water in a large heavy saucepan. Cook until the sugar is completely dissolved, stirring constantly. Cook to 290 degrees on a candy thermometer; do not stir but wipe the side of the pan with a wet cloth to remove any sugar crystals. Reduce the heat so that there will be no discoloration of the syrup. Cook to 310 degrees on the candy thermometer. Remove from the heat.

Add the oil of peppermint and food coloring and stir just enough to blend. Spoon enough hot syrup onto a greased pan to make the size lollipop desired. Insert the stick into the hot syrup. Repeat with the remaining syrup and sticks. Let stand until cooled completely before removing from the pan.

A Thyme to Remember
The Dallas County Medical Society Alliance, Dallas, Texas

Call it music therapy. Call it reminiscing. Regardless of the label, the Junior League of Wichita Falls' Goodtime Singers project is just plain toe-tappin' fun. Since 1976, members have traveled with homemade instruments (and a few real ones, too) to nursing homes around the city. They entertain residents with song medleys from days gone by. The smiles, hugs, and sing-a-longs make true music for the soul. For a few minutes at least, the volunteers make days a little brighter, problems a little smaller, and the "good ole days" not so long ago. Goodtime Singers is one of the many projects supported by funds generated from their cookbook, *Now Serving*.

Ice Cream Muffins

1 cup vanilla ice cream, softened
1 cup sifted self-rising flour

Preheat oven to 350 degrees. Put paper liners in muffin tin. Combine softened ice cream with flour in medium-sized bowl; stir until moistened, do not overmix. Fill liners 3/4 full. Bake for 20 minutes or until inserted toothpick comes out clean. Very good with honey-butter.

Stir Ups
Junior Welfare League of Enid, Enid, Oklahoma

Cowboy Candy

Serves 24

12 whole honey or chocolate graham crackers
6 squares white almond bark
1/2 cup creamy peanut butter

2 squares chocolate almond bark
2 squares white almond bark

Line a 10×15-inch pan with foil and coat with nonstick cooking spray. Fit the graham crackers in a single layer into the prepared pan. Combine 6 squares white almond bark and the peanut butter in a microwave-safe bowl. Microwave on High until melted, stirring occasionally. Spread over the graham crackers.

Melt the chocolate almond bark in a microwave-safe bowl in the microwave and drizzle over the white almond bark layer. Melt 2 squares white almond bark in a microwave-safe bowl in the microwave. Drizzle over the chocolate almond bark layer and swirl with a wooden pick, if desired. Chill for 10 minutes or until firm. Break into pieces and store in an airtight container in the refrigerator.

Marshes to Mansions
Junior League of Lake Charles, LA, Lake Charles, Louisiana

Gobblers

1 (16-ounce) package chocolate sandwich cookies
1/4 cup red hot cinnamon candies
1 1/4 cups malted milk balls

1 (16-ounce) container chocolate frosting
1 (10-ounce) package candy corn

Separate the cookies, leaving the cream filling intact on 1 side. Attach a red hot candy to each malted milk ball with a small amount of the chocolate frosting to make the turkey head and body. Attach each turkey body with some of the chocolate frosting to the center of each cookie half with the cream filling. This forms the base of the cookie. Spread the inside of the remaining cookie halves without the cream filling with some of the remaining chocolate frosting. Arrange the candy corn with points facing outward along the outer edge of the frosting to form the tail. Attach a tail perpendicular to each turkey body with the remaining frosting. Store, covered, in the refrigerator until just before serving.

Note: This is a great project for the children while you are preparing Thanksgiving dinner!

Made in the Shade
Junior League of Greater Fort Lauderdale, Fort Lauderdale, Florida

Popcorn Balls

1 cup sugar
1/4 cup dark corn syrup
1/4 cup water
1/2 teaspoon vinegar

2 tablespoons butter
1/8 teaspoon baking soda
1/2 teaspoon vanilla extract
2 quarts (8 cups) popped corn

Mix sugar, corn syrup, water and vinegar in a medium saucepan. Stir well. Boil without stirring until the mixture reaches the hard-boil stage. Add butter and boil until the mixture spins a thread when dropped from a spoon. Remove from heat. Add soda. Stir in vanilla extract. Pour over popped corn. Rub hands with butter and form popcorn balls. Store in an airtight container.

Add Another Place Setting
Junior League of Northwest Arkansas, Springdale, Arkansas

Fool's Toffee

36 to 40 saltine crackers (1 sleeve)
1 cup (2 sticks) butter
1 cup packed dark brown sugar
2 cups (12 ounces) milk chocolate chips
1/2 to 1 cup chopped pecans

Line a 10×17-inch baking pan with foil and coat the foil with butter. Arrange the crackers in a single layer with sides touching in the prepared pan. Combine 1 cup butter and brown sugar in a saucepan. Bring to a boil over medium heat, stirring constantly. Boil for 4 minutes, stirring constantly.

Pour the butter mixture over the crackers. Using a wooden spoon, spread the mixture evenly over the crackers. Bake at 350 degrees for 5 minutes. Sprinkle with the chocolate chips and let stand for 2 minutes or until the chocolate chips soften. Spread the chocolate evenly over the prepared layers using a knife or metal cake spatula. Sprinkle with the pecans and press lightly. Chill for 30 minutes or until set. Break into pieces and store in a covered container in the refrigerator.

Note: Saltine crackers may seem like an unusual ingredient to use in a toffee recipe, but do not be "fooled" into thinking this is a mistake. This secret ingredient makes the toffee much lighter and crispier than using graham crackers. Teenagers love to make this candy. Makes a great gift for teachers, coaches, or friends.

River Road Recipes IV: Warm Welcomes
Junior League of Baton Rouge, Baton Rouge, Louisiana

Fresh Fruit Pizza

1 (20-ounce) roll refrigerator sugar cookie dough
8 ounces cream cheese, softened
1/3 cup granulated sugar
1 teaspoon vanilla extract

Assorted colorful fresh fruit (strawberries, kiwi, peaches, blueberries, etc.)
1 (10-ounce) jar peach or apricot jelly

Early in day: Preheat oven to 350 degrees. Lightly grease round pizza pan or jelly roll pan. Cut cookie dough into 1/8-inch slices; seal dough edges together to make crust (dough expands when baked, so leave a little space at the edge of the pan, unless the pan has side). Bake until light brown, 10 to 12 minutes; cool.

In bowl combine cream cheese, sugar, and vanilla; mix until smooth. Spread over cooled crust. Arrange fruit in decorative pattern on top of cream cheese mixture. Heat jelly until slightly runny. Carefully spoon over fruit to glaze. Refrigerate until ready to serve. Variation: Add 1/2 teaspoon of your favorite liqueur to cream cheese.

Tampa Treasures
The Junior League of Tampa, Tampa, Florida

Contributors

*A League of Our Own ...
From Blue Jeans to Ball Gowns*
Rockwall Women's League
Rockwall, Texas (2006)

A Southern Collection Then and Now
Junior League of Columbus
Columbus, Georgia (1994)

A Sunsational Encore *
Junior League of Greater Orlando
Orlando, Florida (1999)

A Taste of Enchantment
Junior League of Albuquerque
Albuquerque, New Mexico (2001)

A Taste of Georgia
Newnan Junior Service League
Newnan, Georgia (1977)

A Taste of Georgia, Another Serving
Newnan Junior Service League
Newnan, Georgia (1994)

*A Taste of the Good Life :
From the Heart of Tennessee*
Saint Thomas Hospital
Nashville, Tennessee (1996)

A Thyme to Entertain
Junior League of Annapolis, Inc.
Annapolis, Maryland (2007)

A Thyme to Remember
The Dallas County Medical Society Alliance
Dallas, Texas (1998)

Add Another Place Setting
Junior League of Northwest Arkansas
Springdale, Arkansas (2007)

An Occasion to Gather
Junior League of Milwaukee
Milwaukee, Wisconsin (2004)

Applehood & Motherpie *
Junior League of Rochester, Inc.
Rochester, New York (1981)

Apron Strings
Junior League of Little Rock
Little Rock, Arkansas (1997)

Art Fare *
Toledo Museum of Art Aides
Toledo, Ohio (2000)

Austin Entertains
The Junior League of Austin
Austin, Texas (2002)

Be Present at Our Table
Germantown United Methodist Women
Germantown, Tennessee (2007)

Beginnings: A Collection of Appetizers
The Junior League of Akron, Inc.
Akron, Ohio (2000)

Between the Lakes *
The Junior League of Saginaw Valley
Saginaw, Michigan (2005)

Beyond Burlap *
Junior League of Boise
Boise, Idaho (1997)

Boston Uncommon *
The Junior League of Boston
Boston, Massachusetts (2007)

California Mosaic
The Junior League of Pasadena
Pasadena, California (2007)

California Sol Food *
Junior League of San Diego, Inc.
San Diego, California (2004)

Celebrate the Rain *
The Junior League of Seattle
Seattle, Washington (2004)

Charleston Receipts *
Junior League of Charleston
Charleston, South Carolina (1950)

Charleston Receipts Repeats *
Junior League of Charleston
Charleston, South Carolina (1986)

Children's Party Book
The Junior League of Hampton Roads
Hampton Roads, Virgina (1984/1997)

Compliments of
Woman's Exchange of Memphis
Memphis, Tennessee (2006)

Cooking by the Bootstraps
Junior Welfare League of Enid
Enid, Oklahoma (2002)

Creating Comfort *
Genesis Women's Shelter
Dallas, Texas (2005)

Cresent City Collection *
The Junior League of New Orleans
New Orleans, Louisiana (2000)

*Down Home Treasured Recipes
from our House to Yours*
West Point Junior Auxiliary
West Point, Mississippi (2004)

Downtown Savannah Style
Junior League of Savannah
Savannah, Georgia (1996)

Everyday Feasts
The Junior League of Tampa
Tampa, Florida (2005)

Food For Thought
Junior League of Birmingham, Inc.
Birmingham, Alabama (1996)

For Goodness Taste
Junior League of Rochester, Inc.
Rochester, New York (1991)

*For Such A Time As This:
A Cookbook*
Park Cities Baptist Church
Dallas, Texas (2003)

From Grouper to Grits
The Junior League of Clearwater-Dunedin
Clearwater, Florida (2005)

Great Women, Great Food
Junior League of Kankakee County
Kankakee, Illinois (2007)

Home Again, Home Again
Junior League of Owensboro
Owensboro, Kentucky (2004)

*If You Can't Stand the Heat,
Get Out of the Kitchen*
Junior Service League of Independence
Independence, Missouri (1974)

Life is Delicious
Hinsdale Junior Woman's Club
Hinsdale, Illinois (2007)

Little Rock Cooks *
Junior League of Little Rock
Little Rock, Arkansas (1972)

Lone Star to Five Star *
The Junior League of Plano
Plano, Texas (2004)

Made in the Shade
Junior League of Greater Fort Lauderdale
Fort Lauderdale, Florida (1999)

Serving Louisiana
LSU Foundation
Baton Rouge, Louisiana (2002)

Shall We Gather
Trinity Episcopal Church
Wetumpka, Alabama (2007)

Simply Sarasota
Junior League of Sarasota
Sarasota, Florida (2007)

*Starfish Café:
Changing Lives
One Recipe at Time* ...
Union Mission/Starfish Café
Savannah, Georgia (2007)

Stir Ups
Junior Welfare League of Enid
Enid, Oklahoma (1982)

Tables of Content *
Junior League of Birmingham, Inc.
Birmingham, Alabama (2006)

Tampa Treasures
The Junior League of Tampa
Tampa, Florida (1992)

Tastes, Tales and Traditions *
Palo Alto Auxiliary for Children
Palo Alto, California (2005)

Texas Ties *
Junior League of North Harris and
South Montgomery Counties, Inc.
Spring, Texas (1997)

*The Bells Are Ringing:
A Call to Table* *
Mission San Juan Capistrano Women's Guild
San Juan Capistrano, California (2007)

The Bess Collection
Junior Service League of Independence
Independence, Missouri (1993)

The Cook's Canvas 2
Cameron Art Museum
Wilmington, North Carolina (2008)

The Cotton Country Collection *
The Junior League of Monroe, Inc.
Monroe, Louisiana (1972)

The Gasparilla Cookbook
The Junior League of Tampa
Tampa, Florida (1961)

The Life of the Party
The Junior League of Tampa
Tampa, Florida (2003)

Toast of the Coast
Junior League of Jacksonville
Jacksonville, Florida (2005)

*Traditions:
A Taste of the Good Life*
Junior League of Little Rock
Little Rock, Arkansas (1983)

Very Virginia
The Junior League of Hampton Roads
Hampton Roads, Virginia (1995)

Virginia Hospitality
The Junior League of Hampton Roads
Hampton Roads, Virgina (1975)

Worth Tasting
Junior League of the Palm Beaches
West Palm Beach, Florida (2007)

* Denotes Tabasco® Community Cookbook Award Winner or
McIllhenny Hall of Fame inductee

Index

RECIPES WORTH SHARING

FRP Books, Inc., creates successful connections between organizations and individuals through custom books.

Favorite Recipes® Press, an imprint of FRP Books, Inc., located in Nashville, Tennessee, is one of the nation's best-known and most respected cookbook companies. Favorite Recipes® Press began by publishing cookbooks for its parent company, Southwestern/Great American, in 1961. Since then Favorite Recipes® Press has grown to be an important and successful division of the company, producing hundreds of titles for nonprofit organizations, companies, and individuals.

FRP Books, Inc., works with many different entities, each with its own unique structure and needs. The company's achievements are directly related to its strong commitment to the success of each customer served. Full support, consultation, and an array of professional services are available every step of the way in the creation, production, and marketing of custom self-published books.

Other FRP Books, Inc., imprints include

Additional FRP titles are
Almost Homemade
Cooking Up a Classic Christmas
Favorite Recipes of Home Economics Teachers
      Desserts
      Meats
      Vegetables
      Salads
      Casseroles
The Illustrated Encyclopedia of American Cooking
My Favorite Recipes, A Recipe Journal
The Vintner's Table

To learn more about custom books, visit our Web site, www.frpbooks.com.